responding to chaos

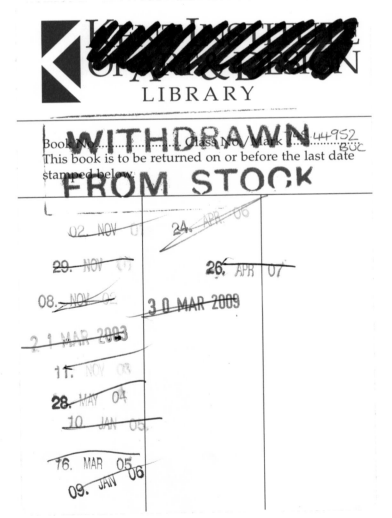

responding to chaos

Tradition, Technology, Society and Order in Japanese Design

David N Buck

SPON PRESS
Taylor & Francis Group

London and New York

First published 2000 by Spon Press
11 New Fetter Lane, London EC4P 4EE

Simultaneously published in the USA and Canada by Spon Press
29 West 35th Street, New York, NY10001

Spon Press is an imprint of the Taylor & Francis Group

Designed and typeset by Sutchinda Rangsi Thompson
Colour separation by Tenon & Polert Colour Scanning Ltd
Printed and bound in China by Tenon & Polert

British Library Cataloguing in Publication Data
A catalogue record for this book is available from the British Library

Library of Congress Cataloging in Publication Data
Buck, David N.
    Responding to chaos: tradition, technology, society, and order in
Japanese design/David N. Buck
        p.   cm.
    Includes bibliographical references and index.
    ISBN 0-419-25110-3 (pbk)
    1. Design—Japan—History—20th century. 2. Design, Industrial—
Japan—History—20th century. 3. Designers—Japan—Interviews.
4. Aesthetics, Japanese—20th century. I. Title.

NK1484.A1 B83 2000
745.4'4952'09045—dc21
                                                    00-024566

contents

tradition   4

technology   52

society   98

order   144

acknowledgements

This book has been an amazing adventure for me, born out of my encounters with designers in Japan. It has given me the opportunity to meet people I had only dreamed of and the inspiration to explore what design could be. Any sophistication in my own design work comes from the lessons they shared with me. So I owe a special debt of appreciation to all of the designers, and their staff, who so willingly gave their valuable time in arranging the interviews in Japan and later during the book's production. Many thanks to them for giving so freely of their time, and for letting me see inside their offices, their projects and their minds.

I am grateful also to the many photographers who so generously gave permission to have their work included in the book and who captured on film the projects' spirit as well as the spaces.

Thanks to the other members of the Gang of Four – Steve H, Dave R and Steve D – for being the sounding board for many of my ideas in Japan and for making my time there so enjoyable; to Keiko Frances Takeuchi for introducing me to the world of literature, a special thanks to Yasuko Tabuchi for always being there, and to T, for saying yes. I am specially grateful to my parents: to my father for sharing his love of the English language and travel, and for showing me that anything is possible, and to my mother for fostering my creative side.

I am deeply indebted to my agent Caroline Davidson for her enthusiasm for this book from the initial proposal on and for her continuing warm support. In what may be a new martial art form of literary callisthenics, she has kept my foot out of my mouth, and steered me, the stranger in paradise, through the world of publishing.

To everyone who has been involved in the book's production; Sutchinda Rangsi Thompson, Sally Carter, Nicola Kearton, Caroline Cautley, Helen Ibbotson, Colin Beck a special thanks.

To Caroline Mallinder, my editor at Spon Press, a special thanks, for her diligence and skill at making the finished book what it is, and most of all for taking the chance on this my first book. ■

preface

This book is both a personal remembrance of my experience, while living in Japan, of meeting and communicating with more than twenty Japanese designers and a collective celebration of their creative craft and dedication.

Responding to Chaos is organised into four themes, Tradition, Technology, Order and Society and their selection post-dated the interviews. I had initially approached each interview without preconceptions to try to discover the person behind the projects and the forces driving their particular design expression. These four themes, recurrently turned to by the designers in interviews, I hope provide a useful way, not just to examine one facet of their individual work, but also to establish key modes of thought in these collective themes. It is worth noting though that most designers' work comfortably spans more than one category and could have been equally happily placed in at least one other. Their placement reflects my own subjective decision and if this at times seems idiosyncratic, please accept my apologies.

I also decided when writing this book that I would choose a thematic approach rather than a disciplinary one. Although in professional terms the categories 'architect' and 'interior designer' may still be relevant in Japan, I have rejected such forms of design nomenclature and instead, I hope, embraced a much more open and expansive approach. After hearing these designers it seemed as silly to talk of an 'architectural' approach to tradition as a 'landscape architectural' response to a social approach to design. The designers' work included in this book easily spans more than just one genre and indeed much of the work has already gone past simple professional boundaries and is pushing back the very edges of design itself.

I hope you will find the following seventeen designers as fascinating to meet in the book as I did in person, and will feel inspired by their creative energy. It would be wrong, however, I think to attribute their extraordinary vision and the quality of their work to a different set of working conditions in Japan. They struggle at times with the same bureaucratic strictures and client vagaries as designers elsewhere – they just seem to be propelled through them by the force of their creative inquisitiveness and in that sense I hope this book will inspire you to pursue your own dreams.

I hope this book offers much more than just a fleeting glimpse of the designers' project work and reveals deeply thoughtful and thought-provoking work that has been responsible for forming a vital part of a unique culture's affair with design.

David N Buck

introduction

Responding to Chaos, a celebration of the diversity of design in Japan, offers an opportunity to meet Japanese designers and the cities that have inspired them. Choosing an interview format allows the reader to share a unique collection of seventeen conversations – ideas, influences, precedents and responses – that span the breadth of Japan's design world. We rarely hear designers themselves speak about their work. We often only meet them when projects are completed, when a summary concerning the final result – the new park, the novel product, the innovative building – is published. By hearing these dialogues in the designer's own words it breathes life into the characters and concepts, into the individual stories and the collective themes it explores. Allowing Japanese designers to speak directly about their work, enables us, through their voices, to see the finished works in context.

This book provides a major survey covering diverse corners of Japan's design world and gives a unique insight into the breadth of discussion in Japan at the present time. Seventeen designers from five disciplines – architecture, interior design, lighting design, product design and landscape architecture – have been selected for this book. Some, like Tadao Ando or Shigeru Uchida, are world-famous. Others, like Kazuyo Sejima and Shigeru Ban, are just starting to receive wider recognition. Juxtaposed among these more established figures are new faces: Kan Izue or Toru Mitani, for example, may at present be little known outside their own profession. As you will find in the following pages, the designers who speak here may have widely divergent approaches, but they all have a clear vision for their work, and speak passionately about it. Covering more than ninety individual projects, this is a compendium of ideas and concepts, completed works and projects that span a range from clocks to computer centres, crematoria to cities in the sky. It provides a rich visual sourcebook of ideas on the cutting edge of Japanese design. The reason for selecting these designers, and what distinguishes them from the thousands of others in Japan, is that they have managed, in a country with deep-rooted traditions, to produce something new. As well as great creativity, they have also had the courage to be outsiders in a society that values consensus over discord, the conformer over the maverick. The very precariousness of their position allows them, and us, a unique view into the world of Japanese design.

Responding to Chaos examines four distinct approaches to design in Japan – Tradition, Technology, Society and Order – revealing how they influence Japanese design from individual projects to the urban scale. These four sections reveal innovative and distinct approaches to design in Japan that cut across professional boundaries. You will hear both architect Kan Izue and interior designer Shigeru Uchida discussing their interpretation of the traditions of Japan; how the concrete geometry of Tadao Ando and the flowing landscapes of Yoji Sasaki are both searching for order in design. Why product designer Toshiyuki Kita and architect Shigeru Ban are both striving for a new social role for design in Japan; and how technology is responsible for producing the wooden structures of Shoei Yoh and the abstract landscapes of Toru Mitani.

The designers will be describing the influences acting on their designs; where they get their inspiration from and in what form it is manifest in their work. How do they respond to the precedents of history, to the whims of clients? Does their work reflect society's values or rebel against them? You may be astonished to hear, for example, that the industrial allegory of Shin Takamatsu's architecture was not inspired by the machine age, but by the spirituality and sheer architectural power of one of Japan's most revered shrines, Izumo Taisha. The interview format allows the conversational text to soar beyond the often published descriptions of individual projects and look in depth at what the designers are searching for in their work, revealing through their answers a unique insight into their characters and how their minds work. These interviews also uncover their views and aspirations, even fears, for Japanese cities.

But why urban Japan? I believe an awareness of their views on the urban conditions in Japan is fundamental to understand fully the context of their work. How do they respond to the chaos of urban Japan? Is there a social message they are trying to express through their work? Shigeru Ban designs low-cost social housing, in paper. Yoji Sasaki's urban landscapes 'pose questions of what is paradise in a modern city, not answers'. Do they even see the city surviving through the next century? Fortunately not all are as pessimistic as architect Kazuhiro Ishii whose catch-phrase of 'Non-City in the City' predicts a future of 'variation, rotation, history, and garbage'. I believe that these diverse attitudes deserve recognition and review.

There is another and equally important reason to include discussions on the city in these interviews. As the world increasingly realises the importance of its natural environment, and makes further moves to protect it, the pressure will continue to maximise the potential of all cities where more of the world's population will reside. With 70 per cent of the country's population in 4 per cent of the land area, urban Japan holds many lessons about urban high-density living, where the forces that act on design, be they economic, social or political, are much more intense. This increasing complexity means that the experiences of Japanese designers hold lessons not just for other Asian cities but for Western designers and cities too.

This book is vital now because it examines Japanese design at an important juncture in time. The country's economic boom of the 1980s produced a surge of interest in land and building, and consequently in design in all its forms. From restaurant interiors to products, from private housing to recreational spaces, design received an unprecedented degree of attention from society. The bursting in the early 1990s of this co-called 'Bubble' economy, has now produced a new environment for design in Japan, one less self-conscious and extravagant, one more introspective and sensitive to a broader range of issues. The dawn of the new millennium has further prompted Japanese designers to re-examine themselves and their role in urban society. I believe that this re-evaluation now demands that their collective work be re-appraised. Examining the current state of design in Japan provides a means of looking back to see where it has come from, and gives a glimpse of the future.

The book that follows is written, not just for professionals, but for anyone who is interested in contemporary design, in art, history, culture, technology, even anthropology, and what these mean in a modern society undergoing rapid change. I hope that the reader will find these urban voices as fascinating as I have. ◼

tradition

I do. Or at least I think I do.

Questions of tradition, like those concerning love, always seem to me the most difficult to answer. No sooner do you start your affirmation than the doubts set in. But in spite of this, the other day I asked myself a tricky question. Just where exactly do traditions come from? They cannot arrive by car because that would be too modern. Alternatively, they cannot come by post it's just far too risky. Last time I sent a Valentine's card it was so far off it almost arrived on Mother's Day. Perhaps they are like fragments of DNA, and just pass naturally, mostly on Sunday mornings, from one generation to the next. It seems such a pertinent question in Japan. There can be few cultures, countries or societies that so wholeheartedly and intensely feel the importance of tradition, with a capital T. This in a way makes it so hard not to be critical of much of the design work that is put out under the tradition party banner – pastiche by the bucketful, history by the bag. Just a plain assertion of a feeling that something – be it wooden architecture or Tamagotchi electronic pets – is all part of the Japanese traditional milieu, is taken as prima facie fact.

The designers' work introduced in the following four chapters is stuff of far greater depth. The inspiration for Kan Izue's unique architectural creations spans early Buddhist teachings to modern mass-produced materials – all creating spaces that improve with age. Shigeru Uchida's interiors embody traditional notions of space but in marvellous contemporary forms. Toru Murakami's architectural aesthetic objects defend the vernacular methods, while Yoshiji Takehara's houses reveal traditional methods of apprehension and experiencing architecture.

For too long traditional images have been a kind of cultural comfort blanket, a romanticised evocation of a past when Japan really did have a closer relationship with nature, families, materials etc. It is a kind of pervasive denial that the destroyers, as well as the preservers, of Japanese culture, have been living there all along. There has been a tendency to avoid taking responsibility for tradition – it has been too much a case of being someone else's fault. The work of the following four designers, I believe, shows that those 'cultured' types with an obsession about the 'value' of tradition – you know the ones who give you the feeling that they would sell up or torch it if the price was right – are missing the point. Tradition lives now. ■

Symbolic Sense towards Space

Shigeru Uchida

「 Symbolic design is strongly supported by the human spirit or mentality and this mental act is created into three-dimensional space as interior design 」

The Hotel Mojiko (1998), Moji City, designed by Aldo Rossi.

'Japanese people have a uniquely intimate relationship with culture'. Chanted like an incantation, it's as though Japan still desperately needs to be reassured that nothing has changed. Which is strange really when you consider the degree to which the country has been influenced by the West in the last fifty years. Some parts of Tokyo now even 'out-America' Las Vegas. This cultural influx and the changes to architecture, as commercial buildings have been liberated by modern – read Western – technology, has had a huge influence on interior design in Japan. The profession has struggled to find its place between the narcissism of collages of traditional Japanese materials and forms – a kind of Japanesque – and a new Post-Modernism of imported fragments of history.

Shigeru Uchida has become Japan's best-known interior designer for convincingly answering the question, 'What is a late-twentieth-century Japanese interior?'. Uchida, who together with Ikuyo Mitsuhashi and Toru Nishioka founded Studio 80 in 1981, has produced a body of work that is unique in the ways in which it produces interiors. These might at first appear to be part of a borderless international style but have actually jettisoned most of the elements that usually

make up that genre and are in fact deeply rooted in the aesthetics of Japanese traditional interiors. It says much for his vision and integrity that he has achieved this most noticeably through a collaboration on two projects with Italian architect Aldo Rossi. In 1989 at the Hotel Il Palazzo in Fukuoka and at the Hotel Mojiko in Kyushu's Moji City opened in 1998, Uchida, as design co-ordinator, held overall control of the project and also designed the hotel interior. What he produced at the Hotel Mojiko was a building where Western

architecture, Japanese finance, tea ceremony aesthetics, international visitors and neighbours all come together to create a place where people can feel at home – but still feel where home was. As Uchida says, 'people cannot enjoy the interior if it doesn't relate to Japan, its culture, and the people of Moji'.

The hotel, Rossi's last completed project which he nicknamed 'the shark', is a 17,689 square metre mixed-use building with wedding, banquet and community halls, offices, 134 guest rooms and two

suites that look out over the harbour through the 'eye' of the shark. But if the exterior, its facade unified by the rhythm of pale-blue square windows, is pure Western – or even pure Rossi – the interior is a subtle fusion of two cultures. The hotel entrance starts with a grand red-sandstone staircase that leads up to a second set of entrances to the lobby, restaurant and community hall. Marked by twin pillars, each side supporting a deep lintel, the entrances are a fusion of Western portal and the *torii* gate to a shrine. The

The lobby of the Hotel Il Palazzo (1989), Fukuoka, is a brooding spatial study in colour and form.

The Hotel Mojiko lobby.

The Hotel Mojiko's Ichiju-an tea room, a glorious celebration of
materials and light.

floor is black-and-white polished marble but is the
design the *ichimatsu moyo*, the checkerboard of
traditional Japan? The ambience of the other spaces
provokes similar responses: just when you think
you have got the cultural reference, another image
appears on the tip of your tongue. But it is the hotel's
tea room, Ichiju-an, that expresses most powerfully
Uchida's sensitivity towards his cultural roots and their
continued relevance to modern Japanese culture, even
in Western architectural forms like this hotel. The tea
ceremony space is enclosed by walls and a ceiling
of cream-coloured *washi* paper (Japanese hand-made
paper). Roughly cut into rectangles, this provides a
slightly blurred sense of depth, you're not sure
whether just distance or time also is being suspended.
The entrance is marked by a purple glass bowl resting
upon a rough-hewn bolt of timber. As light filters
through the paper *shoji* screens it casts a slowly
rotating oval of purple light on the floor that reflects
the changes in hue and intensity of the outside light.
The scene is so peaceful that the only movement
is particles of silence floating through the space.

It is this aesthetic sensitivity that really captures
your attention in his work. Long after any intellectual
discussions of design style or influence, of techniques
or forms have faded from your memory, you are left
with images of just what quality his designs are.
I sometimes think that all the discourse in design
on questions of style – is Modernism dead or alive? –
serves merely to distract us from the much more
difficult but much more important question of whether
the design is actually any good or not. What sets
Uchida's work apart from others is not just that he
matches Japanese traditional spatial aesthetics with
contemporary forms and in contemporary 'Western'
buildings, but that he does so in designs that are of
such consistently high quality. Maybe everybody could
do it. But everybody doesn't.

So often this East–West interaction has been fraught
with misunderstandings. Just look at the Impressionists
and Japanese oil paintings of the same period. You
see their influence in our work and our influence in
theirs – it frequently looks like there was a real
dialogue there – but when you actually listen to what

they were saying, it reveals a relationship devoid of true cultural understanding.

But to see Ushida's work as a stylistic endeavour, even if a successful one, would miss out the other aspect of his exploration of cultural identity, the designer's role in defining and creating perceptions of what constitutes the 'social group' in Japan. When he first opened his own office in 1970 at the age of twenty-seven, Japan was still in a period of rapid growth. With the social unrest of the late sixties behind it, the country was at the beginning of a period of greater individual freedom, both economically and socially, that created a new, more open environment for interior design. Uchida calls this early period, 'the war against society' as he, and fellow conspirator Shiro Kuramata, designed bars where people met not as members of professions or groups, but as individuals. The rampant economic growth of the 'Bubble' period produced a new environment for interior design in Japan, and Uchida has now moved from creating places for the individual to meet to places where 'small societies' of individuals and families can gather and engage in dialogue.

Encompassing social relationships, traditional aesthetics, contemporary functions and symbolic spaces, Uchida's work touches all corners of the Japanese cultural cross while answering – what often seems the Holy Grail of design in Japan – the search for a contemporary 'Japaneseness' in a culture that has been influenced so assiduously by Western icons, aesthetics and techniques. If you are asked to define the periods of modern Japanese interior design, just tell them there is only one: the Shigeru Uchida period. ■

You have written frequently about Japanese historical notions of boundaries and space yet, when I see your work, I cannot find a visual reference to these Japanese ideas you talk about. How important is Japanese identity to you as a designer?

I feel that Japanese history or culture does not consciously direct my architectural style. Nevertheless I believe its spirit pervades my work, as something fundamental which has been instilled inside me. I have never used Japanese designs or vocabulary at all, yet I feel that my culture colours my work subconsciously, and that is why many foreign designers say that my style is typically Japanese. Like almost all Japanese designers and architects since the Meiji Restoration in 1868, I have been educated in the Western style. To begin with, I was in the same position as many other people learning to design, and as a result of this immersion, I wasn't aware of Japan at all at that time. Indeed, I was making an effort not to be Japanese. Thus, in the beginning, I was in the same position as many others in that I felt that I was working within a global culture, and therefore I was consciously trying not to appear Japanese in my style. However, the fact that what I produced were ultimately Japanese designs suggests that culture runs extremely deep.

Jun'ichiro Tanizaki in his book *In Praise of Shadows* (1933) was expressing what he thought was a historical Japanese aesthetic regarding light. But if we look at the Modernism of, say, Richard Meier, it's the opposite approach of architectural interiors expressed through an aesthetic of pure white, pure light. When you are designing interiors, which do you feel greater affinity towards?

To tell you the truth, I like both. However, most Japanese intuitively understand the aesthetic of *In Praise of Shadows*.

I'd like to ask you about Longleage (1997), the nail salon in Tokyo, where I felt your design was possibly influenced by Neo-Plasticism or Russian Constructivism in its use of planes of colour and lines of light.

At the Longleage Nail Salon (1997), Tokyo, Shigeru Uchida used both colour and line to both define and congeal the spaces.

First I would like to talk a little more about light itself. I believe that we Japanese have been intuitively expressing the aesthetic of *In Praise of Shadows* through our use of natural light in our living spaces. However, after modernisation, a different vocabulary has been introduced and I feel that this must be due to artificial light. I think that artificial light is very attractive, so that is why I wanted to see how much I could absorb this new vocabulary and then use it in my art. If, through my use of artificial light, a spiritual element of Russian Constructivism is present, I feel that it must be something that is universal – an awareness shared by all modern people, whatever their region or history.

Could you talk a little more about that design?
Although I have mentioned that there is a universal vocabulary, in a particular field there is a very Japanese vocabulary. What I am referring to here is how to erect partitions. The reason why partitions are placed there is to separate the three elements of space. In particular, the Japanese perspective does not tend to divide spaces with actual walls even if they are used in three different ways. For example, if you have space A and space B and you divide the two clearly using a wall, then they are obviously separated, aren't they? A and B's functional differences are then distinctly split. However, in Japan, the spaces A and B are both separated and fused together. This inherent notion of space has been used for a long time. Therefore, since this feeling has seeped into me, I do not see A and B divided in a strictly physical manner. So my approach is, in one sense, to present the two spaces as implicitly intermingled, and yet the two are still distinct. I think it is quite important how the spaces A and B are divided. Under these circumstances, we often divide spaces in accordance with our awareness and our sense of the aesthetic. For example, suppose you erect four poles, and then place sacred straw festoons across them. Although it is not a wall at all, the fact that the space between the four pillars becomes sacred – a place where God is present – is made use of in our ceremonies. The fact that we divide two spaces is thus a very

perceptual matter. So Nail Salon's truth may become more obvious in various places. That is a specific characteristic.

When you look at the work of some architects you can often quickly detect some historical precedent that they have been influenced by. But looking at your work, I cannot find the precedent. So where do your ideas come from?
This question brings me to a very interesting story. The person who made us aware of how we Japanese interpret 'Japanised' space was Donald Judd. Indeed, this story may go back further. Since the Meiji Restoration, many Japanese artists have made a great effort to bring together Western and Japanese design characteristics. They tried really hard to find Japaneseness by doing this. However, I feel they were in a period that did not fully understand exactly what Japaneseness was, in terms of the principles of Japanese design style, and in the context of a modern society. Thus, during this period, we have often built and designed by adopting the traditional vocabularies which the Japanese are good at, such as straw *tatami* mats or *shoji* partitions or *sukiya* style. However, although they put a great deal of effort into their work, the reality is that the traditional Japanese stylistic vocabularies are different when compared to the modern. In this way, all these new conditions and styles have followed from the old. However, the design awareness possessed by the Japanese is not of clear cut stylistic vocabularies. Rather, what is important for us is how we furnish a space, or how we feel towards it. What I have noticed is that, as I explained earlier, partitions are used very differently in Japan and in the West. Second, we are a nation that sits on the floor. This is a very important point. Third, in our living space it is our custom to remove our shoes. These three issues are very important to us.

Regarding the Japanese use of partitions that we were made aware of, I was reading one of Donald Judd's books. Initially, I thought Judd was referring only to his own minimalism and sculptural artwork in relation to that theme. However, he was commending the way in which his work was installed at an

exhibition. I had thought that Judd expressed himself fully so long as his artwork was exhibited in minimalist form without focusing heavily on the installation side. However, the important point to him was actually the way in which objects were arranged, or what was behind objects but could not be seen. Thus, he placed great importance on how to arrange objects and how to relate them to each other. When I was considering the relationship between an artistic object and its surroundings, I came to realise the following, 'Japan is completely different from the West on wall-setting or wall-erection methods or the way objects are laid out.' We had been using our own Japanese setting methods without being consciously aware of it. The material used can be concrete, aluminium, iron or anything. In other words, when we look at how things are going to be arranged in a room, I think that a fairly Japanese style of layout will be implemented. In this sense, I think the architecture of Tadao Ando is quite *sukiya* in style.

I'm interested in your mention of Judd because he uses seriality or sequentiality frequently in his work. Is this related to your use of stripes?
That's right.

The base of architecture, or a common thread that runs through the history of architecture, is often said to be a search for order. What are you searching for in your work?
This is a very important issue and I would like to talk about two aspects of Japanese architecture in relation to it. However, the concept of order, which Western architecture possesses, does not exist in Japan. With regard to these two aspects, then, there are two typical architectural styles in Japan. These are the *sukiya* and *shoin* styles. The *shoin* style has certain units that have to be combined and co-ordinated according to a fixed definition. The *sukiya* style does not fit into a schematic order, but instead it is an architecture that should abandon the order. If this order can be defined in a wider sense, it is the question of how to create a building that matches the feelings of those inside it. Thus, the *sukiya* style

of design seen in tea houses has freedom as its theme. If you look at this concept in a negative way then it allows you to do anything, in a simplistic manner, wherever you wish. Or, if you see it from an overall point of view, there may not be any order at all. Let us take urban planning as an example. In the West, the planning scheme may include architecture in the form of units to fill in a defined project area. However, in Asian urban planning, the *sukiya* style, with its primary message of being free, makes freedom appear randomly in the city – that is how Asian cities are formed. However, if you ask me whether this is an incorrect method for urban planning, I cannot totally agree. I believe that it takes a substantial amount of time to complete a city. However, if we are to go into more detail, the subject will become very lengthy due to the regional situations and all the other aspects involved. So, the real question is why the city has developed in this way.

One factor increasingly apparent in the Asian city is the threat of it becoming a theme park. Whereas in the past, culture or function was the basis, now it's entertainment which is cheapening the focus of design. How do you feel about the Asian city, or of entertainment as the focus of design or development?
I think everybody is very confused about how to deal with modernisation. I think that Japan was the first to adopt modernisation. I believe this is why we have really created chaos in the city. As you already know, Japanese culture has been created by its interactions with cultures introduced from outside Japan. I believe the first such introduction was in the sixth century from China and all those outside influences were modified and became Japanised over the next two hundred years. In that period we transformed several foreign styles into a Japanese version, one of which was that we should take off our shoes which changed our living style. So the question of this becoming 'horizontality', perceptually, is a very important issue for understanding Japanese culture. Hence, over these two-hundred-year periods we changed. It was during the Kamakura era, which I believe was the twelfth

century, that a new culture was introduced from China again. Over the course of two hundred years after that introduction, various aspects such as new technology, completely new and different cultures, and traditional Japanese culture were fused, and new cultures, including a culture of tea, were born. It has now been about 130 years since Western culture was introduced, hasn't it? So, in seventy years from now, which makes two hundred years, we will definitely create our own Western style!

Does that mean you are optimistic about the city in Asia or in Japan?
Just a moment! I think it will change slightly more. Sometimes I think we can never go back again, but at the same time people have started to be aware of what is happening and perhaps if it improves then we can change things slowly. Such drastic change actually happened in the post-war period. The changes that took place in the fifty years after the Second World War, rather than in the Meiji era, occurred with amazing force and speed. So, from the Meiji era up until the pre-war time, there were no significant changes from the Edo culture [1600-1867]. So, I guess that in about fifty years the culture will be sedated.

I visited the Hotel Il Palazzo again recently. Has that concept of a design-centred project been replicated elsewhere? Have you been design co-ordinator for similar projects since then and did that project fundamentally change the role of designers in Japan?
That was a very symbolic project and so no other project can be compared to it. Hotel Il Palazzo may have been well understood by the intellectual classes but the general public may have had a rather different idea. The four bars was a very important theme for me at that time. They were like four different designs for me in co-ordinating this project, and I used them to elicit the differences in background and the differences in individuals or in ethnic groups. However, I cannot help thinking that some people interpreted this element as a pattern, or reproduced it, or considered it quite lightheartedly, exhibiting it in various public places. I regret that it consequently became a kind of

The Hotel Il Palazzo rises above the surrounding groups of low-rise buildings. Its travertine facade, articulated by columns and cornices of green steel, a homage to the principles and precedents of the West, is the home to Uchida's lush interiors.

design typology, despite my belief that design should be truly free, using various types to reach out to different people. Moreover, what I wanted to do was to expand the possibilities of design. I would like to talk about this in relation to Rossi, as the situation is very similar to that of the recent Hotel Mojiko. When I look back to Rossi's work before the sixties, and his work of the sixties or early seventies, there is a great deal of similarity to mine. After that period Rossi and I changed direction. However, the reason why I feel comfortable working with him is that we share a closeness in our basic sense of, and views about, architecture. A very important adventure in design is to create something new after obtaining and assimilating foreign things. Either Aldo Rossi had to construct something in Japan, which is very foreign to him, or I had to receive Rossi's idea of design and at the same time create something new for interiors. We both had to do very foreign and new things, and I feel we were given the opportunity to be adventurous.

A series of three collapsible tea houses named Ji-an, Gyo-an, and So-an (1993).

The interior of Gyo-an exudes a kind of paranoid restfulness.

The hotel's windowless facade appears its strongest feature and I've heard that it was a comment on the social situation at that time in Japan, the so-called 'Bubble' period. Although, as on that site, you had a riverside location, perhaps you didn't want to look at it, perhaps you didn't want to comment on it. In your other work is there a social message hidden, something that you are trying to say to modern Japanese society?

I believe, in many ways, that design inevitably contains a social message. The direction of my message after that period seems to have changed significantly, in particular from the beginning of the seventies. At the beginning of the seventies, we were fighting against the relationship that existed between society and the individual. In general, as a society becomes more industrialised the uniqueness of the individual is almost lost. This happened at the beginning of the seventies in Japan. We recognised that individuals have various abilities and the potential to create, and as we wanted this to be widely recognised we sought to emphasise it. That's how things were then. This is why Shiro Kuramata and I were constantly building drinking bars – *sakabas*. The *sakaba* was like a sort of guerrilla headquarters for us. They also functioned as a salon for the intellectuals. There, people would chat, discuss, get to know each other; and then they would leave the bar and re-enter society to express themselves. It was that kind of centre. Naturally, I call it 'The era of the bar'. There, regardless of their particular professions, journalists, designers, artists and engineers used to gather for a drink as *individuals*. It happened very spontaneously. This kind of fighting lasted quite a while, but in the eighties we started changing our strategies. Before, we had been fighting against the relationship between society and the individual, but later, in the eighties, the time came when we had no choice but to use the uniqueness inherent in each individual as our main issue. So, my theme is not the grand one between society and the individual. Instead, my theme is the relationship between the individual and their surroundings. In other words, society understood as a community or family, and how they and the individual influence each other. This is mostly my current theme.

Consumerism seems such a strong force in Japanese society. For a product designer, Japan should be heaven. Do you feel in heaven?

I think it is a deceptive kind of consumerism. Consumers do not choose products – in most cases they are forced to select them. For instance, how many calculators do you have? Without realising, you may have five or ten. One is enough. In the same way, many unnecessary items are being produced around us. As for the question as to whether industrial designers are very happy, there are situations where designers are not allowed to free themselves to be creative. Under certain circumstances, some people have already decided that the market for creativity does not exist at all. To my eyes, this kind of market, where creativity is involved, doesn't exist. Many things are produced by an accumulation of misunderstandings, right through from the production stage to the point where the product is completed. For instance, your tape-recorder is not made by designers, but by the market – by the sales division. But actually this market is non-existent, it is something virtual that they created. When you decide what kind of object you will be designing during the production stage then a lot of misunderstandings arise.

One of your earlier projects was a series of three tea houses, Ji-an, Gyo-an, So-an (1993). How did you find that process of designing something which has a strong identity with Japanese culture? Is this something that you would like to do again?

The greatest thing we have lost in Japan is ceremony. Ceremony is not only found inside the framework of the tea ceremony. In Japan many ceremonies took place in the four seasons of our daily life. I think it was ceremony that provided various types of functions that linked or fused people together socially. The saddest thing is the fact that all of the ceremonies have been lost. By the way, we had a tea ceremony using these three houses in the New Year. What was moving was the serene way in which one person received the tea, and then the next person poured the tea and received the other person gracefully with their hands. When they came out of the tea room, their faces were lit with reverence. In other words, my understanding of this incident was that they must have felt that the meaning of the ceremony was there. I felt that even in a tiny tea house we were made to experience something significant. The flow of time has become too horizontal in modern society, hasn't it? Time is not at all horizontal but continuously moving in society while being divided into symbolic and ordinary time. The amount of symbolic time available has lessened a great deal.

Architecture for the last thirty or forty years has been obsessed with the question of style, for example, Modernism versus Post-Modernism. But style is actually one of design's most easily communicable aspects. How would you categorise your work and are you interested in questions of style or identity?
There are no clear-cut styles in any artwork I have designed. My view is that I am given the chance to be engaged in extremely abstract work, referred to as interior design. In particular in interior design, as far as I'm concerned, I have been fortunate to have concentrated on abstract work, regardless of my location. Of course, I would not say that all my interiors are in this form. However, when you think about how abstract things are really upheld, I can say that it is spiritual. Interior design is about how to put a person's spiritual condition into three dimensions. I believe an architect addresses two issues. One of them is how to produce architecture both in daily society and in our living spaces. The second issue is to what extent architecture can accommodate socio-abstract characteristics, whatever form it takes, or its location in our lives. The first issue has added elements, such as new technologies, as well as regional particularities, nationality and special characteristic values. As we are fully engaged in these everyday, it is understandable that things change. When we design and build such things, a projected order may be necessary, to a certain extent. I think various styles are produced out of these dilemmas, or through discussions. On the other hand, however, if I could explain architecture in the abstract style, I feel contemporary architects have weaknesses in the order

or the relationship. Architects are trapped in the middle of these issues. Despite the fact that they have to solve daily tasks, some architects want to do abstract creative work. On the other hand, whatever the demands of the abstract creative work, their daily routine interferes. So, this is their weak spot. Therefore, more symbolic work should be done regardless of everyday routine or order. If this is done, you will realise what constitutes ordinary life.

I feel that Japan has now reached a point where it requires further urban planning. Asian countries were formed in this way because abstract style buildings are abundant. Green areas have always existed. Hence their relationship remained harmonious without any need to consider urban planning. However, as buildings are being built so rapidly one after another, nobody can tolerate them any longer. So, Western-style urban planning has become necessary. However, when such planning was not required, it was very pleasant not to have to think about it. The city itself was like a large park. National cultures arise through a continual process of interaction with each other. As a result they often come to share certain character-istics. This is clear when we consider that Japanese culture was really born from its exchanges with both Chinese and Korean cultures. For some time now, Japan has been experimenting with ideas and practices originating in the West and in modern times. As a result we Japanese cannot deny the fact that the culture we are currently creating is quite modern and Western. Yet although our present Japanese culture is modern/Western, many Japanese people continue to draw on Japan's own spiritual culture. In many cases they appropriate Western ways from a Japanese perspective.

They still consider these Western influences to be part of their own cultural baggage, you mean?
A culture's uniqueness, and especially that of its regional localities, is brought about by those who receive and use it. Even if these people have the same cultural identity, they will also be different from each other. To give an example, the Hotel Il Palazzo, built in Fukuoka and influenced by the local people's

perspective, would have been different had it been built in a northern province of Japan such as Sapporo, or in an Italian city. These buildings were necessarily influenced by the endemic local culture. The Hotel Mojiko may also give the impression that it is totally Western. This is understandable, since the hotel building was developed jointly with a great Western architect, Aldo Rossi. The story behind this hotel is that its makers strove to represent a symbolic town such as Moji, which captures both the modern and the Westernised Japan, in a hotel. However, it was also the West that was viewed by the Japanese culture of the Meiji era, and it was the West seen from the perspective of what was then current Japanese culture and lifestyle. Nowadays, and one hundred years later, such Western elements still evoke a sense of nostalgia.

How were you able to express this in the Hotel Mojiko?

The Japanese element that I used for the Hotel Mojiko has been expressed in terms of the functions of places. Although its form and design draw on Western models, the reason these have been transformed using a Japanese style of expression was simply to express Japan's aspirations towards Western ideals, as it perceives them, and its need to assimilate these. The hotel is in an architectural style born in the West. Many design-related vocabularies that suggest the West have been used. Nevertheless it must be noted that these were applied in a distinctly Japanese way. This is due to the fact that ceremonies, wedding receptions and family gatherings, which have been carried out since ancient times, take place in this type of space. A culture's traditions, customs and history do not die quickly. Even if there is a Western type of space in present Japan, the activities which take place there are essentially Japanese. In the light of this, what I attempted to create for the Hotel Mojiko design were ways to enable such ceremonies to be carried out naturally. Arrangements that accompany the Japanese life style are presented in various places – one of the hotel's most striking features is a tea room which is called Ichiju-an. This tea room is a special means used for communicating in Japan. In general,

a tea room is not an indispensable place in a hotel project. However, the reason we dared to have this kind of special space was because we wanted to integrate the hotel with the people of Moji. In general, hotels exist for a guest population that comes and goes. The goal set by this hotel, however, was to create a symbol of the Moji people and somewhere where they could relax and communicate. Taking this into consideration, a tea room was built both because of its importance in Japan at large, and to ensure the hotel was able to integrate successfully into its locality. In addition to this, there are ceremony rooms that represent a Western space using Japanese concepts and styles. The guiding principle behind the design of this space was not the appearance of the ceremony room itself. It was focused rather on the approach to it and the psychological path to the ceremony. In our country, we adopt a method to pass through a spiritual space, expressed as an 'empty area', in order to go into a holy place. This is expressed in a *roji* that is seen in a tea room, and in a *sando* leading to shrines and temples. The 'empty area' is a place for a spiritual silence in order to create a transition from a secular space to a holy place; it is seen as a very important place in our culture. This was also taken into consideration in the hotel design and interpreted in a Japanese way while adopting Western style.

How did you design the spaces to accommodate contemporary functions?

The many spaces prepared for ceremonies are used variously. On one occasion there may be a party, on another a symposium, or a concert, or even a family ceremony. The spaces are different from those which have a fixed use for a particular function; they are based on the Japanese concept of a space used for many purposes which has been current since ancient times. For example, the specific feature of Japanese space can be altered by simple partitions. They can be open, closed or divided. This allows various different arrangements for each ceremony's particular needs and occasionally it may be required by a change of season. For this purpose, the Japanese space must be constantly *utsu*. *Utsu* is an ancient Japanese word

and indicates an emptiness, or vacancy and nullity. The state of emptiness means that a space does not have a fixed style and that it can contain various ceremonial occasions. The spaces created at the Hotel Mojiko were heavily influenced by this concept of changeable use. It must be emphasised that, although the building has spaces styled in a Western manner, many of the activities which take place there are of a specifically Japanese nature.

How do you express this essentially Japanese spirituality in your work?

True interior design is not ultimately concerned with its own visible forms but with the spirit they manifest and communicate. The outer style is thus a locus where a sophisticated psychology is reflected. In Japan the essential force that is crystallised in the architecture expresses aspirations towards Western culture, awe and reverence towards unseen objects, and also respect towards history. And so it becomes the archi-

tect's endeavour to create a collective experience, not an object; the important point about style being how it is experienced. In other words, the experience of smell, feeling, time and air fall into this latent architecture rather than into that of a visible style. The Hotel Mojiko appeals to the core of Japaneseness in the Japanese. So, while adopting styles drawn from the West, it is designed to appeal to those coming from a Japanese perspective through its subtle arrangement of the space.

Do you see your own Japaneseness expressed in your work?

My works can be quite diverse. At first glance, some are very Japanese; some of them have been the result of elimination and reduction, which is traditionally Japanese; and others are executed in a Western-influenced style. Among these various buildings the Hotel Mojiko reflects an attempt of mine to locate an interpretation of Western architecture right inside our Japanese culture. ■

The Hotel Mojiko's Ichiju-an tea room is a wonderful alchemy of vivid monotone and subdued colour.

SHIGERU UCHIDA
1943 Born in Yokohama

Education:
1966 Kuwasawa Design School in Tokyo

Employment:
1970   Established Uchida Design Studio
1973-   Lecturer at Kuwasawa Design School
1974-78 Lecturer at Tokyo University of Art & Design
1981   Established Studio 80
1999   Guest Professor at Sapporo University

Major Projects:
1977   'September' Chair
1983-86 Boutiques for Yohji Yamamoto including Y's Superposition
1985   Japanese Government Pavilion for Tsukuba Expo.'85
1988   Itchoh Restaurant, Tokyo
1989   'August' Chair
1989   Nijo-Daime Tea Room
1989   Hotel Il Palazzo, Fukuoka
1989   'Dear Morris' Clock
1991   'Come Rain & Come Shine' Chests of Drawers
1991   'Dear Vera' Clock <1989> for Alessi
1992   'Vertical' Series Cabinet
1993   Ji-an, Gyo-an, So-an Collapsible Tea Rooms

Interviewed in his office in Tokyo on 19 February 1998 and by correspondence 8 April 1999

1995   Bay Roost Bar, Osaka
1997   Kobe Fashion Museum, Kobe
1997   Longleage Nail Salon, Tokyo
1998   Hotel Mojiko, Art Direction and Interior, Kita-Kyushu
1998   'Paper Moon' Lamp

Awards:
1981   Japan Interior Designers Association Award
1987   Mainichi Design Award
1990   Best Store of the Year Special Award
1990   Shokankyo Design Award '90 Grand Prize
1993   First Kuwasawa Design Award
1998   Japan Inter-Design Forum Award, Excellent Member Award

Exhibitions:

1986   Uchida Furniture 1986, Gallery 91, New York
1988   Kagu Tokyo Designer's Week, Tokyo
1989   Shikimi, Three Nijo-Daime, Tokyo
1995   Method Remembered, Spazio Krizia, Milan

Publications:

Uchida, S. (1986) Residential Interiors, Tokyo: Shinchosha
Uchida, S. (1987) Interiors of Uchida, Mitsuhashi & Studio 80,
        Tokyo: Rikuyosha Publishing
Uchida, S. (1988) The Era of Chairs, Tokyo: Kobunsha Publishing
Uchida, S. et al. (1990) Hotel Il Palazzo – A City Stimulated by
        Architecture, Tokyo: Rikuyosha Publishing
Uchida, S. and Oki, K. (1994) Japan Interior, Vols. 1–4, Tokyo:
        Rikuyosha Publishing
Uchida, S. and Rossi, A. (1996) Interior Design Uchida,
        Mitsuhashi, Nishioka & Studio 80, Vol. 11, Germany:
        Taschen
Uchida, S., Rossi, A. and Matsuoka, S. (1998) Mojiko Hotel, Aldo
        Rossi, Shigeru Uchida, Tokyo: Rikuyosha

Aesthetics that improve with Age

Kan Izue

「 I wanted to destroy, to hammer a big nail into the traditional Japanese way. I wanted to make a renaissance of the tea room so I chose the naked woman!」

Sen-no-Rikyu (1522–1591), the father of the tea ceremony, died a tragic death four hundred years ago. But even if he were alive today he still might not rest easy, haunted by the question: what has happened to my legacy of aesthetic simplicity epitomised by the tea house? The other traditional arts of Japan are certainly not faring well these days. *Ikebana* (flower arranging) is wilting; *sumi-e* (ink painting) is now a fossilised art reduced to drawing landscapes you'd be hard pressed to find in China, and the tradition of wooden architecture has moved in two short generations from Ise Shrine, rebuilt as a symbol of purification every twenty years, to 2 by 4 prefabricated systems that probably won't even last that long.

Even some people who took heart from the early seventeenth-century Himeji Castle becoming a UNESCO World Heritage Site are wondering aloud whether the traditional architectural aesthetics – so influential they helped forge Modern architecture 12,000 miles to the west – are really still alive in Japan. When was the last time you heard of an architect devoted to the unprofitable subject of aesthetics? Or the use of cheap materials when

Bou-Bou-an (1994), Nagoya.

there's money for expensive ones? Or the reconciliation of industrialised production with traditional arts?

These are important questions for contemporary Japanese architecture and the answers can be provided by architect Kan Izue and his zinc-walled tea room Bou-Bou-an. Awarded an International Academy of Architecture Prize in 1996, Izue designed Bou-Bou-an, a 10.6 square metre space, as a contemporary reinterpretation of the traditional wooden tea room – reviving Rikyu's aesthetics in the cheapest of industrial materials. Huddled adjacent to a factory, at first glance, the tea room appears as an inconspicuous, low garden shed, its curved vaulted roof echoing the crown of a nearby cherry tree. Step a little closer though and you get a hint of its modern materials. Walls made of corrugated slate board, the cheapest waterproof board more at home as warehouse roofing, cast vertical bands of alternating light and shadow. That half-ghost, half-mirage structure seems to capture the ephemeral quality one associates with the tea house.

But go inside and Bou-Bou-an reveals its contemporary heart: zinc sheets, old newspapers, iron H-beam, drain cover checker-plate. A reinterpretation of the traditional aesthetic of *shin-gyou-sou* based on the life phases of Zen Priest Ikkyu (1394–1481), Izue's unique usage of cheap industrial materials makes the traditional aesthetic experience available and up-to-date. With new wooden tea houses now occupying the dubious distinction of the world's most expensive architectural square metre (costing up to ten million *yen* or £50,000), it might be tempting to conclude that Izue's design for Bou-Bou-an at five million *yen* for the whole building lies far from the traditional aesthetic.

History suggests otherwise. Tea houses were originally built from broken branches, ash-covered walls and salvaged boards. If the great architecture of the West was the architecture of kings and gentry, then Japan's contribution to world building was the *sukiya* style for the common people. Izue's work is a great affirmation of the power of applied thought. But beyond returning tea house art to the budgetary realm of ordinary people, does Izue's work have a broader message for Japan's modern concept of architectural and urban 'beauty'?

The architect stresses the need to distinguish between two Japanese terms for beauty he believes are mistakenly used interchangeably; *kirei*, which connotes a 'clean' beauty that subsequently gets dirty and needs replacing, and *utsukushii*, the beauty he explains as 'being like a Japanese pickle that improves and gains flavour with age.' The modern emphasis on *kirei* has had a huge influence on the urban condition

of Japan leading directly to the widespread 'scrap-and-build' mentality. It is an economic beauty that has made the stock exchange, but not cities, shine. In a world of finite resources and spiralling maintenance costs, Izue claims that what Japan really needs from now on is a cultured aesthetic beauty of *utsukushii* architecture.

There is a certain irony in his proposal of what sounds like a Western methodology to preserve Japanese aesthetics. His notion of preservation as valuing the survival of old buildings is what has made the existence of traditional architecture an integral part of successive periods of 'modern' architecture – in the West. It is Japan, after all, that rebuilds Ise Shrine, its most renowned shrine, every two decades in a cycle of rebirth that has kept the tradition, but not the original building, alive for a thousand years. Rather than seeing, as Izue claims, Japan as a modern victim of scrap-and-build, perhaps it was the originator of it.

But if Izue's work at Bou-Bou-an seems too esoteric or too specialised a project type to really test his aesthetic theory, then an earlier project, the Hotel Liberty, is a fascinating contrast. Forget aesthetics, the function is completely contemporary: if the tea house was the meeting salon in Ikkyu's age, this is something to which contemporary commoners are able to relate, a love hotel. Sandwiched between a highway and river embankment in downtown Osaka, the roughcast area now seems a backwater of the city's industrial legacy – the kind of place that looks and smells like it probably had a glorious past, but has now faded way past sepia and is into grey scales. Towering up out of the ground, the building's metallic facade is a curious cocktail, one part soft natural forms with graduated shadows, one part violent intrusion into the cityscape. It seems to be both a natural extrusion up out of the site and a codified series of sexual metaphors: like an early Lauren Bacall, although it stays fully clothed, it makes you believe something is just about to happen. Izue's rhythmic curves for the building's exterior were created from aluminium sheeting, interrupted only by the windows of the restaurant incised into the seventh floor. Both this hotel and a later project, the Zinc

The Zinc Restaurant and Gas Station (1995) is 1,546 m² of organic metallic revelry. One corner of the ground floor of the triangular site houses the gas station with parking for twenty-five cars, the two restaurants on the second floor are topped by the third-floor hall.

Hotel Liberty, Osaka.

Restaurant and Gas Station (1995), explore the organic nature of industrial materials. The dichotomy this represents is more closely related to the whole question of aesthetics than might at first seem to be true. It forces you to see that there are two sides to materials that frequently get confused: the harsh reality of their industrial genesis and the image that shadows them of cheap, clean, common goods, one step away from trash, and the fact that they are the contemporary incarnation of Ikkyu's aesthetics of common goods, for common uses, for common life. The 'traditional' wooden structure of tea-house architecture is a warm and comforting illusion to be sure, but finally no more than that. The aesthetics that Ikkyu spoke of were not connected with history but rather with the apprehension of materials and the experience, not the image, associated with their

use. Both Bou-Bou-an and the Hotel Liberty illustrate not only the range of Izue's work, but just how important it is in Japan. It combines two seemingly intractable opposites that have bedevilled so much of the 'tradition' debate there: it is much more traditionally 'Japanese' than the work of other architects trying to interpret historic notions of space, and yet profoundly individual.

Whether he is right in thinking it could be a hundred years before the real value of his work is realised is difficult to say, but let's hope Izue's designs are a step towards recapturing the original beauty of the arts of traditional Japan – often lost today in the rarefied pedigree that surrounds so much of the 'cultural heritage' – where it ultimately matters much less how you made it, than how you find it. ■

What is the driving philosophy behind your architecture?

In essence my architecture is the architecture below zero. I want to tie Japanese traditional beauty with Japanese modern-day architecture and I believe that Japanese culture or beauty is related to a negative sense. Everywhere in the world, including Japan, uses advertising, so it now seems – superficially – that there is a positive answer to everything. But my idea of Japanese beauty is a kind of opposite one, a negative feeling, a beauty below zero. Japan has this aesthetic history that goes back 1,200 years and so for people to understand my concept of beauty will probably take until the next century!

This is a negative feeling towards what?

Well I'm going to talk about that later! Do you know the German philosopher Max Picard? He wrote a book entitled *The Silent World*. The book started with the following phrase: that the essence of God is silence, the essence of human beings is words. He also said that, although this might sound strange, God was a

kind of silent type! The last part of Japanese aesthetics is silence. So to summarise, there is a kind of line with talking as a positive action and on the other minus side, silence as a kind of internal language of the heart. Japanese people intuitively understand this idea of silence. Basho Matsuo [1644–94], the most famous poet from the Edo period, wrote the following poem that everyone studies in elementary school: 'how still it is here – stinging, into the stones, the locust's trill'. Which means in a quiet place even the small sound is very powerful.

Sen-no-Rikyu, the father of the tea ceremony, when asked to explain the aesthetic of the tea ceremony, recalled the poem of the Heian period poet, Teika Fujiwara [1162–1241],: 'when I look around, there is not even a flower, red leaves there. I'm in a rush mat hut on the beach, what a plaintive and lonely evening, isn't it? I feel an indication of late fall'. If we just cut the poem into sections then from the first two lines everyone would imagine the scene of shimmering autumn leaves. But the next phrase, 'I'm in a rush mat hut on the beach', is negative and rejects that image. However, it isn't completely rejected and some of it is retained in the brain. The next phrase 'what a plaintive and lonely evening, isn't it?' creates the image of a very poor dwelling. And 'I feel an indication of late fall' creates an even lonelier image. But the mind subconsciously superimposes the image of the flowers in front of that poor building – it is a kind of silence isn't it? It exists only in the mind. That poet wanted to decorate the image of that poor dwelling with the image of flowers, and I would like to take that philosophy and translate it into architecture.

Do you know *suibokuga*, a form of calligraphy painting? In the sense that there is no colour, it is a minus or negative aesthetic. It's a kind of negative beauty that asks Japanese people to imagine the colours behind the black and white of the painting. So *sumi-e* is one of the negative aesthetics, as are the aesthetic of the tea ceremony and *haiku* poems according to Ikkyu. There is also the beauty of *ikebana* and when you go to a tea house there is always a single flower at the entrance. There is a Japanese saying: 'thick but thin, thin but thick'. The Western way with a lot of flowers, a great volume of flowers, is a kind of positive beauty, but the Japanese way with only one flower is the negative aesthetic. It's not the volume of flowers but the heart of the flower you can find, and also the heart of the background scene. So I have mentioned flowers and art. Next, do you know *Noh* theatre? The main theme is usually after death, the image of the devil or a ghost. When people see the *Noh* performance they think it was good but they slowly forget and a year later they cannot remember the story, but still remember it was good. So in all forms of art, in Japan, it is always a minus world, a world of negative beauty.

Since the Meiji Restoration in 1868, we have been influenced by a lot of Western thought and it has made us lose something, including the negative Japanese mentality of beauty under the influence of these positive aesthetics. So instead we are moving forward towards positive things which have been created under the influence of Western society including, for example, advertising on TV. Japan now is a country obsessed with money. Like people who

have eaten so much that even delicious food isn't appetising, they have forgotten those spiritual things. When I was a kid, a long time ago in Japan, people had a more spiritual sensibility than today's young people. Young people now often forget to say thank you or pray facing Buddha at home, which they used to do before eating. Young people have forgotten to appreciate what they have. This is the result of too much food and too much money. This has made Japanese people forget everything that used to be of Japanese traditional mental beauty, the negative feeling. As a result, a very light – I mean in a spiritual sense – type of building is appearing in the architectural world here, like the prefab houses that sprung up after the earthquake in Nishinomiya and Kobe, in 1995, which symbolises that Japan has lost that mental quality. Those prefabs have no spirit, and no nationality.

Although you say that negative or simple beauty is a traditional Japanese aesthetic, the aesthetic of Modern architecture in the West was to make a clean table swept clear of all extras. Haven't you been influenced by this aspect of Modernism too?
Yes I have been influenced to a great extent. That's why I mentioned Max Picard, you know the guy who said that the quality of God is silence. In the world of art I would say I have been influences by Mondrian and Rothko, and in terms of architectural influences I would say Mies. But the point I was most influenced by from Western architecture was that of *chinmoku*, silence. People want to make silent architecture, to make silent cities. But what is silent material? What do you think?

How about Richard Meier's white spaces, where the colour is extracted to remove the material's quality, leaving only the pure silent experience of space?
Well white is a colour, not a material, but what is silent architectural material? I have spent quite a lot of time philosophising about this. [What is silent architectural material?] Do you know the expression 'to keep silent like a stone'? Stone is a silent material, it's used for gravestones. Churches, old Greek buildings

were all stone. The Parthenon is made from stone. Silence equals God, so stone equals God, so stone is a representative of silent materials. So stone is a silent material, but stone architecture made from aggregated small stones is in one sense poor, in the same way that Japan in some senses is wealthy but is in reality poor. We cannot now make something gorgeous by using stone, but there is 'man-made stone'. It is unclad concrete. If we use compacted concrete it is harder than cheap stone; so concrete is the silent material. It has the potential as an architectural material.

Among silent materials in Japan, we have the traditional *kawara* or clay tiles. But I need to explain a little bit more about what I mean by silent material in order that you may understand fully. I have to explain the real meaning of potential. I want to ask you what the difference is between culture and civilisation. It's a difficult question – even most university professors cannot answer it – no matter how many times you ask them! But in Japan, as in all other countries, people want to be cultured, no one wants to be civilised. But if you ask them the difference they cannot answer. No one is clear about the difference, no one knows the difference between them, so they cannot make cultured architecture or a cultured city. The philosopher Tetsurou Watsuji [1889–1960] explained the difference in simple terms. He said civilisation is taking vegetables from the farm and adding salad oil to them directly – it's a one-dimensional taste. Culture is to take the vegetables, put them in a box, cover with a stone, and leave them for a few weeks or months to make pickles, and the taste will change and become more mature. They will have a hidden taste. That hidden taste is called culture, cultural potential. So what is the architectural material that has a hidden taste? Stone and bricks are old materials and so they contain a hidden taste, but in the modern world we have to use glass, steel, concrete, and metal. But there is civilised metal and cultured metal. Copper is originally a red metal but after a few years becomes green – so it means after a few years the hidden taste is revealed. Steel is originally black but after half a year becomes metallic brown. So these materials become 'cultured

materials'. But stainless steel, you know that shiny stuff, is a civilised material. It doesn't reveal anything with age.

There is an important point related to this, the 'Bubble' economy has burst and so has maintenance. Without maintenance and just left alone, these materials will become more beautiful, like the temple architecture of Western Europe with its sculptured stone, copper and lead. The older they become, the more beautiful they become. Usually if people look up the word *furubiru* in the dictionary they use the two characters of 'get old', but that is a mistake. They should write it this way – using the characters for old and beautiful – so things become beautiful as they age. It means that they have potential.

Kirei and *utsukushii* are also two words for beauty that linguists misunderstand. No matter which dictionary you look them up in, they have always got it wrong. I think of *kirei* and *utsukushii* as being quite different. If something is *kirei* then if it becomes dirty you have to throw it away. It's the same story with the world's cities, they became *kirei* but they haven't become *utsukushii*. To become *utsukushii* they have to get beautiful as they get old. When people visit Europe or China, they always go to look at temple architecture. This is because the temples are made of brick, or tile, or copper, and so have become beautiful with age. If you go to Kouryuji or other old temples anywhere in Japan they are covered in bacteria. Dirty, but beautiful. The essence of *utsukushii* beauty is to gain beauty with age. The essence of *kirei* is dirty. It has become a question of sanitation! It's the same with prefabricated architecture, once it gets dirty it has to be thrown away. Nobody wants to give them a preservative order! We have to do the type of architecture that becomes beautiful with age; at least we have to make public architecture this way because it's society's common heritage. For economic activity, the *kirei* type of beauty is better: scrap and build; it's a question of money. Our housing or government buildings have to be *furubiru* from now on or we will all be in trouble. Now prefab housing is finished after ten years – even without an earthquake – but for buildings to last a hundred or two hundred years they must be the

Sited on the corner of the canal, the Kawara Tile Museum, Omihachiman (1995), is the central focus of a conservation area. Moreover, it is an embodiment of Izue's philosophy of recapturing the beauty of traditional materials to create architecture that improves as it ages.

Even the details of the paving at the Kawara Tile Museum are an expression of the *shin-gyou-sou* aesthetic.

type that acquires beauty with age. Big company's buildings may be *kirei* but they are never *utsukushii*. If we carry on as we are then Japan will be finished.

How did you become involved in the Kawara Museum?

Before we talk about the Kawara Museum there is one more thing I would like to say. In Ohmihachiman, a town just outside Kyoto, Boris, a missionary, came to Japan to teach, and while he was here he constructed a few buildings. The essence of God is silence, I mentioned previously, and the essence of Japan is silence also. Boris's Western architecture is well suited to the *kawara* architecture of Ohmihachiman. The reason they are compatible is that they have the same potential for silence. So architecture is to philosophise! And philosophy is architecture. I think this explanation enables you to understand my design policy. In the architecture I make, the architectural materials, light, smells, colours, brightness, darkness, all lead to one point – silence. *Kawara* is a silent

material. These *kawara* were from the Hanshin earthquake and I used them to pave the paths. These *kawara* are gods. After the Kobe earthquake people only appreciated these broken *kawara* for their function to keep off the rain, not for their cultural value, nor their aesthetic value. At the Kawara Museum I wanted to show these broken *kawara* as beautiful objects in their own right, so that is why I used them for the paving there.

There is the background of silent aesthetics to *kawara*. An old priest called Ikkyu made the aesthetic of *shin-gyou-sou*. There was a war in Kyoto with two factions, one in the north and one in the south. Yoshimitsu – who built Kinkakuji, the Golden Pavilion – wanted to have Ikkyu killed but was stopped by his mother. Instead, Ikkyu was forced to become a priest. As a priest he lived in Daitokuji Temple in Kyoto and was forced to obey many harsh Zen rules, until he was twenty years old – it was the *shin* type of lifestyle, very disciplined. He left Daitokuji at twenty and joined the common, worldly life outside, and his character became softer: *gyou* type. In later years he became *sou* type, he lived with a blind younger woman, forty-seven years his junior, a life of freedom. *Sou* means freedom, *shin* means severity, and *gyou* is an in-between state. In this way, aesthetics were decided. His calligraphy changed from *shin* to *gyou* to *sou* – although he described it as his lettering getting worse! But joking aside, he was led that way by aesthetics. Anyway, the front side of the museum is *shin* type, strict and bound together. There the *kawara* are bound together by steel strips. Do you know Zeami [1364–1443], the founder of *Noh* theatre? He said silence is beautiful. From movement to rest, from rest to movement, the time space between them shouldn't be vacant. Art is used to make this intermediate spatial interval interesting. For the exterior *sou*, or free space, I used grass instead of something with a strong form like a pine tree. So it implies freedom. The Kawara Museum garden has a large carp playing in the paving pattern – it's between *shin* and *sou*, and represents *gyou*. This is what Ikkyu said should be interesting. Well that's the background to the concept of the Kawara Museum. The site, in an old area of the town, was originally a *kawara* factory and there was a proposal to tear it down and replace it with an apartment building, an idea completely opposed by everyone who lived nearby. So the council decided to buy the land and build a *kawara* museum there instead, and they held a design competition that I won.

Old *kawara* had a water absorption capacity of between 7 per cent and 15 per cent but modern *kawara* have a water absorption capacity of zero, or at most 3 per cent. Why is it bad for them to take up water? It is because in Japan's cold winter, pores in the tiles hold water that then freezes, expands and cracks the tiles where the surface stretches. So that water absorption capacity has been reduced. What is beautiful about *kawara* is the aspect of co-existence with nature – this is another area where Japan is going wrong, all this recent talk of living with nature. Old *kawara* always had moss growing on them. Because they absorbed water, they could harmonise with nature, and had a flavour about them because of it. Modern tiles, those with zero absorption

capacity, absorb neither water nor human emotion. My house in Kyoto is sixty years old but it never leaks even in heavy rain. Old *kawara* were tender towards people in sense and feeling. The other point is that the old material *kawara* were made from gave them a patchy colour. These days this patchiness is considered as evidence of low quality. However, a man called Heihachi Fukuda said that what makes *kawara* interesting is precisely this patchy colouration. With the new tiles which use a different process, the 'quality' has increased, but they are so even coloured they look as though they have been painted. They may have improved in quality but their essential character has diminished. If they have no blurred colour then they have no culture. These new *kawara* with no character and water absorption, are you really going to use them to make a *kawara* museum, I asked? I thought I would be sure to lose the competition, but I won! The straight and narrow approach to the museum represents the *shin* type, the stoic type, strict type, so there are no beautiful flowers present; instead just simple, black bamboo, the type that doesn't flower. Plants are also divided into *shin-gyou-sou*. And in order to make an interesting space that fits with the philosophy of *shin-gyou-sou* I put a weeping cherry tree here with an old type of lantern to capture the mood of the old licensed quarters that were around there. Thus the architecture itself is governed by *shin-gyou-sou*, the outside spaces and circulation routes are also *shin-gyou-sou*, and the plants, *shin-gyou-sou*, so my policy is that everything must be divided into the three stages of *shin-gyou-sou*.

But when your architectural work is based on this one policy, how does that relate to the functional reality or requirement that the spaces must also satisfy? Isn't there always some limitation born out from the function?

Oh yes, just one of them by itself is no good. Because they are in fact separate. Bou-Bou-an is a tea room I designed and for which I won an IAA Prize, and again it is divided into *shin-gyou-sou*. For this project the budget was also very limited. Usually this type of space in Japan would cost 100,000,000 *yen*, even a cheap one would be 50,000,000 *yen*. The tea room is probably the most expensive architecture in the world. But the client only had 5,000,000 *yen* – to build a one billion *yen* building. I told them that I couldn't build a tea ceremony room, but I could build a tea house. Adjacent to the site was a warehouse which was made of what we call slate, the cheapest material in Japan, and so I used it not to make a *chashitsu*, a tea ceremony room, but a *chagoya*, a tea house.

At the entrance we used checker plate, the material they use for drain covers or manhole covers, you know, with a non-slip surface – it's a cheap material too – and also broken *kawara* tiles from nearby housing. In terms of Japanese aesthetics this corresponds to the *shin* type aesthetic. For the *sou* type space I used old newspapers, and I told my secretary to fetch some from nearby hotels. It was no good getting Japanese newspapers because they would just be read as news-print, so in order for them not to be read I picked up French, Korean, Russian and English newspapers, which I then stuck on the walls. *Sou* means freedom of speech. So that is why I used newspapers as representative of freedom of opinion for the *sou* type. In the *shin* type space I used an iron H-beam onto which I poured *soya* sauce to make it start rusting. Iron, which I said earlier is one of the silent materials, changes to a rusty-brown colour over time and releases a hidden 'flavour' of age. So that is *sou* type space. Between *shin* and *sou* we need an interesting space, and as you can see there's a nude photo of a woman stuck here and without it the space wouldn't have been interesting or sophisticated at all. The question is why is there a nude here? Katsuichiro Kamei, the philosopher, said 'religion makes woman wear many clothes, Renaissance makes woman naked'. I wanted to make a renaissance of the tea room so I chose the naked woman! I wanted to make a renaissance between the *shin* and *sou* periods, a renaissance of the tea ceremony. I wanted to destroy, to hammer a big nail into the traditional Japanese way. Usually the tea room is very expensive using costly materials and craftsmen, but I used only very cheap materials. The H-beam I used cost only 1,000 *yen* for the whole thing. I wanted to shock the traditional way of Japanese architecture.

Because of the expense involved, traditional Japanese things have started to die out. But originally Sen-no-Rikyu made the tea ceremony for the common people, not for the privileged, the aesthetic of the poor people was the tea room. From the mountain's broken branches, or parts from shipwrecked boats, and ash from burnt wheat – the materials for the tea room were those that poor people had access to. The origin of aesthetics in Japan was the tea room for the poor people. Great architecture all over the world is the architecture of kings and the upper classes. Japan was the only country to make *sukiya* architecture, to make aesthetics for the poor people, and the original creator was Sen-no-Rikyu. But now it's reversed and only the very rich can afford *sukiya* architecture. It has become like those *ryotei*, high-class restaurants. I wanted to return the tea ceremony to the ordinary people, to say to people that you don't need high-class stones or high-class columns to make a tea house but that you can do it with zinc plate. You can do it with old newspapers. You can use old broken tiles for the garden. Anything you can get your hands on. I wanted to show that there is nothing cheaper to use to make a tea house. I wanted to discover the potential, how to put that spiritual potential into these cheap materials. This is a meditation space. For that, do you need expensive materials? For my tea house I didn't use even one carpenter. It's the world of silence. Usually the tea room is dark but this one is bright because of its materials but it will gradually get darker – *furubiru*, beauty that increases with age – so that's why I used these materials.

But wouldn't you like to explore the potential of expensive materials?

This type of cheap architecture is very challenging. To use expensive materials, of course you get the expensive space. If you use high-grade materials – of course it looks rich. Everyone in Japan thinks that zinc board and these cheap materials are boring. But to reveal the beauty of these boring materials, that's my power and capability. That is art. Of course if you use marble you create a place of high quality but to show the potential of these cheap materials is my

The alcove in Bou-Bou-an's metallic interior.

The old newspapers at Bou-Bou-an make a collage evocative of Tai-an, Sen-no-Rikyu's famous Kyoto tea room. Just visible in the distant corner of the alcove is the feminine form that Izue used to express his hope of a tea-ceremony renaissance.

architecture, my architectural skill. I say 'to make something interesting from something that is not interesting, now that is really interesting'. This notion is one important Japanese aesthetic. This is made possible by thinking about the heart of the material, something interesting inside, not the surface. There is a mentality or emotion within us that is drawn out by making something interesting from old newspapers and slate board. Do you know the Yoshimoto Comedy troupe?

The one that includes the director of the film *Sonatine*, Beat Takeshi?

Yes. Well that type of interest is just surface interest, like using marble in architecture. But the aesthetic of making something interesting from something that isn't interesting, now that is an emotional interest. Thus there is superficial interest and emotional interest. The main concept of my architecture is to create something with that emotional aesthetic. That's what I want to say. ■

KAN IZUE
1931 Born in Kyoto

Education:
1957 Bachelor of Civil Engineering, Ritsumeikan University, Kyoto

Employment:
1951   Worked as an architect in the technical art section of Kyoto University
1957   Entered Takenaka Building Contractors
1976   Established Kan Izue Architectural Design Office
1984   Lecturer at Osaka Municipal University
1991   Reorganised company into Izue Architectural Design Office
1992-94 Director of the Architectural Association of Osaka Prefecture
1992-94 Director of the Japanese Architectural Association
1991-99 Lecturer at the Osaka University of Fine Arts

Major projects:
1977   House in Marugame
1982   House in Sakasedai
1989   Tokyo Chikuyo-tei
1991   House of Clouded Moon
1994   Zinc-walled tea room 'Bou-Bou-an', Nagoya
1995   Kawara Tile Museum, Omihachiman
1998   Zen House

Awards:
1984   Grand Prix at the Japan Interior Design Award for the House in Sakasedai
1990   Grand Prix at the Commercial Space Design Award for Tokyo Chikuyo-tei
1991   Yoshida Isoya Award for Tokyo Chikuyo-tei
1996   Special Prize at the International Academy of Architecture for Bou-Bou-an
1997   Gold Prize at the 9th Iraka Award / Prize of the Minister of International Trade and Industry

Kan Izue was interviewed in his office in Osaka on 14 June 1997

Exhibitions:
1988   Exhibition of the Architecture of Kan Izue, Gallery Ma, Tokyo
1998   World Architecture Triennale, Nara
1998   Contemporary Architect Exhibition III

Publications:
Izue, K. (1981) *Detail of House Design, Tradition of Suki and Modern, House works of Izue Kan*, Tokyo: Kenchikushiryokenkyusha
Izue, K. (1984) *House House*, Tokyo: Gakugeishuppansha
Izue, K. (1986) *Izue Kan, Flowers of Burai*, Tokyo: Maruzen
Izue, K. (1989) *A Separate Volume of New Architecture, Series of Japanese Modern Architects, Izue Kan*, Tokyo: Shinkenchikusha
Izue, K. (1996) *Beauty of Sukiya*, Tokyo: Kashimashuppankai

Snapshots of a Residential Tradition

Yoshiji Takehara

「 I believe that it is a vital part of architecture to make connections between past and present 」

Perhaps it's the lack of open space but Japanese TV uses houses as locations for everything from suburban dreaming to murderous mayhem. And then there are the ads. Watch a week of TV there and you will see housing packaged up in pursuit of sales of everything from soap to sin, and back again. But you would have to be a couch potato with your own private Idaho to find houses that look traditional, but use contemporary materials, feel contemporary, but are deeply wedded to traditional notions of space.

The purists might blame the influx of 'Western' materials that have destroyed the traditional preference for wood, while others see the start of the problem as a younger generation who love high-rise living and comforts any creature would dream of. Ask Yoshiji Takehara, Osaka architect, founder of Moo Architecture Workshop and winner of the Togo Murano Award in 1996, and you get a very different answer. Forget form and function, he has developed a highly original approach to housing design that reinterprets Japan's residential traditions.

At the Yamasaka House II (1985) in Osaka's Higashi-Sumiyoshi Ward he designed a three-floor house for a couple with two children. Completely occupying the 149 square metre site, the building offers a benign facade to the street. Punctuated by an abstract arrangement of small square and rectangular windows and openings, it nevertheless has a kind of warm, earthy familiarity to it – like Picasso might paint the face of old uncle, not beautiful exactly but friendly and dependable. Inside, the house plan is divided by a cross, the rooms connected by a courtyard and series of open-air terraces that bring light into the interior and give sufficient 'distance' to the family's rooms. Made of exposed concrete, wood flooring and with large frosted-glass windows the house seems more modern inside than consciously historic. So where is the tradition?

It might not readily be apparent from the building's plan, but the ambiguous space of the terraces, or *ma*, is vital in making the spaces Japanese. In traditional houses there was a main room and separate *hanare* with the circulation around a *doma* – literally an earthen space – or courtyard. It is an historical type that would be hard to use in multi-storey housing now, and so Takehara has reinvented it, readapting the house plans to a modern style of living that brings the Japanese feeling held through history to contemporary life. This kind of uninterrupted, interconnected space that doesn't have a real function – and so has been

driven out of most modern prefab housing – Takehara surprisingly believes is closely linked to Modernism. Rather than the literal historical referencing of Post-Modernism, he believes Modernism's reductivist mood of uncluttered spaces, makes it easier for *ma* type space to be achieved, and for him to realise what he calls his 'Modernism for the Japanese language'.

For the Higashi-Hiroshima House (1997), the 525 square metre plot gave him a much more extensive site to work with. For the family of five he took a much more liberal, and literal, approach to '*ma* connective space'. The two-storey structure has five main rooms that enclose a courtyard on three sides. Outdoor routes, covered but usually open at one side, divide but link the spaces via a series of walls, screens and openings. The surprising complexity of the routes this creates would make it a great place to set a *samurai* drama – you could hide whole regiments around the corners and never be seen. Looking out from the room interiors you see fragments of views of other spaces and the garden. Sometimes in contemporary concrete and glass, sometimes in more traditional *tatami* and stone, this layering of both materials and time means Takehara's version of architecture is powerfully different: usually you just get one without the other, very rarely both. His inspiration for this project was the Kouhouan in Daitokuji Temple, Kyoto. It's the type of architecture where you have to go around outside – even if it's cold – on a long path to get from one room to the next. Suddenly, yet finally, you turn a corner and arrive.

Applied flexibly, Takehara's new take on tradition effectively tackles the thorniest part of trying to be a modern traditionalist. You cannot try to turn back the clock without looking dated, alternatively you end up looking like a little Post-Modernist if you do nothing but quote. Not just in these two projects but in all his work he has the good grace to let history speak for itself, and the good sense to let the architecture be contemporary.

So much for the past. What about the future? Takehara hopes to make a new type of *ma* space that reflects sociographic changes with smaller families, weaker ties. He is now proposing a new type of

Yamasaka House II (1996), Osaka, looking back to the street from the end of the roji.

The Higashi-Hiroshima House (1997), courtyard seen through the low window from the entrance.

collective housing with *roji*, or courtyard spaces for neighbours or different types of family group, extending the Japanese tradition in a new way. Driving his reinterpretation of tradition is both a sense of loss for the past when materials gained beauty with age and a belief that architecture's role in society is to make something beautiful and permanent.

His work is very different from those bastions of kitsch Japanese space, the bars and snacks that lie littered around the streets of all cities there. Their Japanesque *wafu* interiors might fool a few tourists, but just using traditional materials without any consciousness towards proportions clearly doesn't work. Materials alone won't keep traditions alive. It's what you do with them. Takehara has discovered something important: the key question is knowing

Higashi-Hiroshima House. The tatami reception room at the entrance seen from the courtyard side.

which deep, significant, and long-standing tradition you venerate, before jumping up and down on its grave.

Certainly there is no shortage of people attempting to keep 'traditions' alive in Japanese architecture. I just wonder if they know what the word 'alive' means. The development of architecture through history has

been to extract the essence of the old traditions and add on a little something new. Takehara's work isn't a conscious attempt to build in a historical style but through combining the essence of traditional Japanese buildings with this century's techniques the final architecture is something new and surprising.

For those architects who work with tradition in Japan there is frequently something anti-climactic about the result. You see their work, read the explanatory text – twice – and still cannot quite feel right about the final result. It's as though a bride throws her bouquet into a melée of single friends, only to have it land short on a mike stand at the edge of the stage. The symbolism just doesn't work if your aim is off. Takehara's housing projects seem to have found just the balance between modernity and mores. Rather like those old Identikit photos of wanted criminals, they only really come into focus when you slightly squint up your eyes. As the images drift in and out of focus, they start to inhabit a floating world where monotone begets colourised early Technicolor, becomes the full Fujichrome: a marvellous picture where history, materials, traditions and space all mix into one.

It might be a little surprising at first that it took a politician to say what every designer ought to know. But when Harry Truman said the only thing new in the world is the history you don't know, he elucidated a truth that, in the search to create something 'new' in design, often isn't too openly acknowledged. At least in Yoshiji Takehara one Japanese architect not just understands this, but expresses it too. ■

How important is context in your work?

Well, when I start to think about architecture I always consider the place the building will be sited and how the structure of the family living there will relate to it, how the family will be able to continue living there, I mean for an extended time. I am studying Japanese architecture so the materials that Japan has available and how they can be incorporated into architecture is the question that is always in the back of my mind. When I first heard your question just now I was struck

The 'connecting space' between the family room and room 1 at the Yamasaka House II.

The Koryocho House. Room 1 seen from the corridor in front of room 2.

by how big the topic was, just how fundamental it was to architecture, but when I actually build something such issues remain as background thoughts and what really is important is what architecture to realise in that place.

By the power of the place are you referring to the actual site or the wider environment that surrounds it?

Many of my projects are in Osaka where the traditional row houses are called *machiya*, other projects in Kyoto are based on their *nagaya* type of row housing. But what is important is that there is a certain relationship between the length of the site, which faces onto the street making a visible contact with the surrounding town, and the depth of the site. The proportions of the building's volume are determined by these two factors but the internal layout – whether to use a *roji* passageway or *nakaniwa* courtyard, whether these open spaces should be at the front or rear of the building – depends on other factors like the site's orientation and the position of the sun. The distance of people's sight lines determines the stopping places or *tachidomaru*, where one would stop and turn. For example, at the Yamasaka House II, there is a *roji* that extends from the street right along the side of the house and gives the impression that the house extends further back. The *roji* is planted with greenery so that the entrance to the house, although physically constrained, feels easy to enter. When you stand in the *tachidomaru* spot and look back, you see the town.

What do you mean by *tachidomaru*?

The meaning of *tachidomaru*, in this case, is to pause, stop and look back. For example, you would not just say hello instantly. You would think about what you wish to say, using the pause to consider. When you build small houses, you measure the space as much as possible. As you think about the space, the place or land itself expands. So, although you consciously think the space is too narrow for people to walk through, you try to make the space appear to expand when people walk in so the space seems much bigger than it really is. Japanese architecture is built that

way. If you go to a temple in Kyoto for example and there is a place you would like to get to, you can never get there directly. You are always forced to move, to walk around, make turns, and through this continuous movement your views change too, and from this process your destination is confirmed prior to arrival. What you first saw and expected as the scene that would greet you is changed through views that reveal themselves as you progress along the route, and this traditional method of design is what I try to incorporate in my residential houses. And at the urban scale when you look at the structure of the town, it first appears extremely dense, but through the addition of these small spaces and ways of movement, becomes a comfortable place to live. So with these passages and courtyards and ways of appreciating of the scene, I try to place my architecture into the city. It might sound strange but I try to build the house as inconveniently as possible. In this house in Nara, the Koryocho House, here too various views are revealed to you as you pass along the *roji*. The land is not naturally narrow, yet I purposely built the houses apart, and made paths between them. To make various things happen as people walk between houses is an essential part of my architecture.

Is this related to the *hanare* type of traditional room arrangement?

Yes. In the old days there was a main room where people lived and a separate room that was reached by an outdoor route. In the centre was an earthen space, a *doma*, where people congregated for various activities before separating again, going off in various directions. So people assembled in areas like the *doma*, *roji* and *nakaniwa*, and this historical pattern continued for generations but unconsciously has gradually disappeared, as it became seen, in a practical sense, as a difficult system to use. As much as it is possible I would like to reintroduce these notions into my houses so that the communication and emotion people had in the past, and have lost, can be reintroduced.

How do you balance the history of Japanese architecture with the reality that there is a body of Modern architecture that is acknowledged throughout the world too, and which exists in considerable quantity here in Japan itself?

Well the courthouse type is a facet of architecture throughout the world, and in Japan too we had this kind of structural composition. Japanese courthouses were quite well developed as a style but when it came to row housing it wasn't courtyards but *roji* that became the method of introducing open space into the arrangement. In Europe it became a patio. But wherever you go you find that openings from the building to the surroundings existed. I suppose there are two rationales for setting basic gardens or courtyards in our domestic houses. One is to protect us from enemies. The other idea of gardens comes from our fundamental way of life. I would like to rethink gardens or paths as reflecting one's life instead of protecting you from enemies. Also I would like to conceive a house plan which suits the current Japanese ordinary family, rather than that of the old houses which were owned by extended families.

To continue this thought a little further, let us look at the example of the Higashi-Hiroshima House, where the site was larger than as is typical. Here I was aware that there was a building and a pre-existing building and there were three elements with a large roof which gave the appearance of it being one house. But in fact, depending upon the route taken through the garden or *roji*, people gather at places with a purpose and I decided to create such a mechanism. The house faces the road and people visiting enter here and turn, so as they pass along this stone *roji* path the sight line continues far off into the distance, so that you can see the greenery that surrounds the courtyard from the entrance. From the opposite direction, the view is of a *doma* space. You look across the corridor, across the courtyard garden, across the stone paving, and see the greenery the other side. This axis continues right through. Light passes along it, wind blows along it, you can see greenery: there are a whole series of numerous senses associated with it. The linear nature of a *roji* enables such scenes to be experienced, if I draw analogies with a camera, in a telephoto way, as you pass along here and arrive at the entrance you

The view towards the
decking from the
approach *roji* at the
Higashi-Hiroshima
House (1997), Nara.

see things through a kind of wide-angle. When you enter this spot, you can see the fallen petals of flowers and when seated can really get in touch with your feelings. Between the two areas of the house is a connecting space – we call it a *tsunagi no ma* – sometimes it may be a courtyard garden or *roji*. So people can go wherever they want in order to get together, but for privacy they are separated. Therefore they gather in the public rooms. It is completely flexible. Sometimes people may get together on the terrace, at other times, or in different groups, it may be the kitchen area. Each house should have a spot called *kaku,* that means core, in which the family can gather. In my designs I consider the various mechanisms of orientation for the family to get there. I can see these mechanisms in the house plans of most Japanese traditional houses. The main example of this in Kyoto in what is called *shoinzukuri*, where there is this linearity of connecting spaces. Do you know the Daitokuji Temple in Kyoto?

Yes.

Well one temple in that larger complex is called Kouhouan, and it has this type of sequence where you go through the entrance, walk around the outdoor corridor – not through the rooms – and then suddenly and unexpectedly you reach your destination. There it is before you. So I use devices in my own work, such as this *tsunagi no ma*, this connecting space, whereby you move through a sequence of spaces to reach your destination. I seriously believe that the intermediate parts of a place play an extremely important role. Through such a system each individual member of the family is able to maintain their privacy, but through using the circulation routes, they bump into nature, and come to feel, how can I say it, the real importance of the family.

I can understand appreciation and affection for those traditional architectural devices, but the reality is that the lifestyle accompanying the use of such spaces has now changed irrevocably. Is the old spatial construction, or composition, still meaningful for modern Japanese lifestyles? For example, you used unclad concrete for this house. It's a twentieth-

century material, even if you use it in a traditional way. Isn't the combination of traditional notions of space and modern materials doomed to be unsuccessful, from both directions?

The bulk of my work is residential. For example, Tadao Ando's exploration of concrete in his projects is very different to my approach. For example, if a wooden construction, from whatever point of view, seems best for a particular site then that is what I will use. But in another case, for reasons relating to the surrounding context or because of the need to provide protection against fire risk, I may use concrete. Or if the site is quite spacious and after considering how to structure the views and spaces, I may want to use a stone wall to create the space. So what I do is to stand at the site and read the situation and from that comes the solution in terms of material, structural system, organisation. Recent housing in Japan so far has just been built, straight off, without much thought. The style of architecture should change as the closeness of family relations changes. For example, if I build the house for my family, my children may not want to take it over as it is. Nevertheless, I want to leave something permanently behind to remind them of the house as it originally was. I suppose ruins work that way. I believe that it is a vital part of architecture to make these connections between past and present. Leaving something behind means that there will be connections. To make many identical buildings that will all reach the end of their life at the same time? What I think is that it is essential, in parallel with such prefab housing, to have some houses where the relationship between family and spaces is carefully explored. It is these carefully thought out works that will bring the traditions to the next century.

Are the dimensions you use related to the traditional *shaku-sun* or are they derived from modern modules?

They aren't the old dimensions but are new ones born out from my experience on site. This floor dimension for example is 3,200. If you use the dimensional method using tatami, it would be, in fact, the standard 3,640. There is one standard traditional dimension that was based on the tatami formula of dividing the

Definition of **shaku** and **sun**:
Originally imported into Japan from China the shaku is the basic unit of Japanese proportions. Almost equivalent to the Imperial foot, its 303 mm can be further divided into sun, each one tenth of the measurement, themselves divided into ten bun. Shaku have a direct relationship to the tatami size (3 shaku by 6 shaku), and can be used in double numbers such as 1shaku1sun, although the standard residential housing units are more usually mixed, like a pillar at 3sun5bun, or 105 mm.

tatami, called tatamiwari. The measurement that we usually use is 960. The next is 1,920. The next is 2,880. The next is 3,840. The dimensions are calculated in this manner. When I want to know how to calculate the dimension, sometimes I adopt half the size of the measurement when the area of available ground size is small, for example 480. I choose the units in this manner, and I incorporate the dimensions I perceive best. This is the same for height, when you stand up or sit down, you check the height of your chair, for example, thus this type of measurement I use in my design work is related to both tradition and function but is adapted to optimise the actual space. After searching through various dimensional applications, it is possible to make spaces more effectively compact. So the dimensions I use have been derived from a unit base extension concept. However, as to whether it is a traditional measurement, it is not because it has been altered by transposing it to suit modern life.

Also do you know that the basis of Japanese proportions is an odd number? A carpenter's square in Japan, the width of the square, is 15 millimetres. Carpenters always use this device, for objects in the flat and for all measurement checks. If the carpenter draws a line with the device, fifteen always remains. So, fifteen is, in fact, the odd number. Fifteen is multiplied by three. In other words, the dimension can be divided. Japanese carpenters in the old days did not have a calculator, they calculated all the measurements in their heads. In doing so, they always used three. So, the measurements for objects have always been divided by an odd number, for example, *shoji* paper sliding partitions. This notion of three being a numerical base also applies to stones. So, for example, you place the first stone, second stone, and then at the third stone you change the direction, turn right or left,

then you might change at the fifth again, rather than at the fourth or second. Although not all cases are strictly in this form, the 15 millimetres of a Japanese carpenter's square effectively functions to a great extent in creating Japanese dimensional style. The figures I use now are mostly based on these kinds of calculation, divisible by three. For example *saburoku-jyuhachi* (3 x 6 = 18). If you use three, all of them can be divided by three.

Is the 'social message' of Modernism, its optimism and utopian hopes for housing, something that you can relate to or are in interested in persuing? Is there a message to contemporary society that you would like to express through your work?

Well one message is that the period is continuously changing, isn't it. What I mean by that is that the family structure, the constituents of a 'family' are continuously changing, and there must surely be an architectural voice reflecting this phenomena. I think that architecture needs to respond to society, through housing. Aside from building up, tearing down, just constructing things in one style like duplicate prefabs, there is a type of architecture I designed that illustrates a different way of living. It makes use of materials that are examples of contemporary industrial goods, within which the 'taste' is inherent. Even if the interior is replaced, the framework remains. Even if a family lets the house to others, the atmospheric effect, or the certain culture that was formed previously, will remain. It is vital that the family is a serious consideration when we carry out work, rather than just simply designing and constructing a building that conforms to society.

What about the aesthetics of traditional gardens?

The way of making a garden for Japanese and for Western people is really quite different. For example, English gardens are more about plants, Japanese gardens have, in truth, more of an agricultural approach. I aim at a fusion between foreign objects, such as stones or gardens including trees, with the architecture. Therefore, I always consider how to create gardens more in terms of their relationship to the architecture than specific details. That idea of architecture's stance towards the city is an integral part of my thoughts. I do not see architectural 'beauty' as a static view of what is most attractive, but rather an experience for the people living there when the surrounding nature is incorporated. The reason why architecture that is three or four hundred years old is better than new architecture is that it has always been and continues to be beautiful and functional. I want to consider how we can achieve this in our contemporary work. It's not so much an objective 'beauty' but that a period's age is something that can be included in what we call 'beautiful'.

How do you feel about the urban condition in Japan?
Irrespective of what the people living there might think, the speed of change is continuing too fast. In the past, time was something that passed more slowly. Forget a hundred years ago, even twenty years ago the speed was so much slower. Despite the fact that people are not aware of the speed of our lifestyle in cities, things have started to move very fast, so now twenty-four-hour running cities, twenty-four-hour service cities, have been created. In addition, the change in commercial goods and the sheer pace of consumer change mean that people themselves feel that they are changing alongside. In fact, living in a city, particularly a city like Osaka with its *nagaya* housing, the relationship between the people living there and the city is being lost. In the old days, people used to have to utilise their spaces very effectively, but this is no longer so. The emergence of convenience stores is the most influential element that has changed the speed of city life. The convenience store is a place where you can buy goods without involving communication with other people. Convenience stores mean that shops have become refrigerators. The stuff that is bought in them is eaten and thrown away the same day. What will become of the town? Will it continue to become the place where everything is consumed within one day? But housing is not so disposable. For me, one part of creating a city is what to do about this speed. If a brake can be applied to this then gradually it can be changed.

Although the city has become chaotic and confused, it still hasn't spread to all facets of living and housing has been exempt. But time is running out and without care the world will be changed irrecoverably. But I believe it isn't too late yet. After the earthquake in Kobe in 1995 everything was decided in an incredible hurry, but why not take time to repair what needs doing? The reason given was that there was a housing shortage, however had it proceeded more slowly then the kind of town that's developing now could have been avoided. So it's a question of proceeding slowly and taking time. Without this, places will become more confused and some very strange cities will be the result. If housing is proceeded with at great pace then prefabs will be the result, identical objects spread everywhere, and the city itself will become separate from the people who live there. That is a huge problem. But if even one example of a better form of housing exists, it will have a great influence and in that sense an architect's social role is significant. If we are asked whether architects can answer socio-architectural questions, I feel strongly that the task of architects in modern society should be to humanise their messages to counter all the fast changes in modern life. There is also one more thing I would like to stress. The notion that architecture can be forgotten about and will still carry on almost by itself without any designer's input is something that I am not very keen on. Architecture is more important than that.

How will housing change in the future?
Well as I said earlier, the plan is changing and the family is too. Families now are becoming smaller and more fragmented and so I would like to make residences that are more collective in style, where two or three 'families' can live together. I mean that instead of an individual house, through connecting courtyards or passageways, a new relationship will be created. Instead of just one's own house in isolation, I believe that a kind of unit exists which was evident in former Japanese communities. Next-door neighbours on both sides was the basic close-knit unit and they offered the gaps between the houses to use as a communal area rather than building their houses in

all the available space. I really would like to design compact, smaller scale old-style communities, residential clusters which are based on this concept. I would like to do this, not in a place with large open spaces, but right in the very heart of the city. Families at the moment are in a very strange situation so in order to achieve this it will take another ten years from now. My aim is to introduce a foreign layout and arrangement of living spaces to more Japanised practices, but I wonder whether it is feasible or not given current individual residential concepts and practice. Rather than have Government offices set out regulations, instead each individual could become aware of their potential themselves. What I want to say is that cities are becoming chaotic and communication between people is disappearing, but in spite of this, prefabricated houses are still being built. I am sure there must be architectural styles which are more suited and I wonder whether there are methods to solve these problems by using an odd number; ideally I think three living in proximity is best.

Is there one phrase that really sums up your architectural work?

It's what in Japanese we would call *ma no kenchiku*, the architecture of ambiguous spaces. I guess it's connected with expressions like *doma*, *nakaniwa* or *roji*. ■

Yoshiji Takehara was interviewed in his office in Osaka on 10 February 1998

YOSHIJI TAKEHARA
1948 Born in Tokushima Prefecture

Education:
1972   Graduated Architecture Course of Osaka Institute of Technology Junior College
1972-75 Research student of Osaka City University

Employment:
1978   Established Moo Architect Workshop, Osaka
1988   Lecturer at Osaka City University

Major Projects:
1985   Kohama House II, Osaka City
1990   Yoshiminosato House, Osaka Prefecture
1993   Tonnosu House, Wakayama Prefecture
1995   Hozancho House, Toyonaka City
1996   Yamasaka House II, Osaka City
1997   Higashi-Hiroshima House, Higashi-Hiroshima City
1997   Koryocho House, Nara Prefecture

Awards:
1996   9th Togo Murano Award
1997   4th Kansai Architect Award
1999   Japan Institute of Architects Annual Architectural Design Commendation

Exhibitions:
1997   Commemorative exhibition of Kansai Architect Award, Kyoto
1997   Survey of Fumitaka Nishizawa, Gallery Ma, Tokyo

Publications:
Takehara, Y. (1997) *Design for Houses of Ma and Kaiyu*, Tokyo: Kenchikubunka / Shokokusha

Defending the Cultural Low Ground

Toru Murakami

「 Architects always seek a new style that they then use to suggest a new style of living – so architecture and society can move forward together 」

North America's igloo, Mongolia's pao, and England's thatched cottage have a lot to answer for – low light levels, cold drafts, poor sanitation and bed bugs. They have also all been partially responsible for giving the expression 'vernacular architecture' a bad name. Used to describe a local style of building in which ordinary houses are constructed, in Japan these private dwellings are simply called *minka*. Formed from locally available materials, their slightly more generous proportions and rougher edges have frequently left them the ugly sister to their thinner and more glamorous relative, the *sukiya* style epitomised by Katsura Imperial Villa. *Minka* unfortunately have tended to become the stuff of historical writings, NHK television period dramas and hobby-horses for the 'move-back-to-the-hometown' movement. This is a pity when you consider that in spite of all the attention in architecture lavished on the bizarre form, the unusual icon and the latest neo-whateverism, the base of the profession, with forty-thousand examples built a year in Japan, is housing.

To find out what has been happening to this tradition we should ask Hiroshima architect Toru Murakami. Over the last twenty years, he has been re-examining the vernacular tradition, and then bringing it up to

The House in Tsuyama (1994).

date. He is the creator of what he calls, in suitably unadorned prose, Modern Minka. Unlike other architects who have flocked to the metropolises of Osaka or Tokyo, he has remained in his provincial hometown, where his house designs have reflected the local style while adapting to the economic realities of the area. Or to put it in the vernacular, low cost. Which means rather surprisingly, concrete. Rather than use wood, the material in Japan that in common parlance is

The rooms, passageways and structures of the House in Tsuyama all appear to float on the thinnest film of water in the central pool. The design seems not just to challenge notions of architecture, but laws of physics themselves.

taken to mean tradition, Murakami has chosen a material that is usually associated with industrial buildings or cheap roadbase. Utilitarian, yes. Aesthetic object? No. He sees in concrete a material that he can mould into pure architectural forms. With good site supervision, concrete – almost any concrete – will meet the required criteria.

But what exactly then are the similarities to traditional *minka*? Not surprisingly, it's all about spaces. In his design for the House in Tsuyama (1994), he used two elements from traditional *minka*; the 3.6 metre module, and a composition of a basic living area combining bedroom, kitchen, bathroom and living room with a *hanare*. *Hanare* were special rooms not for daily use that were separated from the main structure. Murakami expanded this traditional concept to incorporate *hanare*: one a ground-floor *tatami* room set in a corner of the building, the other the second-floor children's bedrooms that were accessed from an outdoor slope open to the elements. The two slightly separate entities fit in with the family's functional needs but also require, like a temple entrance, a sequence of spatial experiences in order to reach them. Unifying these autonomous spaces is a series

of cantilevered aluminium louvres that project out over the central courtyard. Blurring views of the surrounding buildings they also dissipate the boundaries between interior and exterior spaces. With the rooms arranged around a central courtyard pool and the reflective unclad concrete surfaces, the spaces constantly segue in and out of focus. The transitions are so seamless it's not clear where one material starts and finishes, let alone what they are. Maybe that's Murakami's great gift here: tradition meets concrete, and they both win. By relaxing the 3.6 metre grid where it clashed with modern functional requirements in the kitchen and bathroom, and retaining the emphasis on horizontal planes and free-flowing, exterior–interior space, he has created a house where industrial materials, traditional aesthetics, twentieth-century living and post-'Bubble' economics are all mixed together and still feel right.

Originally *minka* were organised in villages of a few hundred inhabitants, perhaps a thousand at most. So how does Murakami relate his modern *minka* to the density of the contemporary city? For the House in Tsuyama, he created an oasis by arranging the main building and *hanare* to enclose a courtyard that is completely occupied by a shallow pool of water. The reflections of the pool bring nature's colour, tempo and dynamism into the house and animate the colourless pallet of concrete, steel and glass. The series of cantilevered louvres then links this internal nature with the neighbouring city, but in a very contemporary, fractured way. The only doubt hanging over his approach is that finally the materials cannot lose their popular contemporary associations no matter how 'traditional' the spatial concepts behind their use. You can only suspend belief so far.

Murakami says his driving design philosophy has been to make architecture as close as possible to an aesthetic object. This is where his work for me starts departing from the *minka* tradition. As much as people in the twentieth century might look back at the skewed wooden columns of earlier *minka* and see an 'aesthetic', let's be honest, there just wasn't any straight wood to hand. Did people three or five hundred years ago, and particularly 'common people', really have the time to develop and appreciate an aesthetic? I doubt it. It was an age when people said, if I should die before I wake up they weren't joking. Haven't other people tried to redraft *minka* to modern social conditions? Of course they have. It's just that they have drawn the line in other places. Murakami's work is both unique and yet

still seems to possess universal qualities. It makes you believe they are no longer inherently contradictory.

Where Murakami is right is in thinking that the lessons we can learn from *minka* are not just nostalgic ones. His *minka* continue to tackle questions of nature, and a social type of housing that ponders questions of aesthetics. His subtle designs make you wonder about the prefabricated box housing you see littering most Japanese suburbs. Their rationale – of low-cost housing suited for 'contemporary' suburban living – may well make economic sense. But their cultural value is precisely zero. When you see them against Murakami's modern *minka* you wonder how they still find buyers. Perhaps the best message from his work is that vernacular architecture can be valid in aesthetic terms and yet still be contemporary. Perhaps it's that cultural traditions and aesthetics aren't just limited to traditional materials. Perhaps more important is that he understands that just asserting the tradition of *minka* is by itself not enough to maintain it. It needs to live now. What do I like best? It's the fact that he wins the battle for urban architecture by capturing and defending the cultural low ground. Forget history, architecture doesn't get any more contemporary than this. ■

You call your work 'Modern Minka'. What a wonderful expression. So why concrete?
Good question, yes why did I? I started making architecture in Hiroshima over twenty years ago and in the city at that time the vast majority of houses were still made of wood. But for wooden housing in Japan you still have to apply an outer surface or skin, it may be mortar or tiles, but I felt rather uninterested in that. Concrete is also a material of nature so I started to use it from my earliest projects and am still exploring its qualities.

Could you tell me about the House in Tsuyama?
The clients had had three buildings constructed before

this house – they were very wealthy and liked to have architecture made – but they didn't actually like those earlier works by other designers so they commissioned me. They were aware of my work from the House in Ajina [1990] that had been published in a magazine they had seen. Anyway, in Japan the vernacular architecture is called *minka* and Hiroshima especially – which is on the Setonaikai Inland Sea, is not a real urban city like the larger metropolises and shouldn't be thought of as an urban city – has its own unique style of housing. Both myself and the clients decided to pursue a contemporary form of *minka*.

The site for this house was much larger than your

The House in Tsuyama's sloped ramp leads up to the *hanare* of the children's room.

The aluminium and concrete elements at the House in Tsuyama seem to have been so refined that all that is left is a mere whisper of their fabrication, but with an overarching aura of their intrinsic qualities until it seems only the phenomena itself is left. Maybe this should be called a *minka* eclipse.

earlier projects so you had much more freedom. How did it transform the design?

Most Japanese houses are based on a 3.6 metre module, so I decided to structure the floor plan around that historical precedent. This house had a core of living room, couple's bedroom, kitchen and bathroom – the basic minimum for a house. Japanese traditional *minka* were constructed of a main living space and what we call a *hanare*. It was a very special room, not for daily use, and was slightly physically separated from the main core of the building. For my design I introduced two *hanare* separate from the other rooms. One, which you could call a basic *hanare* room and the other which was the children's bedroom on the second floor. This was also a kind of *hanare* because the approach to it was from outside and there was no glass along the walkway edge to access it before you entered the room.

Is this square plan a traditional *minka* layout?

This is a kind of model or ideal plan and so it was not typical in traditional *minka*.

Historically houses were arranged around an earthen open space. Why did you decide to have a pool in the centre of the courtyard?

My architecture is colourless, I never use colour, and as the building itself is unclad concrete and uses colourless materials and finishes like white paint, metal or glass, I wanted to bring the colour of nature, the vibrancy that surrounded the building, directly into the house. I would like to interpose a complete silence,

be a good expression but in *sukiya* architecture the materials are thinner. In my case, many of my clients are ordinary citizens, working people. When I design their houses, I therefore search for an expression of new space, and use this to guide my selection of the materials and the creation of structures. At that stage, keeping the costs down is extremely important. This type of efficiency is essential to the design of *minka*. What is most important is that we study the most advanced construction design for its applications, processing and the joint work which can utilise modern material performances at their maximum, while also obtaining a light and transparent space.

Your work is influenced by traditional architectural notions but you use modern materials, how does that work? Aren't you concerned you might end up with fragments of tradition, like a kind of rustic Post-Modernism?

I think that because I emphasise horizontal lines and planes you can feel the building's traditional mood. Also it is open to the outside and especially to the courtyard. The interior and exterior spaces are mixed and that is a very traditional Japanese idea. It's traditional yes, but in a very conceptual sense. It is an entirely different story from referring to a traditional architectural style or order through the method of Post-Modernism.

even one that may be considered as emptiness – in the sense of oblivion or an emotional emptiness – even in these busy city residential houses. I want it to be implied in a simple, solid geometric form of triangular parallelepipeds, with silent space as a void by incorporating an inner quad.

When I met Shigeru Ban he called your work, with its thin columns and emphasis on horizontal open planes giving flexible space, Modern Sukiya. Do you feel this a true depiction?

Well that might be true. But really, as I said before, I think of it as *minka*. Contemporary *sukiya* might also

The House in Okayama Fukutomi (1991) seems to have sailed dreamily by, floating above the chaos of the surrounding town, docked in a small green pool at the end of a suburban road.

The wings of the House in Okayama Fukutomi's roof, part aesthetic intention, part sculptural form, are both unique to the house and yet intensely evocative.

If you want to create architecture that relates to traditional architecture, then why not use wood instead of concrete or modern materials?

It's something of a misconception that wood is a low-cost material. If you construct a building of concrete, even very cheap concrete, then it can be made very accurately, and finished to a satisfactory standard. For wood over a certain standard of material you can make an excellent house. But if you choose cheap wood it's impossible. For posts, for example, wood needs to be of sufficient size and you just cannot get around that.

You use a 3.6 metre grid. Is it related to *shaku* or old measurements that were derived from the human scale (like the *tatami* was the size for one person to sleep)? As Japanese people's proportions are changing in accordance with dietary habits, isn't there a case for this re-examination of traditional *minka* to reflect this new reality? Shouldn't you choose a 3.8 metre grid or a larger module for contemporary housing?

Well I believe that Japanese people can still feel intuitively the dimensions of 3.6 metres that relates to the *tatami* module, not just in the horizontal plane but vertically as well. But in my housing I don't use the 3.6 metre grid exclusively but mix it together with larger dimensioned spaces for the kitchen or bathroom, for example, where that better suits modern lifestyles. Though I pursue efficiency in my own way when designing and constructing buildings, rather than quoting Japanese traditional architecture, I believe the result is a similarity in atmospheric sense. Also when 3.6 metre module boards are used, for example, in the construction of concrete framework, there are systematic areas which fit economically using 3.6 metre modules. This is the reality of the situation which Japanese architects, not only myself, cannot ignore when we design architecture in Japan.

You want to bring nature and natural light into the house through the use of a courtyard but also people say the courtyard type is a response to the chaos of urban Japan. What do you think of the urban situation in Japan?

If you look at this site at the House in Tsuyama there is a six-floor office nearby and what is at present vacant lots surrounding the house will in the future be built upon – a kind of imploding chaos. So to counteract this reality to some extent we need enclosure. So I opened the glass to the garden and outside city and used a series of slits in the walls so there is a kind of ambiguity, it's not only closed but also open in places. I used louvres to create this effect, to hide views from the buildings and also to create shadow.

You said your architecture is the aesthetic object? What do you mean by that?

Well from the very start my hope was to make beautiful architecture, and yet I also understood that architecture cannot be just an object in the way that sculpture can. People have to live in architecture, it's the primary function, so it cannot be just an object. But in spite of this I would like it to get as close to it as possible. Even if people live in my buildings my architecture should be an aesthetic object, for me. From the client's lifestyle or the environment, from the site and location, I can imagine the forms, and from these two I can make what I call 'pure architecture'. When we think of residential houses in the current environment, a 'shelter' – which could be quite primitive – could be reconsidered. Also I would like to rediscover a pure meaning of shelter. I see it as consisting of tension between the outside and inside of the environment in which architecture is located and it symbolises one aspect of the era and lifestyle. Then, I would like to produce an environmental object using minimum materials that would not involve consumption, in order to achieve a gentle and soft ambience.

My experience has been that aesthetics and function are at opposite poles. How do you bring them together?

That's difficult! It's become an obsession for me, to think about this!

I was delighted by your design for the roof of the Okayama House (1991). It's so simple and yet a compelling, beautiful solution. Where did this idea come from?

The site faces the approaching road as the site sits on the axis of a T-junction. I wanted to make a deck at the end of this street. And at this site the ground conditions were very poor and the requirement was for the cost to be kept low, so both the piles and the foundations are flat concrete. I needed to place the house kind of resting on the soil, kind of floating. I made the house balanced on both left and right sides of the site – I called it a ship in the swamp – and so the roof is a kind of sail. I wanted to make a large roof overhang, deep eaves, as most Japanese houses used them, with a central space of compacted earth or *doma*. With the roof design, a vague or ambiguous area is created which gives either half an outer area or half an inner area. In order to provide the feeling of extension in the limited space of a room, and also to achieve a centripetal effect as well as providing reasonable shade in relation to azimuth and the sun, the roof has notches for the sky. The decks and the road are divided by a mobile glass screen and the indoor activities are gently transmitted to those who pass by the road via this screen.

Why the curved, vaulted roof?

I first used the vault roof at the Atelier in Sakamichi in 1988 where it was a very low-budget project and one where we needed to make as big a volume as cheaply as possible. The reason it is cheaper is because usually for architecture to enclose a volume you need four sides but this had only three dimensions and a roof, so it was cheaper. Also for a thin roof, the curve is structurally stronger than a flat roof of comparable thickness. Before the vault I used to use gable roofs, but because of the symmetry at the top if there is even a very small mistake in construction it is immediately obvious. With a curved roof it is much less noticeable.

The spaces in these houses are very open. Is it habitable? Is it functional enough for residential architecture? Not that I am denying its beauty!

The courtyard is semi-open so this room is defined by a private room and the semi-open space so it's not what I would call open. There are also roll screens to draw down at night and to provide privacy.

The image of concrete is as an industrial material, it has weight but not lightness in the popular imagination. How do you see concrete?

I make concrete thin in places, so, for example, at the end of walls that are visible, it is 150 millimetres thick, but otherwise in invisible places it is 300 millimetres to give adequate structural support. It's not how concrete is made but rather how its quality as a material is shown that is important.

Modernism in the early twentieth century was interested in social housing. Does your work have a message, perhaps a political or social one?

The social situation and design situation are always changing so I think one function of architecture has to be to make a new style or new image. Architects themselves seek some kind of new style and after having discovered it for ourselves, then we can suggest to society how to live in this new style or how to make use of this new building form. It's only after this that architecture and society can move forward together.

Are you optimistic about the city in Japan and about Japanese architecture?

Fifty years have passed since the war and Japanese society can now begin to think about the city. When I make a small residential building I first think of making a small oasis in the city and then think about how to connect that oasis with the surrounding city – so it's very important for us to make architecture. I don't just want to make a concrete box in the city, devoid of all connections. Existing rows of stores and houses in cities have created a sort of landscape scenery, and I suppose, if I add my architecture then a new scene is created again. So my approach is to decide what the form should be. For example, if I imagine when I enter the building, I think of what form to cut out and the outside landscape scene. I consider what sort of building it should be given my architectural principles. So I feel that to design and construct buildings is to produce a new scene.

Do you think your work is Modernist in the sense of a rational plan or Modernism in the vein of the International Style?

The Atelier in Sakamichi (1988), designed for a pottery artist, is pure, distilled serenity.

I don't belong to a particular category, I just build my own style.

If you look at the work of Carlo Scarpa you can imagine how his mind worked. How does the design process work for you?

I start thinking from the site, how to make architecture in this location, in this environment and combine it with my belief – or hope! – that it should be an aesthetic object. It is very important what can be seen outside from the interiors and the surroundings. This is the most important thing for me. Sometimes the project goes through many changes, for others the first idea is accepted. The Atelier in Sakamichi or the House in Okayama were my first inspiration.

Have you been influenced by Post-Modernism, or Modernism, in your work, in addition to traditional architecture? Are the quotations you use in your architecture related to Post-Modernism's search for meaning or relationships with history?

It is not Post-Modernism. When I start a design, at first I think about the form in the environment. It should be a very rational plan, because the building is a kind of object for life. Japanese traditional housing which was made of wood was very rational, because it was suited to Japanese customs or seasons, the Japanese environment. Steel, glass, concrete, the materials of my architecture, they are now all very common materials found anywhere in the world. When I use such ubiquitous materials in Japan I believe I should make my architecture suited to the immediate circumstances or the environment or period in Japan. Compared with other countries, in Japan, concrete is a very accurate material because of the skill of the carpenters who, familiar with wooden architecture, can make very accurate concrete form work. If I designed something in the US or Europe I couldn't make this type of accurate architecture. ■

TORU MURAKAMI
1949 Born in Imabari Ehime Prefecture

Education:
1972   Department of Architecture, Hiroshima Institute of Technology

Employment:
1972–75 Shozo Uchida Architectural Design Office
1976   Established Toru Murakami Architectural Design Office
1992–96 Affiliated Professor, School of Engineering, Hiroshima Institute of Technology
1998   Professor, School of the Environment, Hiroshima Institute of Technology

Major Projects:
1980   House at Suzugadai
1980   House at Koi
1982   House at Kurose
1983   House at Ono
1985   House at Takata
1986   House at Deshio-I
1986   House at Hongo-cho
1987   House at Deshio-II
1988   Atelier at Sakamichi
1989   House at Nakayama
1990   House at Ajina
1990   House at Shikigaoka
1991   House at Okayama Fukutomi
1993   Nakagawa Photo Gallery
1994   House at Tsuyama

Toru Murakami was interviewed in his office in Hiroshima on 22 January 1998

1995   Notre Dame Seishin University Center Building
1995   Office D
1996   Aji Town Office
1997   House in Imabari
1998   Atelier in Hijiyama-honmachi

Awards:
1990   Seventh Yoshioka Award for the House in Nakayama
1990   The Second Japan Institute of Architects New Designers Award for Atelier in Sakamichi
1994   Architectural Institute of Japan Design Prize for the Series of Houses including House in Ajina
1997   Education Minister's Art Encouragement Prize for Freshmen for the Planning of Aji Town Office

technology

It's no coincidence that Ridley Scott's *Blade Runner* (1982) was inspired by images of Tokyo. Just think of it. Notions of a future city, based on an already existing one. It says as much for Japan's technological prowess as the Empire did for Britain's economic ambitions that what might seem a spurious notion soon warps beyond philosophy to become hard-baked reality. Nothing can shake the image of Japan as a technological powerhouse. Technology seems to have more profoundly infiltrated society than any other post-war factor, it almost equals Buddhism and Shintoism in the fervour of its believers. And the design work that it has inspired has at times seemed to be more consumable than the technology that inspired it in the first place. It doesn't matter how bizarre the form, or how futuristic the imagery, in Japan at least, it could always find a backer and a market niche. It almost reminds me of the advice that one 1940s standard's composer gave to another – 'carry on being uncommercial, there's a lot of money in it'.

But as the work of the following four designers shows, the reality of technology-inspired design is stuff of much deeper metal than a superficial glance might suggest. Like a Sonny Rollins calypso, it starts off seemingly familiar enough, but by the time the piece is over you have been taken on a journey you can never quite forget. Home is no longer where the heart is. It's where it believes it one day could be. Shoei Yoh's architecture responds to the forces of nature, but then gives it a post-Darwinian twist. Technology sets his work free from any established notion of genealogy and produces a new form of architecture that really hasn't been selected from any known species. Part organic extrusion, part technological vessel, it is more portent of future form than any sci-fi film I've ever seen. Not surprisingly some of the designers' work has been infused by the spirit of Modernism. Both landscape architect Toru Mitani and architect Waro Kishi see Modernism's enthusiasm for technology as still offering the potential to realise new forms and focuses for design in Japan. But if that is the departure point then the destination is certainly new. They may taxi down a runway lined by Le Corbusier and Alvar Aalto, but once they start ramping up, they roar past the old icons to take us on a glorious journey of discovery. Kishi's work builds on Modernism's structural base to find a new way to bring open space to urban architecture. Mitani's landscapes use technology to rush us on a journey – backwards – to places where a spiritual communication with the landscape is possible. Lighting designer Motoko Ishii's work is a marvellous celebration of technology showing how, like a Spielberg vehicle for time travel, it can take people back to an earlier, even primitive, relationship to light, and forward to safer cities for the future.

The image of Japan as a technologically-based society is not a form of outside psychoanalysis but is widely believed by the Japanese themselves. So in a sense the technology-inspired work of the following designers is not just a personal story, but is also the story of Japan in the twentieth century. ■

A Modernist listening to the Earth

Toru Mitani

「 If you feel something but you cannot tell what it is, it's a spatial experience, a landscape architecture experience 」

It cannot be easy being a landscape architect in Japan. No sooner does this new profession discover a common voice than it starts to slur its speech. And nowhere is this more noticeable than in the debate concerning Modernism. Long after the architectural profession had finished with form-follows-function, its relevance to the design of urban landscapes is still being contested. After all they say, the nearest you get to a real function for landscapes is recreation. Modernism had produced a rash of great architecture of course. But it was a style that was subsequently adapted, unsuccessfully for the most part, to landscape architecture. What had been the spatial purity of functional architectural forms in the landscape became barren tracts of open grass. Too often what had been planned as flexible space became dead space.

But Toru Mitani, a Harvard educated ex-architect, is one Japanese landscape architect who is sure of the relevance of Modernism to landscape architecture. Exhausted by the endless quotation that he felt defined Post-Modernism, in his landscape projects since returning from America, he has explored how Modernism's abstract concepts of space can provide

a suitable compositional tool for the landscapes that new technology is now delivering.

He is certainly one of the few landscape architects in Japan to embrace both new technology and civil engineering. This is so crucial in Japan where post-war environmental history has been a fight where concrete battles geography, and wins. From river flood-control systems, to breakwaters, to roads slicing through 60 degree mountain slopes, civil engineering 'culture' has pervasively changed Japan's landscapes. There's now less wilderness and more engineered nature. The development of landscape architecture as a profession in Japan has been hampered by its unwillingness to cosy up to civil engineering, where the land is still 'fresh'. Too often it has attempted to align itself with the more glamorous 'design' profession of architecture, thus reducing its role to a minute one. Mitani both understands and embraces the reality that civil engineering presents a great field for landscape architects as well as a chance to really influence the environment on a much wider scale. Japan as a country is 60 per cent forest, 80 per cent mountains and has the world's largest number of man-made islands. Put these together and you can see where landscape-architecture-as-engineering could start to exert real power.

Like many of his recent projects, the Kaze-no-Oka Crematorium Park (1997) in Oita Prefecture's Nakatsu City is concerned with establishing, through an assemblage of simple forms, opportunities for an intimate contact with the earth. The 3.5 hectare site contains a crematorium and funeral hall by Fumihiko Maki with Mitani responsible for the design of the park, a place providing a quiet ceremonial atmosphere for visitors and a recreational space for local families. Instead of styling the design from any conventional symbolism of death, he created a bold and irrepressible hymn to the sacredness of the site. The site is located at key

the park from a simple 'site', into a sculptural space. Animated by the black clothes of funeral worshippers the space has a taut serenity. During early site work they found third-century burial mounds, proof that another, earlier, civilisation had also understood the beauty of what Mitani calls 'ground graffiti'.

Within the simple oval form, the metaphor of orientation gave rise to a series of benches. A pun on the geographical term, benchmark, and marking the direction of the twelve Chinese Zodiac signs, each bench has a seasonal message in old Chinese script, while in the central dip is a 'wind bench'. Located over a small well, an underground wind bell creates subtle sounds modulated by changes in the wind direction.

crossing points in the city with an old shrine directly east and renowned mountain top to the south. With a nod to the area's extensive ruins and tumuli, he made orientation and a celebration of the earth the two defining characteristics of the park.

A shallow concave grass oval, about 112 by 72 metres, was excavated into the site. Slightly tilted, it cuts off views of houses to the south, while the north ridge holds the crematorium structures that appear as fragments of walls and towers beyond the sculptural green dish of the landscape. Strengthening the perception of orientation are stripes of alternating stone and gravel, cut into the oval's grass like bar codes on a giant pack of vegetarian food. They convert

'The wind bench's small sounds and use of old script are deliberate' says Mitani. Rather than pushing people to read his landscapes, he tries to hide something that they can think about for themselves: 'We need physical experiences, real experiences, and we landscape architects have to make chances for that'.

In some ways the profession of landscape architecture in Japan is caught in a contradiction. It wants to establish its own voice in the design world, but seemingly cannot move too far away from the vocabulary of the garden tradition without losing its roots. One way to escape that has been the route Mitani took, via an American university. Home-grown landscape courses now tend to be housed in engineering departments

The Kaze-no-Oka Crematorium Park (1996), Nakatsu, Oita, with Fumihiko Maki's building part submerged in the landscape.

The Kaze-no-Oka Crematorium Park. The Wind Bench and lines of paths emphasis the orientation of the oval.

where landscape is seen as a more environmentally friendly version, but only slightly so, of civil engineering, or in a faculty of agriculture where it is frequently reduced to a kind of planting design with non-edible species.

He is to be applauded for being able to get his projects – filled with metaphors, suffused with hidden meanings and subtle nuances – actually built. It is so hard in Japan with any clients, and particularly public clients like those of the Crematorium, to get these essentially personalised views or opinions built in a country that so values consensus. Consensus has a warm fuzzy glow about it but in Japan it means less meeting of minds, more middle ground. Mitani probably deserves more credit for being able to realise these ideas than he does for having them in the first place.

Perhaps it is best to think of Mitani's technology-inspired Modernism not so much as a reaction to Post-Modernism the movement, but to a larger force in contemporary life, the architectural version of which was only a small part, the prevalence of image over meaning. As recent Hollywood movies, such as *Pleasantville* (1999), acknowledge much of what we see is not so much a representation of an experience, but a representation of a representation, a quote not from life, but from celluloid. This is not just a Japanese movement but a world-wide one where people are increasingly searching for reality among the images that we are told now pass for experience. In a sense, Mitani's Modernism may be less concerned with

design per se but rather with delivering through the medium open to him, landscape architecture, an opportunity for people to really experience something from their encounter with his work. In a sense it doesn't matter what emotional interaction they have with his work or whether any of the crafted concepts are communicable, but rather that they present a forum for experience itself to take place.

I just feel curious at times that he doesn't seem too interested in nature, either as a process or even a reservoir of landscape scenes. His designs are clearly a fruit of man's endeavour. Maybe that is his architectural background talking. Maybe it's the lack of an accessible natural environment in Japan to be influenced by. But he does realise that design has a social role, a power to influence society and not just be influenced by it. Too often in Japan landscape architecture has seemed to suffer from a kind of green, social narcolepsy – it had answers for every-thing you wanted to know about designing a modern society, but then forgot to ask. Mitani realises that the profession needs to sharpen its teeth and tackle more contentious issues like the maintenance of open space. As he says of Japan at the moment, 'people don't nurture the trees, just enjoy them'.

If in the early part of this century Modernism was too easily satisfied with the ability to create functional spaces with forms to match, Mitani's work demon-strates, in Japan's 1990s landscapes, it won't be sated without place, intention and spirituality too. ■

What motivated you to move from architecture to landscape architecture?

It was in 1985 just before the 'Bubble' period. People in Japan were proud of their urban life and the development of Tokyo when I got into landscape architecture. I was a student in the Department of Architecture and Post-Modernism in Japan which seemed to be when endless quotation, endless manufact-uring of vocabulary, form and sign was in a kind of boom. I couldn't see any hope in such a

design attitude, so I decided to escape from Tokyo to the US and from Post-Modernism to landscape architecture. When I came back to Japan in 1990 I was surprised to find the situation was still the same, some seemed to regard a chaotic situation as a kind of tradition in Japanese culture. The logic of many architects was very self-contained, I felt, then I recognised my interest in landscape may help open a door. Now watching the architectural design world from the outside, from landscape architecture, I enjoy myself attending to the creation of urban open space.

Modernism was associated, initially, with new materials giving rise to new forms. But there are no new materials in landscape architecture, and certainly nothing as profound as the changes wrought on architecture by the cantilever or curtain wall. Do you think that Modernism, except in compositional terms, has some relevance to landscape architecture?
It is true that we are still using the same grass and trees as the nineteenth-century gardeners. However we approach landscape in a different way. I was impressed when I visited Michael Heizer's *Double*

Negative [1970] in Nevada: it pretends to be an ancient ruin but actually is very modern, I mean very contemporary, because the space is made by a machine. The materials may be the same but the technology of forming the land and composing the landscape is totally different. This is the result of today's technology. We may not have found any new materials, but a century ago we started life with new technology. In Japan, for example, most of the mountains are cut down by machines into ugly forms. I'm not sure if it's ugly or beautiful but technology is definitely the form of our culture – surveying, levelling, benchmarks, forms made very exactly by laser beams. We need to be conscious of the process of how our landscapes were born – new materials, new design tools.

Let's talk a little bit about function.
I guess most people usually think that functionalism didn't occur in the field of landscape architecture although it was the core of modern architecture. But, in fact, it is the landscape that has been recomposed from the point of functionality or efficiency, and especially open space. The form of contemporary spaces is the result of pursuing how efficient it could be for mass traffic systems, and modern technology has made it possible to reform the urban landscape for this functionality by means of raised highway networks, underground transport systems and so on. Rural landscapes have also changed in terms of functionalism. For example, the shape of ocean waterfronts or the shape of river lines is today the form of flood control. The landscape where we live is more or less like that. I believe we designers should find the possibilities of these new forms and new space and embrace them.

So are you optimistic for the future of landscape architecture in Japan?
Yes, but only if people can see these new types of forms from the viewpoint of aesthetics, then see the technology as culture. If people just think it ugly, we designers are compelled to hide those shorelines and riverbanks with traditional conservative gardening techniques. Isn't it odd? I see a good life style as being like this: when you start a new life in a new room, you pay something for a good table and chairs because they are necessities. A poor life style is like this: you pay the minimum for those necessities but hang an expensive picture on the wall to show the room's landscape as rich. Unfortunately, I think the Japanese landscape manner today is still like the latter.

Japanese people often say they have a close relationship with nature. But Japan frequently seems, to Western eyes, to be dragging its feet in environmental issues. What do you think about nature and ecology?
The word nature contains two different meanings for people today. One is used by so-called ecologists to mean the ecological environment, and the other is the meaning used by literature. The former – ecological environmentalists – see nature as an object. It is the modern style to think in such a way. It treats our

Double Negative (1970), Nevada, by Michael Heizer. Taken by Mitani in 1988.

The model of the landscape of the Kishiwada Condominium, Osaka, with the buildings removed to show the inter-relationship between the 'figures' and background. Designed by Toru Mitani and Hiraki Hasegawa (1994).

Model of the Shinagawa Mall Cherry Blossom Project (1992).

planet as being one system – man controlling natural systems from the outside. On the other hand, the word nature still has a literal association that means something outside of us. Japanese people may still persist in considering themselves as part of nature. As Rousseau lived in nature, so nature was always the largest being which was beyond control. People prefer that there is an unknown realm of nature instead of studying all parts of it. I don't mean environmental control is not necessary but I think most modern societies feel a kind of frustration that we are as large as nature. It is a closed system without an open door. As a designer what we can do is, while controlling the environment, make people feel nature as a larger being outside of us and show how small we are.

From the 1980s onwards many Japanese architects talked about 'dealing with chaos'. Many landscape architects feel that if architecture is chaotic then conversely landscape should be non-chaotic – plain, simple, ground figures, for example. What do you think about the role of open space in the city, or landscape architecture's role in the real urban situation?

If I use the words figure and background and describe landscape in terms of the former, then we live in a kind of spatial balance between architecture and open space. For example, in small towns in Italy, open spaces like plazas are sometimes very functional, utilised for festivals. The plaza is the core of the city. The landscape itself is the figure and architecture is the background. In a good city, architecture and open space are equal. In Japan today, most people, and even some architects, think of the open space as background, just a dish for the architecture, and so consequently they don't like to pay much for it. So what I'm always trying to do, initially in real projects, is stress that the open space is the figure. One reason I use these formal or very designed forms is that I'm trying to make people discover that the ground can be the figure. In this project for the Kishiwada Condominium in Osaka, working with Coelacanth Architects, the courtyard design is a kind of pattern of function; underground parking lot structures that show their head on the ground, and space created by itself. In this space the delineation of figure and background appears in response to how they are actually used. When a series of paths is used as the route for a festival, it is a figure. When kids make their own playing rules from these green pads, a different area is the figure and other areas drift into the background. I think that a rich urban landscape must be like that. It doesn't mean chaos as you mentioned it, but flexibility and complexity.

I think Japanese cities are visually chaotic because no matter how small the architecture, every client wants their building to have its own voice. Unfortunately what you end up with is a visual equivalent of free jazz played badly, every building shouting with a different voice. Maybe the landscape's role should be silence.

I totally agree with you. Quietness, simplicity are some of my goals. But I still hope quietness could be an impressive figure. When the clients start to talk about simplicity, or quietness, it unfortunately sometimes means a very naturalistic design with a lot of green and trees.

Part of Modernism was utopian, architecture was a social profession with a clear message. Does landscape architecture have a special role in society?

Yes. Common space is the key to people realising what the social system is. For example, street trees are a typical landscape loved by the public, but they are usually unconscious that it is the result of paying taxes. In the exhibition of the Shinagawa Mall project, I made a kind of story using cherry blossom which is very popular in Japan. People don't maintain the trees, they just enjoy them and throw away a lot of trash which the government comes to clean up afterwards. My proposal at Shinagawa Mall was that one cherry tree should be allocated per family. If they maintain it well for a year they get the right to occupy that cherry tree for the best flowering season, plus their name is carved on the floor at the foot of that tree. In such a way people would realise that communal space is the

integration of private efforts, I hope. I also designed its detail to show that the process of private maintenance creates the characteristic urban landscape. In modern society, roles are divided too much. Rethinking design of the common open space could help to solve this kind of estrangement.

Japan has a long history of garden art, it's Japan's most recognisable landscape tradition. But do you find it relevant to the modern profession of landscape architecture?

I'm not a historian, just a designer. So any traditional garden style and Modernism are the design sources I can learn from. For example, people talk a lot about maintenance for a contemporary park design, but not for the traditional garden. There is a great approach to maintenance in the traditional garden style, for example, at the Silver Pavilion, in Kyoto, where the sand garden is raked into a stripped pattern. When they rake the sand to remove leaves they make the pattern automatically so the maintenance itself was a part of the design already. The large sand mound known as Moon Dike in the same garden is now viewed as part of the traditional style but I guess it was just a sand mound to keep sand for maintenance. The forms are the translated forms of maintenance, forms of function.

Shusaku Arakawa and Madeline Gins designed Yoro Park (the Site of Reversible Destiny) in Gifu Prefecture (1995). It's the opposite to your subtle way. What do you think of this project?

It has good and bad sides I think but one positive aspect is that it stimulates the realm of landscape

Yoro Park – the Site of Reversible Destiny (1995), designed by Shusaku Arakawa and Madeline Gins. Taken by Toru Mitani in 1997.

The raked gravel of Daisen-in Temple, Kyoto, is alleged to be a metaphor for the ocean and islands. But, in fact, this is the result of maintenance with rakes and additional piles of sand.

design in Japan. It questions and challenges the Japanese common sense of what a park must be, and shows that public space is not just a functional tool but is part of art. What I don't feel comfortable with is that the design looks a little like Disneyland. Arakawa quotes a lot of themes and stories and compels people to read into the landscape. I don't want to push people to read my landscapes. The feeling and impression of the space is most important to me. If the impression is good then people will come back again and maybe on the second or third visit they will find something they don't understand and so will return some other time and try and read it. I like it when people need time to get to know a place. I'm interested in the abstract concept of Modernism rather than the explanatory manner of Post-Modernism. Developing a consciousness of what the place is, isn't done through the vocabulary but through physical experience. Once a designer starts thinking about a

place or space sincerely, I don't care if it is Modernism or traditional, it doesn't matter to me.

Landscape architecture publications in Japan often feature projects with complex written explanatory text. But when you visit the sites it's almost. impossible to experience or feel those meanings. I wonder what leads them to torture their work with such verbal explanation?

What you feel is very important and sometimes it must be, what should I say, unsolved. If you feel something but you cannot tell what it is, it's a spatial experience, a landscape architecture experience. If you can talk about it and explain with words then we don't need space design, we just need books. You are right to point out that the Japanese design tendency is inclined towards such a form of narrative, so they sometimes lean towards the Post-Modernist attitude. But the Modernist attitude is to raise questions and present a very abstract experience. At the Graduate School of Design, Harvard, I was impressed by the fact that when students presented their design concept, sometimes they just made a line on the paper and said this is my concept. In Japan, students bring a lot of text and make a speech to explain their concept. At this point, I would like to extend the discussion to what we can learn from traditional gardens, which are usually explained in relation to symbolism of garden elements. We learn that this is a tortoise, this is a crane, this is a tiger's footprint, so we tend to think that such a narrative meaning is significant for those gardens, but actually it is not. Why it is beautiful is that the space is beautiful. It is a fascinating mystery for me why Japanese garden masters used such icons as the tortoise, tiger – sometimes even dragons! – to bring the spatial ideas to their disciples. The Japanese had never seen dragons or tigers – they are imaginary animals of course – but they still persisted in using them. I guess it's a kind of key, how they tried to bring these spatial ideas to the next generation. They didn't explain design meanings by words, they just used imaginary icons. So design must be logical but shouldn't be narrative.

When Fumihiko Maki invited you to join the Kaze-no-Oka Crematorium project, was the building design already completed?

No it wasn't. And in fact Maki continued the design process until the end of construction – it's one of his great qualities I think. Sometimes he even made extensive changes while the project was on site. Anyway his attitude is very open to the staff in the office, to co-architects, landscape architects, interior designers. For the crematorium I initially had the inspiration to make a huge earthwork, something like the stone rings in England as a kind of celebration of the earth. I wanted people visiting here to be aware of geographical directions and to feel the relationship of man and the earth. At first the earthwork was a circle but during the design process Maki studied his architecture, the size and form of the earthwork kept changing and finally my circle became an oval!

Why did you use a metaphor of direction?

I discovered that the site is geographically related in a particular way to the oldest known shrine in Japan and to a mountain peak. When we started construction we found a real tumulus. One exciting part of landscape architecture is that we are drawing 'ground graffiti' for future generations. So this project is my graffiti. The tumuli are from the second or third century so when people read an explanation of these ruins, they will think about the long period of time and how people are just a transient part of it.

You used white for paving materials at this crematorium and in many other projects. Why?

I often use white and people say it's not a very naturalistic attitude. The point I am interested in is how the form works to make a sense of space in the open landscape. The white line I used is a kind of instrument for observing the effect of forms in landscape. In the crematorium project the path is not just a path but an abstract line of the earthwork. Without the parallel lines crossing the grass it may be just concave, just earth, just the ground. But now with these lines it is a space.

Does the dish's curvature have a particular meaning?

I started to think in that way but I gave up as I decided it doesn't really matter. For example, people feel direction as a physical experience but this kind of connotation they just read as a text and say, 'ah, but

The Kaze-no-Oka Crematorium Park. The curved bowl of landscape is emphasised by the striated path patterns that lead the eye towards the 'ground graffiti' of the ancient burial mounds in the background.

The approach to Harima Town Centre (1998), Hyogo, is a celebration of engineering-as-landscape, the clean-cut forms emphasised by the linear planting. Designed by Hiraki Hasegawa and Toru Mitani.

I don't like it!' Designers sometimes make use of such features as a form of 'story making' but I tried to make this curve to give the best spatial experience. That attitude I learnt from Maki. The physical experience is more important than the narrative for me.

What response did you get to the crematorium project?

Many people have told me they found it interesting and actually the citizens liked it. This project is very Modernist, just grass and trees, and when the design was first shown people said it was very Tokyo-like, urban park-like. But actually they need it because in their rural area most of the open space is rice fields and they do not have real open space they can use. It may look like they have many oppportunities to commune with nature, but actually they don't. People didn't know the relationship between the old shrine and the mountains so I wove in a little story about orientation and I hope they will be proud of their town.

You have explored how to express the land, its form, its tactility and texture in other projects too.

In the Community Centre at Harima, in Hyogo Prefecture [1998], which I designed with Arata Isozaki, I tried to intimate the existence of an aesthetic aspect in a typical civil-engineering earthwork. I treated it as a kind of design element by creating shallow slopes to convey a strong feeling of up and down movement like the gardens of Villa D'Este in Tivoli. I was interested in showing how the mountain was cut as a sculpture-like form. People usually cannot see this kind of civil engineering from an aesthetic point of view, but I think it's an important part of the common contemporary landscape. I listen constantly to the earth. How should the earth's form be shown? To return to the crematorium project, this is just a very shallow earth dish but the idea of shallowness is very important. It gives a sense of tension to the earth surface. I learnt this from F.L. Olmsted's campus designs. Its intentions involve space rather than merely a site. ■

TORU MITANI
1960 Born in Numazu

Education:
1983   Bachelor of Architecture, University of Tokyo
1985   Master of Architecture, University of Tokyo
1987   Master of Landscape Architecture, Harvard University
1992   Ph.D. in Architecture, University of Tokyo

Employment:
1987   Designer at Child Associates, Cambridge, Massachusetts
1998   Visiting Professor, Department of Landscape Architecture, Colorado State University
1989   Designer at Peter Walker & Martha Schwartz
1990–95 Senior Designer at Sasaki Environment Design Office
1998   Partner of Studio on Site
1996-   Associate Professor, Department of Environmental Planning, University of Shiga Prefecture

Major Projects:
1993   Garden for Novartis Pharma K.K., Tsukuba Ibaraki
1994   Isar Buro Park, Halbergmoos, Germany
1997   Kaze-no-Oka, Nakatsu, Oita
1998   Landscape for the Town Centre, Harima Science Park City, Hyogo
1999   Garden for Setonaikai Broadcast Station, Takamatsu, Kagawa

Toru Mitani was interviewed in Hama-Ohtsu on October 18th 1997 and by correspondence on 14 April 1999

Exhibitions:
1990   Art Space Symposium
1992   Landscape Design: Nishi-Shinjuku, Tokyo, Osaka Business Park
2000   Our Heritage Imaging Future: Harvard University Graduate School of Design

Publications:
Mitani,T. (1988) 'American Landscape Architecture' SD 8808
Mitani,T. (1990) *A pilgrimage in the Landscape*, Tokyo: Maruzen Publications
Mitani,T. (1992) John Beardsley, *Earthworks & Beyond* (Translation), Tokyo: Kajima Institute Publications
Mitani T. *et al.* (1994) 'Plaza', *Space Design Series* No. 7

Architecture that responds to the Forces of Nature

Shoei Yoh

⌈ Technology must be consumed and refined. If it is just limited to architectural forms then it doesn't make sense. It must be for consumers and available to millions of them. People consuming products like the electronic pet Tamagotchi, that's the way it should be ⌋

In 1926, the world of architecture was irreparably changed when it collided – literally – with the world of transport. The Barcelona tram that ran over Antoni Gaudí ended a life that had produced some of the world's most inventive buildings. The idiosyncratic designer of the Casa Batlló, the Güell Park and most famously the Church of the Sagrada Familia, Gaudí was a creative genius of structural design. The curvilinear forms he used for his structures may have appeared to be irregular but, based upon the paraboloid, hyperparaboloid, and even the helicoid, they all had their origin in nature. It was a revolutionary design experiment that has occasionally since been imitated, but never continued. Until recently that is. In a series of projects over the last decade, Shoei Yoh, a Fukuoka architect and Professor at the Graduate School of Keio University, has liberated his work from the geometry of conventional architecture by creating what he calls 'Phenomenological Architecture': building structures that respond, literally, to the forces of nature.

In 1992 for the Galaxy Toyama Gymnasium in Kosugi, he created a topological roof surface of varying thickness that floated like a transient cloud formation over a forest of concrete columns. Seen against the backdrop of adjacent mountains its rippled surface has an inherent calming effect, as though the harsh fractal outline of the peaks has been weathered down to curves. It seems less architectural structure, more sedimentary form. The water-based analogy is further reinforced in the interior spaces where the roof structure's maze of branched trusses dip and rise as they flow across the gymnasium in a fluid celebration of roof architecture.

Yoh created his topological roof design, quite simply, with a creative stroke of genius. Whereas in conventional roof structures, flatness in the face of varying loads from wind and snow is achieved by differing the thickness of the steel supporting the roof, he increased the depth of the roof itself to accommodate the varying pressures between the columns from snow loads. This gave the roof an asymmetrical form directly determined by the natural forces of snow and one that also reduced to a minimum the amount of steel needed for the roof structure.

If the Toyama Gymnasium was about melting the roof structure into fluid forms, two years later he went

one stage further and completely liquefied the roof until it oozed down past the columns and formed a folded canopy. The Naiju Community Centre and Nursery School (1994) looks like a cross between an upstart volcano and an organic sculpture. Nestling among a grove of trees, its primitive-looking form was created from bamboo mesh and concrete. A square net of bamboo, like a brown lace handkerchief, was hung over a temporary central post that supported its weight, the folds naturally appearing after the net was stretched down and anchored on to the foundations. This tensile bamboo structure was then loaded with wet concrete which, when the post was removed three weeks later, became a concrete compression shell. The folds in the 'cloth' made entrances and alcoves, the bamboo net still visible in the interior spaces makes you feel as though you are miniaturised inside a traditional Japanese woven bamboo basket. Yoh's design moves beyond naturalised forms for roof or wall elements and instead is a continuous surface that bends, warps, melts, oozes and meanders. It's less a building than a mysterious covering. The dimmed, creased, interior is both cultural familiar and yet slightly intimidating. Bond could chase a villain in here for weeks and never find him.

Both these buildings in Naiju and Toyama were made possible through extensive computer simulations yet seem incredibly natural and have a serene, perhaps almost primitive aura. It is a fascinating dichotomy. The same sort of feeling you get on a beach in late autumn when you're not quite sure which way the balance is strongest. Fiery autumn or warm winter? Here, nascent innovation or decaying naturalism?

Yoh sees technology – which has allowed him to get closer to calculating natural forces of snow, wind, and earthquake movement and so realise his new structural forms – as a necessary scientific development, but insists it must be the right kind. The Pompidou Centre, Paris, for example, gained world-wide fame as an architectural dream realised through high technology, but a technology so specialised it has never been used again. Yoh perceives Japan's technological energy as not being channelled into architecture but commercial ventures. Available. Consumed. Affordable. And that wonderful name, Phenomenological Architecture.

I guess the only cloud hanging over this new direction is that there must come a point when the forms are so warped from our understanding of what constitutes architecture that it will cease to be the most applicable word to describe these habitable structures. In that sense what now seems a bright new technological shift may, in retrospect, seem like the beginning of the end. A new beginning, but one

Naiju Community Centre and Nursery School (1994), Fukuoka Prefecture.

Naiju Community Centre and Nursery School: four phases of construction.

associated with a death. Or perhaps in the future Yoh's work, like that of Gaudí's itself, will in spite of its undoubted creativity be so far away from what we are capable of understanding as architecture that it will remain an eddy in the swirl of history. I hope not.

It's hard to believe that it is nearly thirty years

since Robert Venturi and Denise Scott-Brown visited Nevada, wrote *Learning from Las Vegas* (1972), and spun the first wheel of the Post-Modern casino. Architectural callisthenics. Topological architecture. The name might not be clear yet but what is sure is that Yoh's work holds great potential for a new direction in architecture. ■

I'd like to start today by talking about some of your earlier projects and, in particular, the Egami Clinic.
It was the first one of four of my Light Architecture series. The site itself for the Egami Clinic [1982] was very small and crowded, confined by a streetcar line along one side and facing east. The client had wanted to be an architect himself and so I had no difficulty getting him to accept these ideas, and in fact he was my collaborator, with a rapport between my ideas and his sympathy. The problem, which was very difficult, was how to get more than 300 square metres of floor space on a 70 square metre property on a site at an

odd angle. The building needed four storeys and on the top floor was a void space for a laboratory. The client was an expert in motion sickness and so I thought of the building from the connotations of ear, nose and throat – which was his background – with the building based on the idea of vibrations. The building's form is similar to the shape of an ear and, from its orientation, lighting slits on the north side give a constant light in the middle of the building for examining patients. So our reasons for designing the building in this form were both physical and visual. When we look at the building from one side it appears to be solid but from the other appears transparent. At night the building's internal lighting illuminates the street surrounding it, an opposite impression from daytime when it appears to absorb light. I was interested in the balance of light between inside and outside.

Has experimentation been an important part of all of your work?
Yes. Well I can say that there are many ideas that I have had in mind for a long time, ideas that take a while to incubate. When I was young I had a few dreams: one was to make a building with 100 per cent transparency; another was to make a suspended building, one that became reality with time. I have always had kinds of predictions for the future in dreams, predictions that finally we can share with other people.

And you have constantly searched for new ways to express the power of light in your projects too?

The Egami Clinic (1982), Nagasaki. Its glass and aluminium zigzag module was just wide enough for a fireman to pass through and provided stiffening for the building's structure.

Yes constantly.

What did this develop from?

Well in 1977 I designed the Ingot Coffee Shop. It was the first time I had experienced the transformation of light from outside to inside. It was a small coffee shop and to avoid using a large air-conditioning unit I looked for a way to cut down the sunlight that entered the space. I thought of having the shop rotated to 45 degrees or using two glass walls – we tried many ways – but finally settled upon chromium-plated glass. It was the first time this product was used and the first time it was glued with silicon double glass planes to a building's steel frame. So this project became a kind of page from the history of glass architecture in Japan. It was the first project where I became conscious of the transformation of light in this way. In the daytime light is just accepted into the building but at night the building itself emits light. Next I designed the House of Light Lattice [1981] for a family home in Nagasaki. As a private residence it needed privacy, so instead of glass walls I proposed stainless steel walls with slits to allow light in and also visibility out.

Ingot Coffee Shop (1977), Kitakyushu.

Stainless Steel House of Light Lattice (1981), Nagasaki. Situated on a slope the house has a structure of 125 mm channel steel bars. The exterior is covered with stainless-steel plates with the slits of light formed by joints of grey glass. The stainless-steel plates and steel frame are joined by silicone rubber.

Oguni Dome (1988), Kumamoto Prefecture.

What were the spaces like after it was finished?
Very powerful. It was just like a silent symphony. The clients were very excited and of course I was too as what had previously just been a dream, was now reality. The light changes every hour, every minute, and so the power of natural phenomena can be experienced at any time. Even stars are visible through the slits at night.

Are your interests in light and light transformation, interior/exterior relationships in any way connected with the traditions of Japanese architecture?
No. I'm not conscious of that. Some critics have tried to make some such connections but there has always been some kind of distance between me and those kind of ideas. One reason for that is that I have never been educated as a Japanese architect. What I know is, I guess, rather limited – *shoji*, Japanese paper screens, and reflections of sunlight. I cannot say that I wasn't influenced by Japanese traditional architecture, I may indeed have been influenced in many ways. It's just that I wasn't conscious of it. The transparency of frameless glass screens connects or unifies the interior and exterior. Visual continuity in space is what I've been trying to obtain, and which has been common in daily life.

So how did you come to architecture?
Well I first majored in economics and while reading a book on sales I found the story of Lux soap. Do you know that when they changed the package colour to gold, sales increased by millions? So this was the first time that I realised that people are not rational, that the ideas we had been taught that the market always determined the price of goods, that mass production reduced costs and led to increased sales, weren't the whole story. I realised from the Lux story that design had the potential to change people's attitudes and, attracted by this, I started interior design, not architecture. But as I like the work of Mies or Philip Johnson, and preferred to use glass to combine the interior and outdoor spaces, I later moved from interiors to architecture.

In architecture one can always talk about style, debate the relative merits of Modernism or Post-Modernism for instance. But how do you describe your work? What is it that you think defines it?
Actually what I have been doing is just what I would like. I concede that Post-Modernism was a kind of reaction to Modernism and historicism but I was never interested in those things, because I thought Post-Modernism was a reaction to the easy-going nature of architecture. In design we always admire the innovator, like Mies; we admire the one who tried first. But the later followers just utilise the preceding architect's work, reproducing Mies's work because it's an easy sell. Mies did it, it's easy to reproduce and

economical. So what I have been trying to do is be responsible for the things I make and to make things that haven't been seen before. Instead of imitating other work, I would like to add something – it's a kind of value – of a new way of thinking and to configure things in a different way. History and tradition are behind us. They are always there but what I am striving for is to make my work, as much as I can, not part of them.

But where do your ideas come from?

Well from kinds of primitive and idiotic impressions if you like. For example, why is a roof always tapered? Do we really need guttering or drainage? When I use glass why can't we eliminate the excess heat we don't use. I have been asking myself those basic and stupid questions, and it's part of scientific development that solves these problems.

What has been a key moment in your career?

The first time I realised the relationship of architecture to social background was at the town of Oguni. The town had too much cedar wood available as the forests were in need of drastic thinning. It was the first time I had really confronted this. I couldn't say I don't do wooden structures. They had a problem, and so what I could do was to utilise the wood that was everywhere in their environment. It was the first time I had thought about how to use this resource. I didn't know about sustainable community design until more recently but I was trying to encourage the children at the primary school to admire or respect their parents or grandparents who had planted the trees. I hoped I could design a building that would utilise this resource that, although it wasn't free, was very commonplace. It could be obtained easily and moreover utilised trees that had grown up over a long period through sunlight and rain without consuming any energy. At that time it was still very difficult to use wood in large structures

because there was no technology to calculate the safety of the building's structure. Wooden buildings are still prohibited by building codes from exceeding 3,000 square metres and limited to a maximum height of 15 metres. It took us three to four years and many experiments, calculations and simulations to develop a system of an epoxy resin that would transmit 100 per cent of the force from the wood to the steel interfaces. So then even if the wood is young or old, the grain large or small, it transmits enough force to the other members through the steel connections. So technology allowed me to design any size building with a wooden structure. To celebrate this and the community's growing pride, we put the primary school students names on each timber member so that they could bring their own children in the future and show them what the community had built.

Could you talk a little about the Glass Station (1993), the gas station project in Oguni?

Very simply it is a glass bubble. The gas station is owned by a concrete company that wanted a unique gas station that would welcome people as a kind of gate to the town. The client generously gave me four times the usual budget for a gas station and I spent about four years on the design. In many ways it is a unique system of a glass bubble and so it was very taxing in terms of fire and building code regulations. The construction company, the glass company, and myself all got together and shared the input so it is a good memory for me, collaboration based on the idea of equal partners.

Why did you start using topology or maybe I should say surfaces. How did that development come about?

Well initially I was very impressed by Arata Isozaki's Barcelona Gymnasium winning design for the competition. Do you know that project? It has an irregularly

Computer graphic of the Glass Station (1993), Oguni, Kumamoto Prefecture.

The Glass Station

The Glass Station is a three-dimensional minimum surface glass membrane, stiffened by a pre-stressed three-dimensional steel net against snow and wind loading. The steel reinforced concrete frame gives 729.72 m² of space for the gas station's pumps, sales room, office space and repair shop.

Four concrete arches, all different heights and depths, are stretched over the corner site and a glass 'bubble' stretched between them. Extensive computer simulations enabled the glass, a material more usually associated with brittleness than plasticity, to resist snow and wind loading. The glass sheets were joined to the concrete arches by a grid of pre-tensioned steel rods and aluminium channels that created the parabolic frame into which the glass, via structural silicon joints to absorb thermal movement, was fitted.

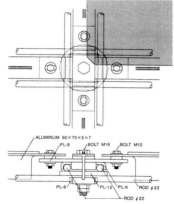

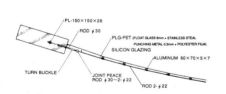

shaped roof. Well four years after I first saw the design I found out that the form was not rational. His irregularly shaped roof was designed that way on purpose. Do you know the Japanese word *shi-i-teki*? It means on purpose or arbitrarily. An arbitrary design with no functional or structural reason, no rationale. So when I designed the Toyama Galaxy gymnasium I focused on the differing pressure forces from snow loading around the columns that resulted from its rectangular plan with its combination of long and short spans. Where there is a long span we need added depth to the beams to maintain that. Dr Matsui, a structural engineer, who had helped me on earlier projects, came up with the idea of placing the columns at random with different thicknesses of steel in the beams supporting the roof structure to make it flat. It means that if we require flatness we have to have varying density. But I realised that if I varied the depth of the truss itself in areas of greater force to correspond to the bending moments, then the columns could be located irregularly, and the truss depth became stiff enough to support the loads. This allowed sufficient space inside the gymnasium, and the depth of the beams reflected how the forces were concentrated. Surprisingly, these snow load deformations gave a visually irregular form, one generated primarily by the weight of winter snow, but one which also reflected the forces of earthquakes, heat, even acoustics. So my fluid topological designs, which I studied through computer simulations, respond to natural phenomena, and most importantly are rational, economic and natural. It is quite different from a Paul Savage structure or other irregular shaped structures, such as Frank O. Gehry's Guggenheim in Bilbao. These may look irregular but my designs are based on scientific or natural phenomena for the result.

I wanted to ask you about landscape, open space and the city.

What I do is emphasise the contrast between nature and artificial figures, and that is why I have frequently chosen abstract and geometrical architectural forms to contrast with the rough forms and irregular shapes of nature. It's not a compromise but a contrast between the two. But in my recent work I have been trying to realise irregular forms and shapes, topological forms which initially look soft and easy to change, but actually are more stable and stiffer than they look. They are like a willow tree against a strong wind – they never break. When we construct architecture we are doing something that is quite different from nature but if we follow the laws of nature, of gravity, of water flow, of snow pressure, then the resultant work will last longer against those very forces of nature themselves. The contrast is more vital. Just like Central Park in Manhattan surrounded with skyscrapers.

Can we move on to the city? Do you see cities as being chaotic and is that an Asian phenomena that Japan should embrace?

Well the density of the city is very high here in Asia and although we don't like it, there is a feeling that it is a city so it cannot be helped. So the high density may be unavoidable but we have to share space and time to get together. It's like a round table – we share the food available, and the community spirit flows from that. If you want something, you take it. I may take something different but we are both sharing the same city. It's the way we live here in Asia and I don't see any chaotic phenomena even if it looks chaotic.

How do you see future urban development in Japan?

I think the density will inevitably become much higher than before. So as we live in increasing density, time becomes limited and space too. So the only way to solve this is to live in higher density communities which means raising the height of buildings. So I take the position that we need to keep diversity, and high density and technology can help. For horizontal movement in the last century we introduced trains and cars, in the next century it will be raised highways using some kind of levitation system or shuttle bus. So by having this raised transportation system it means that people can enter buildings at well above ground level or underground as well and then disperse by going up or down. Without this raised transport system people can only go up, for a hundred or two hundred floors. These raised transport nodes allow

bipolar movement, reducing transport time within the building and, with these traffic nodes naturally forming sites of communication, they become plazas where people can exchange information, buy goods or find entertainment. So we will have an 'aerial city' at this raised level not down on the ground as now. There may still be underground transport systems but the ground level itself will be kept open and free for the environment. Other-wise there would be chaos at ground level. With this method the natural environment will remain largely unaffected by the built developments and will increase the amount of open space in the city compared to what we find in present day Japan. The open space will be more like that of nineteenth-century cities before the development of the car. More like community space than just space for physical movement.

In England in the sixties they tried this idea of streets in the sky, but it was abandoned with the realisation that many social problems remained unsolved.

Were they purely residential buildings?

Yes.

That's why. In my proposal there is a mixture of commercial and residential. They should be mixed with no segregated zoning. In my Yokohama 2050 city

Yokohama Daikoku Pier
Aerial City (1992)

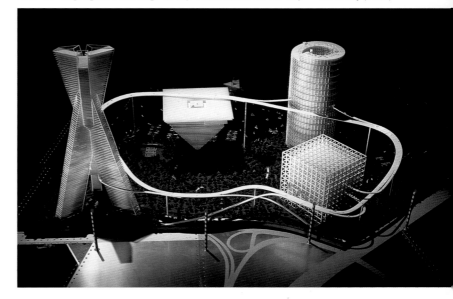

project [1992] every building has a different function but the ground floor levels are all open, liberated to the public. Concert halls and casual recreation facilities, public buildings and those that people want access to will be at ground level so that people can walk on foot rather than use a vehicle. Social, cultural and physical activities will be nearby so that time and space can be reduced. For Japan with its history of earthquakes what we need is architecture that can deliver alternatives, other choices that can be used without energy supplies, as a kind of life-line that could last for 200 days and allow people to survive. I still think that the only solution for Japanese cities is to raise the buildings higher and higher and leave the property open to the public with trees for common use. Some designers have just proposed taller buildings as tall as 1,000 metres but it's nonsense. Without the high-level approaching access I introduced in the 2050 Project, it just doesn't make sense. The sky access in the middle of its height makes a node or an interchange of the city, reducing the number of elevators.

Could one problem of your vision for buildings in the future be the one that the Metabolists encountered with their 'long-life' buildings, that they will quickly become dated by the very technology that makes them possible in the first place? Instead of flexibility and recycling the reality could be scrap and build as it's more economic to tear buildings down to accommodate new technology than to fit it into existing buildings.

Metabolist Movement: *The Metabolism Movement was started in the mid-1960s by Kisho Kurokawa, Yukio Otani and Kiyonori Kikutake as a reaction against Modernism where the building's completion was the end of the process; a set of clean photos for the magazines, followed immediately by oozing decay. They instead stressed structure and proposed flexible planning within a building, often around a central core, so that new uses could be incorporated as functions and lifestyles changed. It was an architectural system that applied the regenerative vitality found in natural systems to allow buildings to 'grow' as they accommodated future changes, leading on to the notion of the 'long-life' building. It relates to part of a wider Japanese social mood where people see themselves as always in the middle of a continuous process, and so makes it seem logical for architecture to be realised as not just space but a time schedule too. Although Metabolism ended up as a commercial style of changeable blocks, this continuity has great resonance for Japan: space, together with process or time, jointly realised in architecture.*

Well one of the interesting aspects of the Metabolist Movement was that they used ideas from nature, not just at the scale of individual buildings but at the urban scale too. So even now in Tokyo you can see in Harajuku, or Shibuya, or Ginza, that the city is a mosaic, buildings constantly change, there is always movement but at different scales and speeds. You can see Metabolism there. I agree that one problem facing architecture is that technology is changing so quickly that the question of flexible use is vital for architects to answer in their buildings. But one solution to this is possibly dimensions. From my observations of old cities like Rome or Paris, what makes those 300-year-old buildings still usable is their proportions. I mean the high ceilings you find in those old buildings gives them a long-life span. They can accommodate people's lives no matter how much technology and social management change. It's universal.

So you are still optimistic about the city?
Yes, I have to be. I think in England in the 1960s there was a great enthusiasm for the idea that technology could solve the problems that had daunted humanity in the past. To make a problem-free future was a dream of that era. But just let me say this. It has to be the right technology. Foster's Hongkong and Shanghai Bank is a typical example, made possible by very high technology, but technology of a kind that is exclusively specialised and expensive because of its limited quantity. Japanese technology by comparison is quite different. It is all commercial technology for consumers, so through mass production the technology becomes tremendously economical and innovative. But Foster's High-Tech, developed for his project as a prototype, has never been used again in the market. A prototype is always fascinating just like my Glass Station. Of course I have been most sympathetic to him and respect him for his concepts, designs and architecture since 1970. I believe that technology must be consumed and refined eventually. If it is just limited to architectural forms then it doesn't make sense. It must be for consumers and available to millions of them. People consuming products like the electronic pet Tamagotchi, that's the way it should be.

Without the economy of scale then the technology will cost millions and be limited in number to one. It doesn't mean I am not interested in high technology. On the contrary I have been always enthusiastic about High-Tech, the most advanced technology.

That's an interesting concept as Japanese society seems very much like High-Tech consumerism.
Industrial feasibility is the only way we can benefit from new technology, like spin-offs from NASA. In the States they quit using trains in California because of the advantage at that time of using cars. In Japan we now have the Bullet-Train which results from us keeping alive the old technology so we can utilise it again at some point in the future. I'm still optimistic about technology in the city because as long as it is available, people will pay for the convenience it provides, and for the opportunities for space and time it delivers. Just like my proposal for Yokohama City 2050. The alternatives must be provided in developing an extreme at one end. As we clarify tensile, compression, bending or sheering forces, we are responsible to the natural phenomena as well as the social changes or the paradigm shift which are the forces affecting our environment. One way or another it is not always a compromise but diversity and multiplicity is the only way to survive in the city. Just like a forest with hundreds of living creatures, constantly changing, with evolutions by accident, the city becomes a salad bowl rather than a melting pot, so the city is kept alive. ■

SHOEI YOH
1940 Born in Kumamoto City

Shoei Yoh was interviewed in his office in Fukuoka on 16 September 1997

Education:
1962	Bachelor of Arts in Economics, Keio Gijuku University, Tokyo
1962	Foreign student grant in aid, majored in Fine and Applied Arts, Wittenburg University, Springfield, Ohio

Employment:
1970	Established Shoei Yoh + Architects, Fukuoka
1992–	Lecturer at Architecture Department of Kyushu University
1992	Visiting Professor of Architecture at the Graduate School of Architecture, Planning and Preservation, Columbia University, New York
1996–	Professor of Architecture and Urban Design at the Graduate School of Keio University

Major projects:
1977	Ingot Coffee Shop, Kitakyushu
1979	Kinoshita Clinic, Fukuoka
1981	Stainless Steel House with Light Lattice, Nagasaki
1982	Egami Clinic, Nagasaki
1983	Glass House with Breathing Grating
1988	Oguni Dome, Kumamoto Prefecture
1989	Saibu Gas Museum for Natural Phenomena, Fukuoka
1990	Pyramid of Sea, Ferry Terminal, Kumamoto
1991	Another Glass House Between Sea and Sky, Fukuoka Prefecture
1991	Karatsu Golf Club
1992	Prospecta '92, Toyama Observatory Tower
1993	Glass Station, Kumamoto Prefecture
1994	Naiju Community Centre and Nursery School, Fukuoka Prefecture
1994	Six Cubes in Light, Kumamoto
1995	Oguni Community Centre, Parasol Centre, Kumamoto Prefecture
1995	Uchino Community Centre for Seniors and Children, Fukuoka Prefecture
1997	Ms Reiko, Tokyo

Awards:
1979	Japan Interior Designers Association Award
1983	Mainichi Design Award
1983	Japan Institute of Architects Award
1989	Architectural Institute of Japan Award
1993	IAKS Award for 1993 Gold Medal
1994	Benedictus Award Finalist

Publications:
Yoh, S. (1980) 'Shoei Yoh, The Form and Esprit of his World', SD
Yoh, S. (1989) 'Shoei Yoh, Ambient Design Matrix 1970–1987', *Kenchikubunka*
Yoh, S. (1997) 'Shoei Yoh, 12 Calisthenics for Architecture', SD
Yoh, S. (1998) 'Shoei Yoh In Response to Natural Phenomena', *L'Arca*

Turning on Japan's Sky Lights

Motoko Ishii

「 I'm not trying to turn night into day. Night and day are different and the earth and its creatures know that. I always try to do something new to make people festive, to allow beautiful light to reach the bottom of people's hearts 」

Twenty-four large xenon searchlights on its upper surface make Osaka Dome seem like a playful space-thing amusing the row houses that lap up to the edges of the building.

Designed by Motoko Ishii, Motoko Ishii Lighting Design Inc (1998).

When Jun'ichiro Tanizaki wrote, in his 1933 book *In Praise of Shadows*, that 'darkness is an indispensable part of beauty' he was doing much more than just offering a personal opinion, he was elucidating a Japanese aesthetic towards light that had been distilled over centuries. In fifty-two short pages, he savaged what he saw as the dazzling influence of the West and trumpeted the beauty of Japanese architecture, women – even toilets – as revealed through the shadows they created.

The aesthetic he described has been a powerful influence on post-war Japanese design from products to interiors to architecture, as each has tried to find contemporary forms that retain this cultural legacy. But Tanizaki's work would surely seem to be the antithesis of the relatively new profession of lighting design. A city boasting a 'light-up', be it Tokyo Tower or Osaka's main Midosuji Street at Christmas, has been taken as a sign of economic achievement, success, even cultural sophistication – a kind of barometer of social standing in Lux. It isn't easy to imagine a connection between the bright neon reality of Japanese cities and Tanizaki's prose, but maybe that is missing

the point. Motoko Ishii, Japan's best-known lighting designer says that the issue is not so much intensity but more the fact that the landscape during the daytime in Japan is very ugly, everybody would agree with that. Any hope of a reprise from the daytime schizophrenic mix of styles is drowned out at night-fall by a sea of neon.

But it is this gaudy night-time environment that Ishii works with, her uniquely sensitive lighting revealing

Tokyo Tower (1989) seen against the summer sky.

The lighting for the Seto Ohashi Bridge uses four-hundred fixtures for each of the three suspension bridges.

The Kanagawa Prefectural Hall was one of twelve post-Meiji era, Western-style, buildings lit up in 1986 for the Light-Up Yokohama festival. Run over a ten-day period, this celebration of light meets culture was seen by 800,000 people.

Designed by Motoko Ishii,
Motoko Ishii Lighting Design Inc.

previously unnoticed nature in the city and illuminating new faces of familiar architectural landmarks. For the opening on 26 February, 1998, of Osaka Dome, a 55,000-seat, 70 billion yen stadium, Ishii's exterior lighting design brought a fresh view to a structure that in daytime has frequently been unsympathetically likened to objects from a UFO to a jellyfish. Rising 74 metres above the surrounding downtown of small factories and tangled streets of row houses, the huge volume of the structure that is so dominant in the day is transformed by Ishii's simple idea for the night lighting. Her concept was to make the unique structure the source for an urban aurora, emitting slanting beams of pink, green, yellow, blue and orange light. The design also accentuated the wavy profile of the building's mid section with 108 metal halide lamps while a single green argon laser shoots out from the building's fourth floor – three years of project planning gave a completely different view from that under daylight.

Ishii's belief in the power of light has been validated by a string of other commissions from Tokyo Tower to the Seto Ohashi Bridge. But when she first proposed the idea of illuminating urban architecture in the late 1970s, lighting was still considered a way to extend productivity rather than helping create an identity for the city, even for those with a rich architectural heritage. Even in Kyoto, long considered the cultural heart of Japan, the nightscape was a huge disappointment. If in the daytime the roofs of shrines and temples and sightlines of mountain peaks were like a stellar map of the city's natural and cultural highlights, at night the city all too often looked just like any other provincial city. Dissatisfied with the city's nightscape, she proposed the illumination of the city's historic monuments to the local government: an idea which, given its originality at the time, rather unsurprisingly failed to see the light of day. So Ishii took her equipment and, at her own expense, travelled around the country and lit up various monuments in the cities she visited, from Kobe to Kumamoto, Hiroshima to Sapporo. The interest this finally aroused led in 1986 to the 'Light-up Yokohama' festival that lit up twelve historic buildings from the post-Meiji Period (post 1912) in a three-week festival that attracted 800,000 people.

Although these new urban landmark projects have brought her high-profile success, Ishii's more subtle influence has been to unveil nature in Japan's urban nightscape by illuminating the natural changes that affect the buildings and urban structures she lights up. The Kansai Electric Power Company commissioned Ishii to design a system for a Sea of Hirama tower that would reveal the changes in natural phenomenon around the landmark through light. Metal halide lamps provide cool blue-tinged lighting for the tower in spring and summer, which changes to sodium lamps in fall and winter to provide a warm-white light. The tide level is indicated by changes in the height of the lighting pattern on the tower's stairwell, tower-top lighting shows fluctuations in the air temperature – red for 0 °C, yellow for 10 °C, green for 20 °C, and blue for 30 °C and higher – with time indicated by stroboscopic lights flashing twice per hour.

Her interest in reconnecting with nature is not limited to natural phenomenon but to lighting up 'natural monuments' within the city too. For Ohtsu City near Lake Biwa in central Japan, Ishii focused on different places within the city in order to highlight the changing seasons. For spring she selected the area around the Miidera Temple, a famous site for blossoms, with its cherry-tree lined approach. In summer the lighting focus was shifted to the deep foliage surrounding Saikyoji Temple, with the landscape surrounding the Hiyoshi Jinja selected to display autumn colours.

Whether Ishii's designs are for built monuments or natural ones, they elucidate simple new views of elements in the urban landscape. What is fascinating is that she uses technology in order to reveal nature and so stop people gradually losing contact with it or just plain forgetting it. Instead of technological advancement destroying nature in its path, through Ishii's work in a curious way, it has become its saviour.

But the spread of electric lighting has also brought some benefits that Tanizaki couldn't have realised. If in his day, light was an ephemeral vehicle for revealing architectural and other forms, now it's a medium which itself can be used to create permanent works of art, the lighting monument. For the Expo '87 in Tohoku, 250 kilometres north of Tokyo, Ishii created a light

monument from a 12-metre-high pole of mirror-finished stainless steel. Eighty 150 watt mercury lamps attached to the surface reduce the harsh form of the pole's outline and give it the appearance of a geometric abstraction of a flower. Like a living form itself it seems to reach towards the sun as though in growth, the sun's rotating light imbibing it with life as it casts off the constraints of gravity. If the neighbouring street trees seem vaguely lifeless at night, the monument, emitting hospital white light from its lamps, now seems to be the living form.

With the prevalence of neon in cities you might be tempted to think that what Japan really needs is not lighting design at all, but rather a stronger finger on the off switch. With houses, stations, streets, department stores, and even parks lit up, it's probably not possible to make a country any brighter. It seems as though brightness has mistakenly been used interchangeably with quality, whereas what is really needed now is to emphasise the quality of brightness. It's a point that is probably more commonly understood than might at first seem – just compare the moody ambience of a five-star restaurant with the brash glitter of your local cafeteria. Highlight doesn't mean high class.

Since opening her office in Tokyo, in 1968, Ishii has been almost solely responsible for creating the profession of lighting design in Japan. Her influence has been so large that it's hard to imagine the profession even existing at all without her. Perhaps when she started her career it seemed that Tanizaki's aesthetic was the only one that was really understood in Japan. Motoko Ishii's contemporary lighting designs may have stumbled upon the real message – that what Japan needs now is not so much darkness and shadows but a new 'culture of light'. It's worth remembering that Edison only discovered the electric light just over a hundred years ago and that like any culture, particularly in Japan, it takes time. Even Tanizaki himself realised the need for an aesthetic to have a contemporary existence when he said 'the qualities that we call beauty . . . must always grow from the realities of life'. ■

The lighting design for Kansai Electric Power Himeji No 1 Power Station changed it from industrial eyesore to landmark, lighthouse, and provider of information: seasons, time, temperature and tide are revealed through the lighting.

For the Expo '87, Tohoku, Motoko Ishii's design turned eighty 150W self-ballasted mercury lamps into a new urban art form – the light monument.

Designed by Motoko Ishii, Motoko Ishii Lighting Design Inc.

Could you talk a little about Osaka Dome?

Over the course of my career I have designed projects from city lighting, to parks and architecture, but in 1998 I had the opportunity to explore lighting giant structures like the Osaka Dome sports and entertainment stadium. These large-scale projects all start with a survey of the city where we try to identify a focal point in the city that is presently poorly lit and illuminate it to help create a unique identity for the city. Every city and even small towns have a characteristic identity – it may have been lost during the recent history of urbanisation or even completely forgotten – which we have to identify and then light up to reveal its character. I was involved three years prior to the

the large and unique structure. The so-called aurora beam was comprised of twenty radiating beams of light in five colours that was created through the use of special filters, while four beams rose up forming a pyramid called the Sky Tower Beam. Each of these lighting elements, and the time calendar, were adjusted by a detailed pre-set program that matched the type of event being held. Together this dynamic concept and state-of-the-art technology has moved the urban nightscape a step forward. I think architecture exists under the light of the sun and, frankly speaking, I think all architects only consider their work in the daytime. They try to visualise how their architecture appears in the daytime. But when the sun sets and the night starts, natural light no longer makes space. So artificial lighting is very important for architecture, space, and people's experience of it.

How did you first become interested in lighting design?

At that time it was very difficult to study lighting in Japan, nobody really knew what lighting design was. I was very impressed to see Scandinavian lights and lamps. They were very beautiful and very natural, and used soft and gentle light. So I went to study and work there, and then I went to Germany, before coming back to Japan and starting freelance, when I began working with architects. At the beginning it was so difficult, very difficult indeed, but I always told myself that even for a young man it would be difficult too to be a freelance designer, and so I worked step by step, hoping that the profession and myself would gradually come to be accepted. When I went back to Japan I met five very famous architects, Kenzo Tange, Kiyonari Kikutake, Kisho Kurokawa, Arata Isozaki and Masato Otaka. I explained both my designs and the nature of lighting design, what I had done in Germany, and what I wanted to do. One day when I finished my talk with Kikutake he brought out a model and asked me for my opinion of the architecture and what I thought about the lighting – this was my first work. A month later, Kurokawa called me to his office to look at a model and after that I was also contacted by Isozaki. Those three architects asked me to

Tokyo Tower
With energy saving prioritised, the lighting power needed to illuminate it is only half that of the Eiffel Tower. Incandescent lamps emitting an emerald green emphasise the silhouette.

Designed by Motoko Ishii, Motoko Ishii Lighting Design Inc.

completion of the Osaka Dome in developing a lighting design that would run continuously throughout the year, not just for the opening ceremony. The lighting had to be suitable for the city, with an eye-catching exterior, but with lighting that wouldn't be overshadowed by the dynamic shape and huge scale of the building. It took a lot of time to develop ideas and to make presentations to the many people connected with the scheme. Then we made more detailed design proposals before making final adjustments at the site. Twenty-four large xenon searchlights were installed on the upper surface to create colourful beams striking up into the sky. Some small flash lights emphasised

The recently restored Osaka Castle (1997) in full moon lighting.

Designed by Motoko Ishii, Motoko Ishii Lighting Design Inc.

collaborate on their projects. This was incredibly lucky and it was just before the Osaka Expo in 1970 when many architects and clients wanted to do something new. So I worked on five projects there. But after that it became very difficult because we had the energy crisis and so almost all projects were abandoned. At first it was difficult to talk about lighting because everyone thought light was just to work by, to do something by. There was no concept that it was a profession in its own right. But gradually I persuaded people. I devised many tests to show how important light is, how it transforms things. In time, people began to understand and dicover the real significance of light. And then this knowledge extended to ordinary people.

Are you satisfied with the progress you have seen?

I'm always happy if I hear ordinary people talking about lighting. For example, once, after I finished work on the Tokyo Tower I took the train to Haneda Airport and there was a young mother with a small child. As they looked at the tower through the window, the mother told the child 'that is the light-up of Tokyo Tower'. That is all the evidence I need of the power of a light-up!

How would you define lighting design?

I want to create something completely different from the daytime, and I always try to do something new to make people festive, to make beautiful light that reaches some corner of people's hearts. To define lighting design? It is to use a light source to create something beautiful. Lighting design is in many senses an international discipline so I don't notice any difference when working in America, Europe, or Japan. The light source itself is just the same. Jun'ichiro Tanizaki's text on the different and unique quality of Japanese light was written a long time ago, these days it is more unified.

I recently visited two of your projects. Osaka Castle, a recently renovated historic building, and Akashi Kaikyo Bridge, a technical feat of modern engineering. What was your design approach for those two projects? Did you approach them differently?

Well Osaka Castle is a very traditional building and is representative of a kind of Japanese architecture. Perhaps you already know the history of Osaka but during the Edo period [1600–1868] there were two capital cities, Edo, now called Tokyo, which was the administrative capital of the Tokugawa Shogunate, and Osaka which was a kind of commercial capital where rice and money accumulated. So Osaka Castle was a symbol of the city's power and influence. But after the Meiji Restoration, in 1868, Osaka's power decreased and so the present local government was determined to remind people of the city's once powerful history.

When I started the lighting design for Osaka Castle in 1997 I wanted to convey a traditional ambience and so I created a program that would seem close to natural light. I think the origin of Japanese light shows a close synthesis with and affinity to natural light and especially the moon. In the historic lighting mood of Japan there is no connection with the stars; but instead people were crazy for the light of the moon. This special characteristic is reflected in traditional Japanese architecture. Perhaps you know that many temples and shrines have gardens with pools that act as giant mirrors to reflect the light of the full moon. At the Silver Pavilion in Kyoto there is a pyramid of sand with a flattened top that acted as a reflector for moonlight. Asian people in general, and Japanese people in particular, have a kind of dream attraction towards the full moon which was developed and enhanced by the traditional nightscape. It's fascinating for me that an expression like nightscape sounds so contemporary but actually has a history stretching back hundreds of years in Japan.

So for Osaka Castle I wanted to create lighting that would be both evocative and suited to a full moon, and also lighting that would remind people of the history of Osaka, would encourage their economic activity through a castle with lights! Warm-coloured lights pour from the castle windows as if a master still lives within, while the exterior white floodlights create a strong contrast between the white of the castle walls and the black roof, giving the form a real sense of three-dimensionality. I used fibre-optics to accentuate the areas of gold leaf and a complex set of annually based programs ensure that the lighting changes with the seasons, bringing alive the festivals of New Year, the Autumn Full Moon, and the Tenjin Festival. The lights, gradually switched on and off from bottom to top, give the final design a warm sense of opulence.

And the Akashi Kaikyo Bridge?

Awaji Bridge is the longest suspension bridge in the world at the end of the twentieth century and so is a symbolic link to the next century and a celebration of one hundred years of technology. The bridge is 4,000 metres long and the span between the two columns is almost 2,000 metres. When I started the design I stood on one shore and looked towards Awaji Island and the other shore was just an incredible distance away. It felt simply unbelievable. But anyway we started to research the project, travelling around by boat, train and car to see how the bridge would appear from all possible directions and viewpoints. It finally took about four years from our first site visit until the bridge was completed and we finished the final lighting adjustment. To design the lighting for the bridge I had four or five concepts. The first was to have a beautiful balance with natural light and to respect that Awaji Island is a very historic place going back to the Heian period [794–1185] and with special links to the Heikei family who had traversed the Akashi Strait between the island and the mainland very often. To express such historical feelings using new technology is very important to me, and conscious that this bridge was the top structural achievement of the last hundred years, my lighting design had to be equal to the challenge! So I wanted to use the very latest high technology that would be completely sincere to people's feelings. There is an area near the bridge that is famous for seafood – red snapper and wonderful octopus for sashimi – so fishermen told me to be very careful not to destroy the surface luminosity level of the sea. As 0.1 lux is the luminosity of full moonlight on the ground, the actual luminous level on the water should be less than that of full moon light, under 0.1 lux.

However, during construction, in 1995, the Great Hanshin Earthquake happened. The client, the Honshu-Shikoku Bridge Authority, decided they would like to

canvas the opinions of many groups in society. In the course of attending these meetings I realised that many local people wanted to have a unique lighting design for the bridge as a symbol of what had happened and as a beacon for the recovery of the city. To counteract the drop in tourism after the earthquake, the local tourist boards wanted the lighting design to help attract more visitors to Kobe. Another opinion to consider was that of the fishermen and also the pilots' associations who were against bright lighting. So through this process of repeated discussions – finally we made about thirty programs for the lighting – the design was finalised. Even the Kobe City Jewellers' Association asked me to make images associated with jewels and so I incorporated the colours of the birth stones, but combined seasonal changes like the cherry blossoms as inspiration. We used a very new type of light, an induction lamp that has three lights – red, green and blue – and with a computer we can make these myriad light patterns and set it in advance, for one year for example. When we design the lighting for such huge structures we always think very carefully about maintenance, so in this case we used high-illuminance, long-life bulbs that can be used for twenty years without being changed. As befits its nickname

The Akashi Kaikyo Bridge (1998), given the monicker the 'Pearl Bridge', uses slightly different hues of white depending upon the season. Time is indicated by rainbow patterns every hour and different birthstone colours on the half hour.

Designed by Motoko Ishii, Motoko Ishii Lighting Design Inc.

of the Pearl Bridge, the white lighting that illuminates the grey towers is given slightly different hues for each season. On the hour, a rainbow pattern decorates the night sky and, with twenty-eight pre-set lighting patterns, there is incredible variety. The illumination of this, the world's longest suspension bridge, was born out of a consideration of peaceful co-existence with nature.

One question I wanted to ask was about the short history of lighting design. If you are an architect in Japan then you have two thousand years of history to refer to but lighting design is a twentieth-century phenomenon. So what do you use to give some context to your work?

Well one aspect of course is natural light. For us lighting designers, sunlight, moonlight, a clear sky, they are all a huge repository of ideas for lighting design. So very often I refer to, sometimes consciously, sometimes not, some image from natural light like a sunset, starlight, elegant twilight. The other aspect is that in Japan we have a very long tradition and culture of lighting. All over Japan from Hokkaido to Okinawa beautiful festivals make use of light and fire. For example, in Kyoto, there is the Daimonji Fire Festival, where fires in the form of giant Japanese characters are burnt on the hillsides around the city on 16 August and everyone says a prayer in front of the light of the fires. They therefore have a huge cultural significance. When I am designing I have an image of some kind of lighting like Daimonji and so a lighting tradition like this is a kind of lighting design text for us.

Tanizaki's book, _In Praise of Shadows_, talks about an aesthetic of darkness rather than brightness, but as a lighting designer do you think in terms of lightness or darkness, brightness or shadow?

I think that the creation of a beautiful sight is determined by the correct degree of brightness. Brightness should be less than 10 per cent and the other 90 per cent should be in a harmony of darkness. But nowadays the city is too bright, especially offices, so we should think about how to have more darkness. For example, in full moonlight the light level is from 0.1 lux to 10 lux. I once organised a very simple

experiment. I found that from full moonlight of 0.1 lux to 10 lux people's eyes can see very detailed changes in the intensity of light and darkness. After 100 lux nobody can tell the difference between 100 lux and 200 lux. After 1,000 lux no-one can tell the difference between 1,000 and 2,000. So after 10,000 nobody can understand the difference between 10,000 and 30,000 lux. It proved that we should be more careful about the illumination level so we can concentrate more on less. So if we use less than 100 lux it means we can save a lot of energy, it's very economical and we can live in beautiful light everywhere.

Does that mean you are not optimistic about lighting design in the Japan of the future?

Oh no. I always believe that the twenty-first century will be the century of light.

That sounds very optimistic! Is new technology limiting your ideas or giving you new ideas?

I always get new ideas when I have new technology or a new light source. For example, when I first saw the latest fibre-optics, a new idea came to mind immediately.

So what are the greatest problems you face as a lighting designer in Japan?

People unfortunately often don't see how important lighting design is. Some people see lighting design as just a device to enhance working conditions. But lighting design has many other properties, to make the environment more beautiful, to bring joy to people, to make something important to us. In the last hundred years Japanese people have destroyed the landscape. Wherever you go on the Bullet Train in Japan everywhere is very dirty, all mixed up, no good at all. Except for a few individual places like Lake Hamana, everywhere is a real mess. So it is my aim to recover Japanese nature and to design a new landscape, with light. I should like to do that in the twenty-first century all over Japan.

In the twentieth-century, architecture has seen a number of movements, Modernism, Post-Modernism,

Deconstruction. Has lighting design been influenced by these styles?

No I don't think so. Perhaps only lighting fixtures have been influenced by architectural movements because they inhabit the world of architectural space. There have been many fashions for fixtures but I think that lighting design that is concerned solely with light fixtures has no meaning at all. The most important thing is light itself. Light fixtures are just a component to deliver the light. In Japan we currently have ten thousand light sources, so many kinds. Not just light intensity discharge lamps but tungsten lamps, high-pressure sodium; some lights will even last for twenty years now. Technology is delivering so much! And it is my hope for the future that lighting should be equal in recognition to the field of architecture. Many people at the moment, probably even you too, believe lighting is subservient to architecture. But when you include natural light, light is the most important component of the whole environment.

It's rather unusual to find a successful female designer in Japanese design. Does that give you a different perspective?

Well that is very difficult to answer because when I work on a project I am not concious of being anything other than a lighting designer. In the beginning, of course, there were many difficulties; likewise many funny stories but each project is a step, whereby if people see good lighting design then the next project will come, then the next one. The stronger people's reactions to my designs, the less severe they will be in regard to the question of my gender.

From the beginning of this century lighting was used to increase productivity. Even now Tokyo offices are full at 10pm. Don't you feel that people have finally become victims of lighting design rather than being released by it?

Well, there was considerable response to the light-up of Tokyo Tower and Tokyo Station. Many people were taken back by my lighting design to the time when they first saw Tokyo Station, so I believe that lighting design in a city can open up and reach people's minds

very deeply. Moreover, when we did these light-ups many people in hospitals looked out to Tokyo Tower and felt that it gave them energy and made them feel better. They saw this tower not as a mechanical structure but as a large luminous candle. I was very happy to hear that. It's not my work as such but I realised that light itself has quite extraordinary power. Not just for Buddhism or Shintoism in Japan, but for Christianity or Islam, many people use a candle for prayer. That is a very basic lighting task. Lighting is a kind of bridge from people's hearts to God.

Energy conservation must become more important in the future. Aren't you worried that lighting design will shrink as a profession?

The opposite will occur. If we use less light then people will understand more about the beauty of light. As I said earlier, the differences between 1 and 100 lux are very big, very clear to the eyes. So gradually people will understand how important lighting is in their life. So lighting design gradually, not rapidly I know, will become more important in people's lives: in their business lives, private lives, family lives.

Do you think that people appreciate your work? I'm thinking of the very slow changes in patterns that you use. Do people have the time to notice them in Japan these days?

Oh yes.

You have been Japan's most successful lighting designer. On a personal level what does success mean to you?

For me to have more chance to do good projects. For example many people knowing my work means that I have more opportunity to do larger-scale work. It's the best thing for me.

Is there some dream project that new technology may help you to realise in the future?

Oh there are many examples. I am constantly talking to electrical engineers and we are always searching for new light sources. For example, we now have many colour temperatures. If they were able to correspond to seasonal changes, for example, cooler colours in summer, warmer in winter, it would be so beneficial. For office lighting or interior residential lighting, can you just imagine how wonderful it would be? People in Japan are very sensitive to the four seasons. We would like to be able to change the colour to suit these seasons. And also think about wires. Now we are limited by the need for lights to have connections to an electrical supply but if we could do away with that, then just like a candle, we could move lights to wherever we needed them.

Will this be possible?
Oh yes, why not? And so we have more and more scope for creativity. In the future why couldn't we have solar panels in the desert and then send light all over the world? If there are satellites in space it is very easy to have solar power, which would solve the energy problems of Japan. There are so many possibilities. Why not use volcano power or wave power? And if LED light sources of just one watt are realised, then 50 watts will be enough for a whole house. It's no problem. ∎

Motoko Ishii was interviewed in her office in Tokyo on 21 March 1997 and on 23 December 1998

MOTOKO ISHII
1938 Born in Tokyo

Education:
1962   Graduated from Department of Fine Arts Product Design Course, Tokyo University of Fine Arts

Employment:
1965–66 Worked for Oy Stockman Orno Ab, Helsinki
1966–67 Worked for Firma Licht in Raum, Dusseldorf
1968   Established Motoko Ishii Lighting Design Inc.

Major Projects:
1970   Electric Power Pavilion, Expo '70, Osaka
1975   Outdoor Lighting Ocean, Expo '75, Okinawa
1981   Royal Reception Pavilion of New Jeddah International Airport
1985   Electric Power Pavilion, Tsukuba Expo '85
1985   Dae-Han Life Insurance Company, Seoul
1986   Laser Performance Osaka '86
1986   Light-Up Yokohama
1989   Laser Art Performance in Europe, Vienna-Brussels
1989   Tokyo Tower Light-Up
1989   Hong Kong Convention and Exhibition Centre
1989   Grand Mall Park, Yokohama, Minato Mirai 21
1990   International Garden and Greenery Expo, Osaka
1990   Light Concert '90 in Kasumigaseki, Tokyo

1990   Fantasy Flash Town, Hakodate
1991   Pacifico Yokohama
1992   The First Japan Expo Toyama '92
1992   Lightscope '92 in Nagoya
1993   Himeji Castle Light-Up
1994   Light Plan in Nagasaki
1997   Osaka Castle Light-Up
1997   Osaka Dome
1998   Akashi Kaikyo Bridge, Hyogo

Awards:
1969   Illuminating Engineering Society of Japan Prize for 'The Diffusion of Light'
1976   Illuminating Engineering Society of Japan Prize for 'The Diffusion of Light'
1979   The Annual Prize for Illuminating Engineering Society of Japan
1984   International Association of Lighting Designers Lighting Design Award for Sanctuary of Shinji Shumeikai
1984   IF Die Gute Industrieform for HYO and LEN pole Lights
1985   IF Die Gute Industrieform for Matoi series pole Lights
1985   International Association of Lighting Designers Lighting Design Award for Daikokudo of Shinji Shumeikai
1986   International Association of Lighting Designers Honourable Mention Award for Cynara Pier, Yokosuka
1986   Illuminating Engineering Society of North America Edwin F. Guth Memorial Award of Excellence for Electric Power Pavilion of Tsukuba Expo
1986   Illuminating Engineering Society of North America Edwin F. Guth Memorial Award of Citation for Dae-Han Life Insurance Company Head Office
1989   Illuminating Engineering Society of North America Paul Waterbury Lighting Award of Excellence for Grand Mall Park, Yokohama, Minato Mirai 21
1989   Illuminating Engineering Society of North America Paul Waterbury Lighting Award of Special Citation for Grand Mall Park, Yokohama, Minato Mirai 21
1990   Illuminating Engineering Society of North America Edwin F. Guth Memorial Award of Distinction for International Garden and Greenery Expo Electric Power Pavilion
1991   Illuminating Engineering Society of Japan Lighting Award
1991   Illuminating Engineering Society of North America Paul Waterbury Lighting Award of Excellence for NEC Head Office Building

1992	Illuminating Engineering Society of North America Edwin F. Guth Memorial Award of Merit for Gifu Memorial Centre and World Lightscope, Hotel New Otani Pacifico, Yokohama
1993	Illuminating Engineering Society of North America Edwin F. Guth Memorial Award of Merit for First Japan Exposition in Toyama '92
1994	Illuminating Engineering Society of North America Edwin F. Guth Memorial Award of Distinction for Rainbow Bridge of Tokyo Bay
1995	Illuminating Engineering Society of North America Edwin F. Guth Memorial Award of Merit for Concert Hall Shizuoka 'AOI'
1996	Illuminating Engineering Society of North America Edwin F. Guth Memorial Award of Merit for Kansai Electric Power, Himeji No. 1 Power Station, Shinsaibashi OPA, and Yebisu Garden Place
1997	Illuminating Engineering Society of North America Edwin F. Guth Memorial Award of Merit for Kobe Meriken Park Oriental Hotel
1998	International Association of Lighting Designers Award of Merit
1998	Illuminating Engineering Society of North America Paul Waterbury Lighting Award of Special Citation for Akashi Kaikyo Bridge
1998	Illuminating Engineering Society of North America Paul Waterbury Lighting Award of Special Citation for Meiko Central Bridge

Publications:

Ishii, M. (1984) *Design for Environmental Lighting*, Tokyo: Kajima Institute Publishing Company

Ishii, M. (1985) *My World of Lights*, Tokyo: Libroport Company

Ishii, M. (1991) *Light to Infinity*, Tokyo: Libroport Company

Ishii, M. (1996) *Journey to my Heartland – Finland*, Tokyo: Japan Broadcast Publishing Company

Ishii, M. (1997) *Creation of Lightscape by Motoko Ishii*, Tokyo: Libroport Company

Ishii, M. (1998) *Light for the 21st Century*, Tokyo: Japan Broadcast Publishing Company

Answering the Question of Modernism

Waro Kishi

「 Architecture changes context, architecture has power itself 」

What constitutes Modernism in architecture is not just a tricky question, it often seems an increasingly futile one. The definition has become so wide, yet source for such intense soul-searching it now almost resembles the Mary Whitehouse definition of pornography – hard to define but I know it when I see it. And when you see the Kim House (1987) designed by Kyoto architect Waro Kishi you would certainly be tempted to define it as Modern. Sandwiched between a gaggle of old row houses in Osaka's Ikuno-ku, the tiny two-storey structure has a fascinating aura of organic stability, as though the structure had risen straight out of the site. It hints at its rational planning with the more public spaces located downstairs. A glance at the grid-like façade, with its open-ended moulded concrete wall panels, will show you its reductivst mood. And with room for a family of six and even an open court-yard, all in 53.43 square metres, it's a celebration of spatial flexibility.

Kishi defines Modernism as a period when there was a belief in a kind of sharing of dreams, but that nowadays it's more 'your dream is different from mine and everyone knows that.' So instead of some universal concept of standardised housing, Kishi has focused his residential architecture on creating what he calls a collection of 'architectural prototypes'. This is based on the concept that there is only one answer to the special situation, even when, like the site for the Kim House, the situation isn't that special. Squeezed among the adjacent buildings, the Kim House is a study in technological solutions to site constraints. A modular steel frame with the facade one span and the depth three was constructed and created around an open central courtyard. In order to reduce work on site and maximise factory production, moulded cement panels and aluminium sash windows were attached to the frame in a curtain wall technique. The facade, a muted composition of deep blue tiles, double window and the exposed ends of the moulded panels has a warm rhythmic almost Mediterranean feel. It's not Kishi's technological solutions that draw analogies to Modernism's roots so much as the irrepressible optimism with which the building expresses the design solution. You really can believe again that technology can deliver architectural solutions even in the most constrained sites. Of course I.M. Pei's Louvre construction in Paris is wonderful, but for me it's incredibly re-affirmative that Kishi's work does not use technology to create some kind of low-cost mock-Georgian-meets-bastardised-Palladian pastiche but has

the confidence to express its identity so self-assuredly. But let's not turn our back on Modernism too quickly here because the Kim House, with its horizontal slabs, vertical wall planes and most importantly flat roof, would seem to be very much part of the story of Modernism.

Kishi admits that the flat roof – or, as he calls it, a roofless slab – was part of Modernism's attack on the history of architecture. But, as he says, from early Egypt until the beginning of this century, architecture had been a story of construction. There might have been changes in the design of columns, or openings in walls, but until Modernism came along, and with its flat roofs reinterpreted the building, architecture hadn't been able to move away from variations on construction and re-examine the basics. Kishi's design for the Kim House is part of twentieth-century architecture's rejection of that concept and instead, like a three-dimensional Mondrian work of art, crafts a building using vertical and horizontal planes and vertical lines; architecture as composition, not construction.

Of course Modernism wasn't an idle aesthetic but rather an architectural dream that was realised through the innovative use of technology. But Kishi's work takes the technological birth of Modernism and drags

it into contemporary urban Japan. His work isn't an overt expression of technological achievement but a quietly powerful adaptation. Other architects' work may seem more related to technology but in a way it's just a kind of post-industrial, post-modern pornography: too much titillating imagery and not enough substance. It's the kind of image of Japan that it is easy to feel comfortable with – technology meets architecture and mutant form emerges. Kishi's work has moved Modernism from its Utopian roots into reality – and a reality for Japan. Let's be honest, those marvellous photos of the Case Study Houses (sponsored by *Arts & Architecture* magazine in the 1940s), set in their landscape idyll, were an expression of an American ideal, not an Asian reality. Kishi's work takes technology and melds it into modern Japan, showing how Japan's technological prowess can solve the practical problems of modern housing. It means that technology isn't actually holidays on Mars, two-hundred-year lifespans, or TVs that change channels from thought waves, but is a reality here, right now.

When you jump up a scale to the city – one area where Modernist theory was conspicuously unsuccessful – Kishi believes he has found a unique way to connect architecture to the city. What is unique in Asia

The Facade of the Kim House (1987), Osaka.

Looking out from the dining space to the courtyard of the Kim House.

and in Hong Kong, where he first noticed it, is that in addition to the horizontal order of the city there is also a horizontal desire. Rather than the clear division between pure public and pure private space that you might find in New York, this horizontal desire changes the pedestrian space to create a new type of 'Asian' urban space. Coupled with this was a hint for the landscape: a landscape very open to the city and, as Kishi says, 'very unstable and so very contemporary'. If someone constructs a new building next door, your 'landscape' has just changed.

Although in the earlier Kim House Kishi had incorporated a courtyard – 'at that time I thought it the only way to live in the city' – he applied his new landscape paradigm at the House in Nipponbashi (1992), in southern Osaka city. On the fourth floor, upper-level dining room he extended the space out to a terrace. Exposed to the city, this open terrace was the family's garden, their interface with nature, escape into the non-human scale, and one that also found a way to accommodate its Asian context. The approach is quite different from Tadao Ando's courtyards that expel the city to shield the occupants from it. Kishi's terraces are like a warm embrace, an unequivocal inclusion – that no matter what the site constraints or context, landscape does matter. The city matters. If other designers preface their work with a 'respect for the

urban context', Kishi feels that even with one small building, 'architecture changes context, architecture has power itself'. For one moment here am I getting another flashback to Modernism? This is architecture with the power to change society?

The whole question of Modernism has been a dilemma for Japan. It needs architecture to have a social conscience as urban design either doesn't have one, or at least has been asleep on the job for the last fifty years. It also needs to sate its desire to build a 'new' future – be it architectural, economic, or technological – while living with one foot in the past. Kishi's work in a way is a key step towards realising that; it is both implicitly Japanese but not traditional, both technically advanced and socially aware. Perhaps the only difficulty his work may face in gaining wider acceptance is that in Japan the popular debate is still obsessed with defining tradition as 'Japanese', heritage as history.

The idea that Modernism needs to find a kind of 'post' situation is not news. Even the idea that we need a new expression that doesn't contain the 'm' word is not news either. What is news is Kishi's approach that breathes fresh air into the debate, and also answers convincingly the question of whether Japanese technology-derived architecture is Asian or Modern. As Kishi's work shows, now it can be both. ■

You opened your office in 1981 in the period before the 'Bubble' started but at a time when Post-Modernism was rampaging through the Japanese architectural world. So maybe I should start by asking, why Modernism?
Actually from the end of the sixties to the early seventies there was a kind of student power movement in Japan and so the situation was quite chaotic. At that time I was at university and there was a sense of confused freedom. The computer was to be the star of the next age, so I entered the Department of Electronics in the Faculty of Engineering. But even the

university soon noticed that I could hardly understand anything about electronics! So after graduation I re-entered the Department of Architecture at third-grade level. On the one side there existed that chaotic situation in society and on the other the myth of Modernism was being destroyed through several publications, not just in Japan but throughout the world. Our generation was searching for a new way, which we found in Robert Venturi's book, *Complexity and Contradiction in Architecture* [1966]. The impact of this book was such that I didn't enter the design studio at graduate school. Annoyed by my limited knowledge of architectural history, I studied the history of architecture instead. At that time the big wave of Post-Modernism was coming and, although I myself didn't believe in Modernism, I couldn't find the right direction. After graduate school I worked for Masayuki Kurokawa, the younger brother of Kisho Kurokawa, whose field spanned from product design, small watches, even ashtrays, to urban planning. He told me to design these things – from product design, to architecture, to urban design – with the same eye. So I went to his studio and I worked for him for three years and I became freelance in 1981 when I began my own practice.

In the early eighties, the masterpieces of Post-Modernism, the AT&T Building by Philip Johnson and Portland City Hall by Michael Graves, were completed. Although I could understand intellectually what they were doing, I didn't like that historical interpretation of architecture. At that time in Japan nobody took an interest in Marcel Breuer or the Case Study Houses, Modernism in the forties or fifties. As it's my tendency when many people go in one direction to go in the other, I went to Los Angeles to see the architecture of Richard Neutra, Rudolf Schindler and the Case Study Houses. And that was the start of my career. Of course now in one sense we are in the age of Post-Modernism because we understand the limitations of Modernism itself – well at least we are in a kind of 'post' situation – but we haven't been able to clearly define the new age yet. In the word Post-Modernism, there is still the word Modernism. So now some people call it Neo-Modernism but in that expression there still exists the word, Modernism.

You said that you found the limitations of Modernism, but do you mean the limitations of the International style?

From the social aspect, Modernism's way is that Mr A and Mr B can have the same dream. So a society where everyone has the same type of dream, from rich people to poor people, is the spirit of Modernism. In, for example, J. J. P. Oud's housing in Holland, or the low-cost housing in Germany in the twenties, the same apartment layout is repeated and connected.

Nowadays we consider this to be a horrible situation, but at that time it was the dream – Mr A can live in that cell and Mr B can live in that cell. The situation has since changed and no one designs only one plan type anymore. These days in collective housing there are so many plan types. It's an acknowledgement that we no longer share the same dream. The limitation of Modernism is that there is no dream we can share. Your dream is different from mine and everyone knows that.

If that side of Modernism, you could say the social housing side of Modernism, is found not to have universal answers, what about other aspects of Modernism, such as its use of new materials or reductivist forms. In these areas is it still alive and relevant to contemporary architecture?

You are referring to aspects of design? For architecture the concept of construction is the basis. My interpretation of architecture is that as we make an unnatural horizontal plane so we must make columns and roofs. We construct the horizontal floor and make the vertical columns and put a roof on it. For myself, the problem of a slab – the horizontal plane, or floor – is the most important but that is my private story. To 'construct' was the basic story for architecture for the four thousand years or so from ancient Egypt until the contemporary age. In twentieth-century architecture, Modernism has been trying to reinterpret that concept and the most important concept is composition.

De Stijl or the Russian Constructivists are in my view, the most important movements in the twentieth century because they wanted to make architecture using only three tools, the horizontal plane, the vertical plane or lines. That was a radical departure from just remodelling construction. Until the end of the nineteenth century, the history of architecture involved changing the design of columns, modifying the design of openings. But our age tried to reject that concept and instead make architecture using vertical planes, vertical lines and horizontal planes. It was, and still is, very revolutionary. We had Deconstruction several years ago – that was a very important trend I suppose – because architecture's problem was considered to

Axonometric of the
House in Nipponbashi
(1992), Osaka.

be construction, so the solution was to de-construct. The De Stijl movement tried to change construction to composition but they couldn't because architecture is architecture, we need horizontal floors and vertical columns. So although the Constructivists and De Stijl tried to say 'no', they couldn't. Post-Modernism is a kind of return to the past, which is a little bit different, but Deconstruction is more akin to the spirit of the Constructivists and De Stijl. They were aware of the problem but couldn't reject the horizontal floor or the vertical columns. That is Modernism I suppose. We tried to say 'no' to the basic concept of architecture but we couldn't! That is the twentieth century for me.

I'm interested in your urban housing projects in Japan because many people say that the urban situation in Japan represents chaos. When you design housing in urban situations like row housing, do you think about the need for order, about the need to respond to chaos?

Actually I gave a lecture in Mexico a few months ago in which I spoke about the city and architecture. I call the urban situation now, the Horizontal Order and the Vertical Desire! That's the present situation. By horizontal order I mean we talk about the city always using plans which show the order of the city, sometimes grid plans, sometimes radial plans. In that order we have the desire to develop and so we go upward and we build skyscrapers, what I call vertical desire. New York is the very typical example of the twentieth-century city, very clear horizontal plans expressed in very clear vertical desire.

But the city in Asia is different. Perhaps Hong Kong is the easiest city to think about, because the plan of the city was created by the British so the grid plan, clear grid plan and infrastructure represent order and like New York there is vertical desire. But there is also something a little different from New York because in Hong Kong there is also the horizontal desire – the billboard. So there is the road that belongs to the horizontal order, there is the building which belongs to the vertical desire, and there is the horizontal desire which is presented by the billboards. So the road space is changing – this is of course a public space –

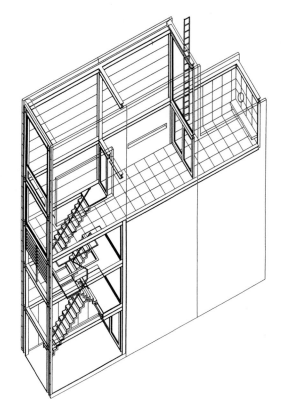

but the billboards introduce a kind of private flavour along the pedestrian way. In the New York city type there is a very clear public space and private space but in Hong Kong – despite the existence of public and private spaces – the pedestrian space has altered in response to the horizontal desire. Is it a private space or a public space? The new kind of space born in Hong Kong is the space of the Asian city.

When you build a house in the big city it is typical to incorporate a courtyard. This feature has a very long history of over one thousand years in both East and West. We have several kinds of courtyard that, as a typology, offer an extremely stable space. On the road everything is happening, but the courtyard is enclosed, it is very quiet, tranquil and stable. While the courtyard may historically have guided the development of the city in Asia, nowadays I think the Hong Kong model is more relevant to urban life – and so my housing is a little bit more open to the city. Instead of a courtyard, I recently included small terraces on the upper floors to create a roof garden. I think roof garden space is more contemporary than courtyards

Facade of the House in Nipponbashi.

Looking out to the fourth-floor terrace at the House in Nipponbashi.

because the space is very unstable – when someone erects a tall building very close to you there is no privacy in your garden. When you sit in the roof garden someone may be watching you and that is a reflection of contemporary urban life, a very new way to think about the city I suppose. I am also very interested in the rooftop annex. On the top of office buildings in Hong Kong there sometimes exists an illegal annex above the skyline of the block. That is the landscape for the people living in that rooftop. The roof is the ground floor and the street is a kind of valley. For us that is the new landscape of the city I suppose. It's very open to the city and a very unstable way of living but it's very contemporary. So several years ago in my early projects I used the courtyard for urban housing, but for projects current my living or dining room is on the top floor of the house and open to the city – of course semi-open to the city – with a garden on top. That is the way of life that Hong Kong taught me.

Several years ago I visited a friend in Hong Kong who lived in a penthouse in a building that was facing Happy Valley, the horse racing track, and we drank and ate on the roof while watching the racing – it was an interesting experience. I could see people were crying and shouting and the horses were racing but it was completely silent except for the sound of the wind. I had never experienced that kind of space before and consider this to be a very urban way to spend time in the city.

Kim House is a famous early project of yours. Were you trying to make a private courtyard space?
Kim House has a small courtyard inside and to the urban fabric it is very closed. It was the old type of urban housing. In those days I thought the courthouse was imperative to life in the city. But, as I said, my experience of Hong Kong changed my outlook and for the House in Nipponbashi, or the House in Higashi Nada, or the Higashi Osaka House, the buildings are open to the city in contrast to the Kim House. That is the story of my architectural development, from courtyard to roof garden, from the closed house to the semi-open house.

Some people say the best designs come from having the most constraints. At the House in Nipponbashi the facade is only 2.5 metres wide, so I wondered about the design process. It seems almost impossible to introduce a comfortable living space into that very constrained site.
Initially I was thinking of using reinforced concrete for the structure and, as the project proceeded the client agreed with my ideas. But for that project we needed very thick concrete walls because of the height, and with the space for formwork panels, the width inside would have been only 1.7 metres. I drew 1.7 metres on the floor of my office in front of the client and asked him: can you really sleep here? Well one week later he said he would try but I was thinking it might be cruel to let him live in that building and so because of the width constraint I finally selected a steel structure that would give an inside width which would be 2.1 metres – still narrow but 2.1 is so much bigger than 1.7 metres. At that time I visited Hong Kong and saw the roof terrace spaces and I realised that the courtyard was not the only solution to urban space. Because of that scale, the 1.7 metre width, the entire architectural space was at a completely human scale. Of course this has advantages but I thought that it would be very hard to live in such a small restricted site when every scale was under the human scale. I couldn't express the reason exactly but I thought that there needed to be one sphere or aspect where the building could have a very high or very wide – I should say non-human – scale to counteract this. So on the upper-floor living and dining spaces I designed a six metre ceiling height. There is no particular reason for choosing six other than as a response to the scale to release the minds of the people living there from a 2.1 metre width and 2.2 metre ceiling height for the other rooms.

Recently I re-read Charles Jencks's book The *Language of Postmodern Architecture* (1977). He said one problem of Modernist housing from the social aspect was the flat roof which is different from the face-like form of traditional housing which has eyes (windows) and a mouth (door). Do you

think that your housing, as a visual symbol, has a human quality even without reference to those traditional housing forms?

I suppose not in the morphological sense. Actually Modernism has been trying to get rid of that type of derived meaning and my work is an extension of that. As I told you in the concept of construction the roof itself is very important, it defines the space and protects people. In Modernism they called it a 'flat roof' but I consider it to be a roofless slab. Modernism doesn't have a roof. So that is actually an attack on the concept of construction. As I told you, architecture needs flat floors and columns and a roof, but Modernism tried to get rid of that. We don't need a roof and we don't need columns, we need a slab, so my architecture doesn't have a roof, it only has a roof garden.

In one of your essays you said that the intention of Modern architecture was to create planes not walls. But was this your intention? What would you like to say as an architect?

There are two architectural approaches I suppose. One is the standard model and the other is the prototype. In my interpretation, the standard is J. J. P. Oud's housing which, as I mentioned before, involves a dream. These days we don't have any shared dreams, yours is different from mine, and so in this age I think the concept of the prototype is very important. The word prototype implies only one response to a unique situation and my housing is a collection of prototypes. In this way, the House in Nipponbashi is the only response to that situation. We can never build the same building on another site. So I call that architecture prototype. They built the standard model in the 1920s and 1930s, but we don't believe in standardisation so I try to believe in the concept of the prototype. Some people say there are no dreams in architecture now but I am optimistic so I try to still believe in the prototype.

I wanted to talk about Modernism and optimism, one part of which was new technology. In 1980s Japan many architects said their work was a

reaction to urban chaos. At the end of the 1990s are you optimistic about architecture and the urban situation in Japan in the future?

As I said, I'm an optimistic architect but not in response to that question! I'm very pessimistic. At the end of the twentieth century a kind of chaotic situation was thought to solve the urban problem. I mean Tokyo was so chaotic that architects thought there was some possibility in that chaotic situation. We Japanese in particular thought that way. And of course the writings of Rem Koolhaas reflect that. I don't believe in that. Of course we can learn so much from the real city, like the situaution in Hong Kong. But I don't know if cities have a future or not. In the 1980s it seemed so futuristic, we Japanese architects considered that the *Blade Runner* type of movie conveyed the shape of the futuristic city, but is that *Blade Runner* type of city really the city of the future? That type of dream is rapidly dying, but we couldn't find a new image of the future city and the computer, or virtual images, never provide us with one.

You used white stone in some houses. Is this an extension of what Richard Meier was trying to do?

I like the very abstract face of the material. I use white paint or a white ceiling, but in another way I like the material as it is. White marble from a distance is just a white plane but when you get closer it is stone. It's the same for a painted steel beam. From a distance it's a white beam or white horizontal material but when you get close it is painted steel. So the material has these two sides of meaning and I want to control these two sides of the material itself.

In one of your recent projects, the roof, I should say, the top horizontal slab . . .

Actually the House in Takarazuka [1995] was a rare project where I thought about the roof. The roof is so difficult to think about or interpret so nowadays I make it a very thin and almost flat feature. However, I was very anxious about this project roof. This is a roof and not a horizontal plane because you cannot go out on it and it is semi-transparent. Light never passes through slabs. I raised the roof because I don't like it to be

The floating roof of the House in Takarazuka (1995), Hyogo.

West elevation of the House in Takarazuka.

supported by columns. According to the concept of construction, the roof should be supported by columns. Using this semi-transparent roof edge I tried to make a connection between the outside space and the interior space.

What have been your greatest influences?
To experience good space or to experience a masterpiece is the best way to be an architect. Every six months I travel in order to experience architecture, from medieval monasteries to contemporary buildings. I like Mies van der Rohe, who defines the twentieth century, our age, itself. I like Le Corbusier who is a genius and always gives me inspiration.

Aldo Rossi said you can't divorce architecture from the life and culture of the city. When you design houses, what is the meaning of context in that situation? Are you making the context?
There was a trend towards contextualism some years ago, in the work of Fumihiko Maki, for example. And of course there is the context in the urban city even in Tokyo or Bangkok. But when you add even one very small building, the context changes. Some people say they respect the urban context and so they put this architectural form into the city, but it is stupid. Architecture changes context, architecture has power itself. It fascinates me that the context is always changing.

In the future, when people look back over your work what would you like your legacy to be? What would you like them to find in your architecture?
Now the biggest concern is the new project I am designing. This may reflect my age but it is too early to think about my past. If the historians in the next century take an interest in my architecture then that will please me. I studied architectural history in graduate school and so I came to understand the pleasure of historians. I mean you go to the book store in the old university where you can smell the dust and you might find an architect who made great architecture but whose name isn't mentioned in the standard textbook. I want to be that kind of architect, like Andre Lucca; no one remembers him but some architectural historians go into a library and discover this great architecture. That is my dream. ■

Waro Kishi was interviewed in his office in Kyoto on 13 January 1998

WARO KISHI
1950 Born in Yokohama

Education:
1973   Graduated from Department of Electronics, Kyoto University
1975   Graduated from Department of Architecture, Kyoto University
1978   Completed post-graduate course of Architecture, Kyoto University

Employment:
1978-81 worked for Masayuki Kurokawa Architect & Associates, Tokyo
1981-93 Principal Waro Kishi Architect & Associates, Kyoto
1981-93 Taught architectural design at Kyoto College of Art
1993   Organised Waro Kishi + K. Associates/Architects, Kyoto
1993-   Associate Professor, Kyoto Institute of Technology

Major Projects:
1982   Kyoto College of Art, Takahara Division, Kyoto
1982   Liquor shop 'Wine Grocery', Kyoto
1984   Interior Design of Japan Tobacco Museum, Kyoto
1984   Mori House, Kyoto
1984   Swimming Club 'Core 25' Kusatsu
1984   Liquor shop 'Yamanouchi', Kyoto
1984   Boutique 'DiMaggio', Osaka
1985   Interior Design of Nagano Natural History Museum, Nagano
1987   Installation 'Cloth and Yarn', World Ancient Castle Festival, Hikone
1987   Kim House, Osaka
1987   Event zone for World Historical Cities Exhibition, Kyoto
1988   Interior design for Toyohashi Natural Science Museum
1989   House in Rakuhoku, Kyoto
1989   Bar Parade, Kyoto

1989	Auto Lab, Kyoto
1989	Tsuzuki Flat, Tokyo
1989	TS chair
1990	Kyoto-Kagaku Research Institute, Kyoto
1990	House in Kamigyo, Kyoto
1991	Yunokabashi Bridge, Kumamoto
1992	House in Nipponbashi, Osaka
1993	House in Nakagyo, Kyoto
1993	Sonobe SD Office, Kyoto
1993	Watch 'Ecco lo!'
1994	House in Shimogamo, Kyoto
1994	Restaurant Sohka, Osaka
1995	Restaurant Murasakino Wakuden, Kyoto
1995	House in Takarazuka, Hyogo
1997	House in Higashinada, Kobe
1997	House in Higashi-Osaka, Osaka
1997	Memorial Hall in Yamaguchi

Awards:

1983	Commercial Space Design Award in Excellence
1987	SD Review Award
1991	Award for townscape of Kumamoto Prefecture
1993	The Japan Institute of Architects Award for the Best Young Architect of the Year
1994	HOPE Award for excellent house in Kyoto
1995	Annual Architectural Design Commendation of the Architectural Institute of Japan
1995	Kenneth F. Brown Asia Pacific Culture and Architecture Merit Award
1996	Annual Architectural Design Commendation of the Architectural Institute of Japan
1996	The Prize of Architectural Institute of Japan for Design

Exhibitions:

1986	Design New Wave '86, Tokyo
1987	Japan Creative, Tokyo
1987	SD Review, Tokyo
1989	Kagu Designers Week in Makuhari, Chiba
1990	Last Decade, Tokyo
1990	Townhouse in Kyoto, Kyoto
1990	City of Yujo, Tokyo-Osaka
1992	Waro Kishi: Architectural Works 1987-1991, Kyoto-Osaka
1993	Tradition and Today, Kobe-Kyoto-Osaka
1993	Trans/Trance Chaos Tokyo, Tokyo
1994	Architects and Models, Tokyo
1994	The JIA Award for the Best Young Architect of the Year, Tokyo
1994	GA Japan League '94, Tokyo
1995	Model for House, Tokyo
1995	Emerging Trends in Contemporary Japanese Architecture, Kuala Lumpur
1996	Emerging Trends in Contemporary Japanese Architecture, Bangkok
1996	Venice Biennale: Sensing the Future

Publications:

Kishi, W. and Kurokawa, M. (1980) Rob Krier, *Stadtraum in Theorie und Praxis* (co- translation), Tokyo: A+U Publishing Company

Kishi, W. (1983) Reyner Banham, *Design by Choice* (translation), Tokyo: Kajima Institute Publishing Company

Kishi, W. (1992) *Waro Kishi: Architectural Works 1987-1991*, Tokyo: Tairyu-do Co.

Kishi, W. (1992) *Critic*, Vol. 1, Tokyo: Daishin-sha Co.

Kishi, W. (1995) *Waro Kishi*, Barcelona: Editorial Gustavo Gili, S.A.

Kishi, W. (1995) 'Waro Kishi 1987-1996', El Croquis 77

Kishi, W. (1997) 'Waro Kishi – Conception/Plaxis', Kenchiku-bunka 7 society

Japanese society was once described as a distant land where everyone has a place and knows it. It struck me at the time as rather at odds with the more harmonious image that I had, where everyone had a place and was content with it. So it seems a pertinent question to ask what exactly is the place of designers in Japan? The reality of the designer's role in society hasn't always been as respected as one might wish. One overarching feature that has permeated all the design professions has been that it operates in a society that is probably much more traditional than we might realise. In the 150 years since Japan opened itself up to the rest of the world, after a 400-year period of self-imposed isolation, the facade of society has changed at an astronomical speed. But the basic social structures or beliefs have often changed at a much slower rate.

In the initial period that Japan opened itself up to outside influences, it imported ideas, including those of Modern architecture and design, quite rigorously. But a gap developed between importing ideas of industrial production and not importing ideas of what makes people happy. Diffused by a seemingly invisible screen, Japan failed to import later ideas of how to correct past mistakes, or even modern ones. Foremost amongst these was the early twentieth-century ideal of the importance of a social facet to design which until recently hasn't really permeated the consciousness of Japanese design. This has been coupled with unusual views towards land. The Japanese traditional notion of land ownership and usage was very much an agrarian one. And in spite of the rapid spread of urbanisation, even in the centres of their largest cities, the Japanese have continued to hang onto a concept of land which is the farmer's notion of an almost sacred and private place. The reality of much of Japan's built form grew out of these ideas of land ownership which, when coupled with the financial hedonism of the late 1980s, too often seemed to form a self-referential view of design in the social context.

The work of the following four designers refutes these long-held parochial notions. Their work is determined to free design from pure functionalism and to strengthen its relationship with society, with urban life, while crafting a new social history and culture for Japan, one that manages to be at once both provocative and reassuring. No one should underestimate the radical departure that Shigeru Ban's paper architecture represents, and yet one feels instinctively draw towards protecting it. Kazuyo Sejima's architectural work moves beyond a simple expression of her concept of new architectural boundaries to fit the new social world, and is a real celebration of it. Toshiyuki Kita's marvellously fluid product forms sweep away tired notions of fashion and evoke both historic memories and future dreams. The metallic playfulness of Shin Takamatsu's buildings are actually a quiet attack on the conservatism of Japan.

These designers' work optimistically embraces a new, much larger, concept of design and fundamentally redefines the parameters of the field in Japan. However, the significance of their works is continuing to be slightly ignored by a still slumbering society. Why are these works important? They are designing the source right here in front of everyone's eyes, undiluted, uncompromised, and almost coincidentally, unconditionally attractive. ■

Adjusting the Boundaries of Architecture

Kazuyo Sejima

「 The real body has changed very slightly, very slowly over time, but outside the human body the environment has changed very dramatically so it is now essential that architectural boundaries be changed 」

Gifu Kitagata Apartments (1998), Gifu Prefecture.

The Gifu Kitagata Apartments (1998) are like a Sergio Leone Spaghetti Western, a great big rolling epic from a genre we think we know well, but actually it is a care-fully crafted homage to a timeless search: in movies for justice, in tower blocks for social justice. The storyline of the apartments designed by Tokyo architect Kazuyo Sejima is like thousands of others: hundreds of people living in close proximity, living rooms stacked in layers like an overblown Victoria sponge. It looks deliciously simple, but can be a hard meal to live there. Her largest housing project to date, these apartments in Gifu Prefecture, designed with partner Ryue Nishizawa, grew out of the project brief, co-ordinated by Arata Isozaki, to invite four woman architects to design a block of a hundred units each, the first fifty of which are now completed. Sejima's design for the ten-storey building looks from a distance like a giant coloured maze inserted into the ground. The ordered rhythm of vertical pillars and horizontal floors usually associated with tower blocks is broken down into a series of zigzag fragments. Sometimes a double-height ceiling, sometimes an apartment's second floor, the unorthodox structural elements express a more flexible series of interior spaces that

helps to break up the scale of the building's volume and reflects the non-hierarchical stance of the design. It's a visual and graphic symbol of the design's social philosophy, to create spaces where new social groups can be born.

At first glance the apartment block shows clear similarities to Le Corbusier's Unité d'Habitation,

Marseilles. He of course was the architect for standard-ised plans with one unit per family – implying through the building's utopian structure the nature of an Ideal Family. Historically of course, he – and to a much greater extent the architects who followed him – was also on the losing side. The tower block is one area of Modernism that is difficult to like. And as experience showed, even harder to live with. What started out as a great idea of clean and safe, light and airy living became synonymous with exactly the same social depravity it had been designed to tackle in the first place. These days, people clamour for the very small-scale, two-storey, back-to-back existence that collective housing was designed to assign to the waste-bin in the first place.

What makes Sejima's design different from the others is that much more than just metamorphosise the structural layout of the building, she has redesigned the social unit too. Instead of being the family apart-ment, the new module has become the individual room, giving the Kitagata apartments a much more varied organisation. This greater flexibility – and a wonderful expression of the design's generosity – allows the traditional and conservative notion of 'family' to be

reinvented to include groups of friends living together or informal associations of elderly residents in a new form of extended family. The structural flexibility that is expressed in the facade is further strengthened as you walk along the corridors. Every room, from kitchen to dining room to bedroom, has a door opening onto the corridor. It is impossible to find the boundaries of where one family meets another simply from the struc-ture. In her design, 'families' are all mixed together, giving a new answer to an old question that aided the downfall of early Modernist attempts at collective housing, how to provide privacy. Sejima believes that if, in the past, people perceived privacy as having strong walls or closed spaces, her new design method-ology offers privacy that is both open and mixed.

Her departure point – of a new world order requiring a new boundary – is a convincing one. So it may surprise people to see how often glass facades appear in her projects. It's a material that often seems in danger of becoming a kind of grey-is-the-new-black of Japanese architecture. Those in the know will know, the rest simply won't care.

Her design for Pachinko Parlour I and II (1993), recipients of a Japan Institute of Architects' Prize, shows why Sejima's work is different. Instead of the gaudy razz of most *pachinko* arcades, *pachinko* is a popular slot machine game, her's is a simple story, writ large in Roman characters that canter across the facade. Not since the heady days of the fifties Las Vegas strip has commercial architecture so adapted to the contemporary urban speed. Half rest-space-lobby, half signboard, the lettering inserted into the glass is sometimes lit up simultaneously, sometimes in fragmented letters, a kind of visual dyslexia for a schizophrenic world. Rather than ornamentation, she inserted an acrylic mirror that produced broken images of the players as they walked past. Like discovering a Roman hieroglyphic tablet in the bottom of your bowl of Won Ton soup, the layering she achieves from a single pane of glass is astounding.

The question of boundaries and just how wonderful a medium glass is for realising a modern interpretation of Japanese traditional spatial intercourse – while maintaining the interior at 28 °C – is of course one that has been tackled by numerous other architects. Where others' flirtation with transparency has at times seemed a curious brew of an almost Stalinist zeal meets anarchist destruction, Sejima's work is held together by an unpretentious fact. It is simply open and human, devoid of any raucous indignation. It seems at peace with itself and with its place in the world. It has a message, oh yes. It's just that it's confident enough that it doesn't need to pick a fight in order to tell you. Where other work that doodles with transparency mostly seems just a little too self-consciously contemporary to be trustworthy, her gloriously fluid spaces and organic spatial sequences seem intensely personal.

The social aspect of her design work appears based upon two main strands. Firstly, she sees the need in contemporary Japanese society for architecture to provide places for people to have direct contact; to meet and talk, face to face, without architects like Orwellian social traffic cops, instructing people how to move around the space. Secondly comes the question of barriers. Permeating all aspects of society from business to personal relationships, there is a penchant for dividing things into boy–girl, natural–artificial, good–bad. This has created sterile spaces that reflect political judgement rather than natural balances. Sejima hopes to create spaces where boundaries are change-able and not fixed, where there is the opportunity and place for people to reconsider their circumstances, and examine the 'feminine' side of 'masculine', or the 'artificial' side of 'nature'. It sounds like an approach that won't win many hearts and minds in Japan. Social strictures, long packaged up as 'cultural' values, have acted as a series of fire walls that have controlled who does what in Japan. Everyone has their place in society and knows it. Can you break down one without risk of an inferno?

The more modern and openly secular Japanese society becomes, the more necessary new concepts for social housing that respond to these diverse groups become. Le Corbusier's and Modernism's grand experiments in the first half of this century produced new solutions, but also new questions. The real quality of Kazuyo Sejima's work is not just realising that the subject of the nature of architectural boundaries is an important issue for Japanese built design, but in answering them so convincingly. ■

You worked for architect Toyo Ito for six years after graduation and then opened your own office. Was there a subconscious dissatisfaction with his architectural approach or a desire to achieve something quite different for yourself?

Well first I would like to say that what I learnt from him was how to make real architecture from an idea. In fact it was the only place where I had any training in realising architecture from an initial concept. As a student I didn't have a strong idea about his work but when I started working for him he told me that he wanted to make architecture like a piece of cloth, by which I think he meant that he thought architecture should cover people like a cloth, softly. But for my own work, I thought I would like to make architecture more freely, not even covered at all. So when I designed my first project, a weekend house called Platform [1988], I selected the wave-form roof. Ito was using the vault roof at that time which covers the space softly but my wave roof doesn't cover the space as such but rather defines it by making a stage where people can move freely, feel free, in fact do anything freely. I didn't want an aesthetic object or to make the space too strong, just to create a place with a covering.

Is there one phrase that allows you to describe your architecture simply?

Perhaps I could say to make a simple place like Platform where people can move around freely and yet at the same time not be instructed as to how to move around the space. Our life in Japan is always ruled or organised around a hierarchy and I wanted to challenge the hierarchy in Japanese society. This is consciously reflected in my architecture's plans that have no spatial hierarchy apparent in them.

Architecture is often said to be the search for order. What are you searching for in your architectural work?

I think we need something like order in architecture, even if only slightly, but not in an explicitly formal sense expressed through a form or object, but through architecture realised in parallel with the environment. What I am looking for in order is not some specific shape but the order of the place or how the people use the site.

Edmund Bacon made a map of Philadelphia using only trees, rivers and landscape elements as a way to emphasise that there was first the natural context before the man-made one in urban design. When you look at a project's context are you thinking only of the built context or are there other things you consider?

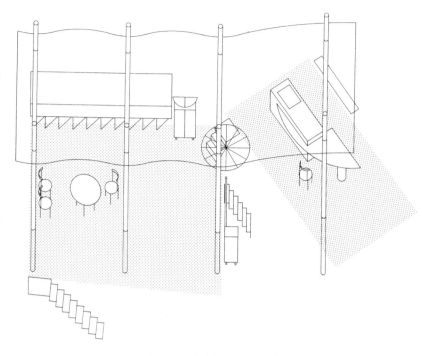

Axonometric of Platform I (1998).

Half of the context is made by real things, or real objects, but half is made by information. So if we visit the countryside, people's way of life is half as different as urban life but half, through the transmission of information, is the same. We all now have the same information on how to spend time, or how to enjoy life, so I think that in terms of context half of the site's context is the real physical area but half is the same all over the world.

The last thirty years in architecture have been obsessed with questions of style. Do you see your work as part of the history of Modernism, for example?

I think of architecture on the premise of modern architecture so in that sense I think our work is in the stream of the history of Modern architecture. If we completely neglect Modern architecture then architecture just becomes regional architecture. I want to discover a new architecture but one that is mixed with Modernism, or at least part of Modern architecture.

Could you tell me a little about the Gifu apartment project?

There were four women designers with Arata Isozaki

The Multi-Media
Workshop, Kuobo, 1997.

acting as the co-ordinator. People said it was like
Le Corbusier's Unité d'Habitation, but I think that in
Unité's plan the unit was one family: one family living
in one unit were connected emotionally and physically
by the space. But in my design every room is one unit
that can be flexibly connected into many types. So the
family as the unit is not so strong as in Le Corbusier's
times. My proposal of many types of aggregations of
rooms means many different groups are possible in
society, not just the old family as understood by the
Corbusian age.

Or the Confusian age?
Yes. 'Family' has changed to a rather different
organisation. So in this respect it is different to the
Corbusian age. One unit is one room so sometimes
friends can live together, or groups of elderly people
who are not related but who would like to share their
life together. It is flexible enough to accommodate
many types or definitions of family. In a sense it is still
slightly like Modernism but it has changed the approach
to architecture and its use. One more important point
I would like to stress is that I think the meaning of
'boundary' in architecture has changed. In the Modern
design age, while glass allowed light to penetrate the
room, the walls resisted people, but they could still
spend time happily between these two materials. But

today even if we make a strong and impenetrable
concrete wall, information still streams into the rooms
and permeates all spaces. Therefore, compared with
Modernism the most striking difference is a new
definition of the architectural boundary. At present I
am studying this from many points. For example at
the Multi-Media Workshop [1997], instead of making
a strong wall we designed two weak walls, or skins.
People select and try to balance their use by opening
only one skin or both. The real body, the internal environment, has changed very slightly, very slowly over
time, but outside the human body the environment has
changed very dramatically. So it is essential that the
boundaries in architecture be changed correspondingly.

In the N-Museum [1997], for example, the client
wanted a concrete volume for displaying Japanese
Nakahechi painting. But if the same concrete volume
was continued through and appeared at the facade
it would form a strong barrier against people entering
and enjoying the place. So our combined glass skin
and polycarbonate skin allowed people to enter from
the garden and also the exhibition place. The M-house
project [1997], is in the centre of Tokyo, near Shibuya,
a very crowded place. It is in a very tight and confined
situation in the centre of Tokyo and so it is difficult to
have privacy. Of course if we constructed a solid concrete volume then the client would have privacy within,
but at the risk of compromising his relationship with
the city. We tried to make the private spaces and the
city spaces more mixed and integrated. We excavated
the whole site – it is a basement floor but above is
car parking, surrounded by houses – so the client can
relate to the city even through the sound of cars above.

In the Gifu housing project, there are many room
types, so as people walk along the corridor they cannot
distinguish the borderline or division of the family unit
and space – every room faces the corridor and every
room has doors. Usually in an apartment corridor it
is obvious from the walls that this area is 'A' family's
and this area belongs to 'B' family. But in my design,
family units A, B and C are mixed, redefining the
nature of privacy. Historically, to create privacy people
made a very strong wall or a very closed space. We
want to find an alternative form of configuration – one

they are comfortable from machines – very numerically – so people feel and define comfort by the data of numerous machines surrounding their lives. Until ten years ago people could feel comfortable without the aid of data to find out temperature or humidity. They always need to be given information by the data, and so seem to be unaware that they are losing control over their lives.

To move back to history again, Modernism itself was very influenced by the traditions of Japanese architecture, then in turn it influenced Japanese architecture. To what extent do Japanese traditional ideas influence your architectural work?
The basic corridor is like a Japanese *en*, which is the name of the original Japanese boundary territory which

The M-House (1997), Tokyo. Its facade offers a taut silence to the city.

A courtyard garden at the M-House.

that is open but where one can seek privacy, or a mixed integration of surrounding context and privacy.

To talk a little more about the M-House; you used corrugated mesh.
Yes. There are three gardens so there is a garden between every room. If we put the garden on the ground floor, then it is visible from the public spaces around the house. Likewise, the basement level, where the rooms are located. These face the garden so they receive light, ventilation and can get the wind and are also very comfortable. The car port is at the road level.

Is your use of a translucent screen part of the history of Japanese architecture? I'm thinking in simple terms of *shoji* (paper partitions).
Yes, except *shoji* are related to shadow whereas I use glass and translucent film. It's not my deliberate intention to try to use Japanese tradition or culture but perhaps my body still recalls my childhood experiences and so in that sense it might be true. I think that in the last five to ten years the Japanese lifestyle has completely changed from when I was a child.

What was the biggest change?
Everyone has forgotten the meaning of the word comfortable. Now people are content to gauge whether

belonged to both inside and outside. I do think about the weak facade or boundary that is the Japanese traditional way and I am always concerned about how to continue the inside–outside relationship.

Do you feel as a female architect that you have some different perspective on design?
I think that the young generation of men and women in Japan are becoming much closer, so the boundary between men and women, like those of architecture is also disappearing.

So which do you think of yourself as first, an architect, a Japanese architect, or a female architect?
I always notice that I am a woman and that I am Japanese and that I am an architect. It doesn't depend on the project but I am conscious of all three aspects of my existence.

Many people say the Asian city is chaotic and that it has now reached its limit, it cannot become more dense, or more chaotic than this. Are you optimistic about the urban condition and the city in Japan?
Regarding the chaotic aspect of the city, I think that it is very difficult to say if chaos is good or bad, so in that sense I am not so optimistic. But at the same time I am not so pessimistic towards the city either. Gradually, the city or architecture alone cannot make the circumstances of what we call the environment. In other words, information or networks create another set of circumstances, so I am interested in a new definition of circumstance for the city. But I think, in Japan, the greatest pity has been the loss of countryside. When I visited Switzerland and travelled by railway for two hours the countryside was very beautiful, but in Japan this situation is very rare. Even the countryside is like a small city. So I think we need a new synthesis of nature and architecture. We are currently designing a landscape which incorporates a glass tree set among real trees. We may look through the glass trees and see the real sky or real trees surrounding it. Sometimes the glass tree looks very natural and sometimes very artificial. I think that we must re-examine our definitions of what is natural and what

is artificial. Once again, I think it is a question of boundaries.

What do you think about nature in the city? Japanese people often say they have a close relationship to nature, but when you come here most people are amazed at the lack of nature of any kind in the cities.
We made the glass trees to indicate to people that we can think about what is 'natural' from many aspects, that 'nature' has many meanings.

Modernism had a social message and we can say a utopian view of the power of design and architecture. What is your message to society?
I think it is very important for people to have direct contact with each other, so I want to create places where people can meet and talk directly, face to face. Secondly, it is important that the boundary is very changeable and not fixed. Especially in Japan, people like to divide things into boy/girl, natural/artificial, good/bad. But everything has another side to its existence, so I want to create places to reconsider whether things are good or bad, and places to reconsider the boundaries of man/woman, or nature/ artificial circumstances.

Why are face-to-face meetings so important?
I believe that cyberspace exists, but on the other hand that real contact is very important too.

What are the major problems that architecture in Japan is facing now do you think?
I don't know, but now people divide architecture very clearly into soft and hard. Architecture is hard but people are gradually becoming interested in only that which is soft. By soft I mean the programme or how to use the space. But I think that division is wrong and so I think about the boundary between soft and hard. Sometimes when we design a public project the government tells us that the soft is already decided so we must design the architecture accordingly. But soft and hard must become more integrated. I am of course aware that it is very difficult for me to say this

The S-House's (1996) corrugated translucent
facade lets light flood in, and out. Arranged
around an outer double-height corridor, there is
equal access to every room; child's, parents'
and grandparents'. This democratic access to
the public space from each room and for each
member of the family, also offers, through
the length of its route, maximum privacy.

as architecture cannot move or is very slow, and I do not reject the idea that the soft programme will change much faster than the architecture does. But this point of integration is the most specific barrier.

Are you interested in the flexible approach that was suggested by the Metabolist movement in the late sixties?

To try to make architecture move is not the right answer I think, because information has a very fast speed. Architecture cannot move – it's a reality – so we should accept this as a positive point, and so then approach the question of how to mix the two sides of its nature. Scrap and build is a different problem.

To move back to the apartment designs . . .

Well we designed four hundred units but at the moment only the first stage of two hundred is completed, fifty designed by each woman. When you look at the facade of my design you can see the double-height edge of the balcony; sometimes this is a double-height ceiling and sometimes it is a second floor of the apartment. One side is a public corridor and the other side is a private corridor which connects to the room and makes it possible for many forms of one family type to exist.

Why did you decide to emphasise the variation in internal planning in the facade?

Gifu Kitagata Apartments.

Due to local government regulations each family unit was required to be divided by the fireproof wall. But we wanted to indicate, even if only slightly, through the facade, that there are many types of layout within the building. Also, every family had an outside terrace and so we tried to make the building's volume as thin as possible to allow people to see the sky the other side of the building through these terrace voids. Every family has one courtyard and in the old days could live on the ground level, but modern housing does not provide a garden or direct contact with the ground. I think the opportunity to experience the atmosphere of the outside is vitally necessary for life. Usually in Japan, people's contact with the outside is a so-called 'terrace' in front of the room, actually a balcony one metre wide. This project is social housing for low-income people but a one metre balcony is not enough to enjoy the atmosphere of the outside, the sunshine or wind. So I designed a garden room the width of the building.

In the 1950s and 1960s this type of corridor in the sky, or garden in the sky, wasn't successful and had many social problems because of poor communication. Weren't you concerned, accepting this project, about overcoming this long history of failure?

In Japanese law this is a rebuild, so we are required to rebuild at four times the floor area of the original. Therefore the programme must be high volume. The public corridor and private corridor is like the traditional space, called *en*, not interior or exterior, and so it provides an opportunity for communication. The Japanese government usually requires us to design community space that can be used directly; for example, creating open space for people like community rooms. But I don't think that is useful for our real lives. As a drawing it is an easy concept for the government to explain to people – this is the community space – but either nobody uses it or it is monopolised by only one person. Usually in Japan the housing has one entrance but on the public side we have one entrance to the dining/kitchen space, one door to the *tatami/* bedroom, and one to the terrace. So I think that gradually not 'families' in the old sense of the word but new families, for example, friends living together, or old people living together, or unmarried couples, will be created. Many new groups will be born out of this space in the future. ■

KAZUYO SEJIMA
1956 Born in Ibaraki

Kazuyo Sejima was interviewed in her office in Tokyo on 18 March 1998

Education:
1981	Master of Architecture, Japan Women's University

Employment:
1981	Joined Toyo Ito & Associates
1987	Established Kazuyo Sejima & Associates
1995-	Design collaboration with Ryue Nishizawa

Major Projects:
1988	Platform I
1989	Exhibition design for 'Transfiguration', Europalia '89 Japan, Brussels
1990	Platform II
1990	Platform III
1991	Castelbajac Sports Shop
1991	Saishunkan Seiyaku Women's Dormitory
1992	N-House
1993	Pachinko Parlour I
1993	Pachinko Parlour II
1993	Exhibition design for 'Re-engineering Tokyo'
1994	Villa in the Forest
1994	Y-House
1995	Police Box
1996	Pachinko Parlour III
1996	S-House
1997	Multi-Media Workshop
1997	N-Museum
1997	M-House
1997	K-Head Office
1998	Park Cafe
1998	Gifu Kitagata Apartment 1st Stage
1998	U-Building
1999	O-Museum

1994	Architecture of the Year '94 award for Villa in the Forest
1995	Selected for Yokohama International Port Terminal Design Competition
1995	First Prize, Kenneth F. Brown Asia Pacific Culture and Architecture Design Award University of Hawaii for Saishunkan Seiyaku Women's Dormitory
1996	Second Prize, Hiroshima City Nishi Fire Station Design Competition
1996	Second Prize, Nagaoka Bunka Souzou Forum Design Competition
1997	Selected for New Campus Center for Illinois Institute of Technology Design Competition
1997	First Prize, Inter Intra Space Design Selection for Multi-Media Workshop
1998	The Prize of Architectural Institute of Japan for Multi-Media Workshop
1998	First Prize, Edifici-mondo: a competition for the recuperation of the antique quarter of Salerno
1999	First Prize, for Competition for the Stadstheater, Almere
1999	First Prize, Hirosaka Geijutsu Gai Design Proposal

Awards:
1988	Kajima Prize for Platform I and II
1989	Tokyo Architect Association Special Prize for Residential Architecture for Platform I
1989	The Yoshioka Prize for Platform I
1990	Honourable Mention La Maison de Culture de Japon, Paris
1990	SD Review 1990 Second Prize for Saishunkan Seiyaku Women's Dormitory
1991	Second Prize for Nasunogahara Harmony Hall Design Competition
1992	Japan Institute of Architects Young Architect of the Year for Saishunkan Seiyaku Women's Dormitory
1992	Second Prize, Commercial Space Design Award '92 for Castelbajac Sports Shop
1994	First Prize for Commercial Space Design Award '94 for Pachinko Parlour I & II

Exhibitions:
1990	Kazuyo Sejima, Panasonic Gallery, Tokyo
1993	Kazuyo Sejima – Twelve Projects, Gallery MA, Tokyo
1996	Kazuyo Sejima 1987-1996, Architectural Association, London
1998	Kazuyo Sejima + Ryue Nishizawa, GA Gallery, Tokyo
1999	Participation in exhibition 'Un-Private House', MOMA, New York

Publications:
Sejima, K. (1996) 'Kazuyo Sejima & Associates 1987-1996' *Kenchikubunka*, October

Sejima, K. (1996) 'Kazuyo Sejima 1988-1996' *El Croquis*, No. 77

Sejima, K. (1998) *GA Sejima Kazuyo Dokuhon*, Tokyo: ADA Edita

Sejima, K. (1999) *Sejima Kazuyo/ Kazuyo Sejima + Ryue Nishizawa*, Tokyo: Shinkenchikusha

Soul Provider

Toshiyuki Kita

「 Design isn't styling, it is the balance between the economy and environment, between people and products 」

Design is the intelligence that drives the product. Without it, all you have is a two dollar lump of plastic! Or at least that's how one wag summed up the significance of product design. And if the image of the Japanese as the world's most committed consumers is true, then the country should be product designer heaven. But for Toshiyuki Kita chasing fashions, or producing new and ever more attractive designs as part of a rising plume of economic growth, is far too narrow a view to encompass his interests and roles. Conscious that since the Second World War consumption has been the main focus for the Japanese economy – and so design – he has combined an idiosyncratic design sense with a strong social philosophy to create 'products with soul'.

Though now dividing his time between Italy and Japan, the product that first launched his international career was 'Wink' (1980). More sofa insect than arm chair, the 'Wink' chair mischievously moved to provide a range of positions. Sitting sideways, straddled, lounged over backwards, it wasn't just flexible enough to suit one's moods, it could actually create them. Typical of Kita's designs, it writhes with humorous undertones and reference to natural forms. The chair's

The 'Wink' chair (1980, Cassina, Italy). Selected for the New York Museum of Modern Art permanent collection in 1981, the back can be adjusted to any angle. The head-rest supports the head and can be bent backwards if necessary. The legs can be extended forward to support the whole body and the covering is easily removed for laundering.

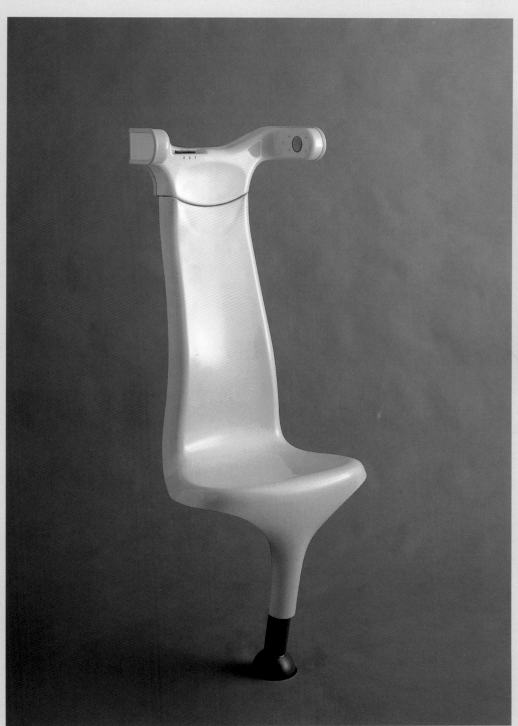

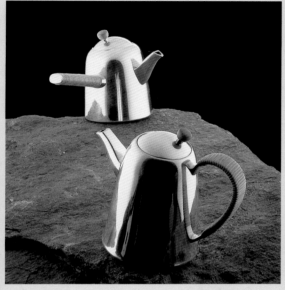

'Cha à la Carte', Kyusu and Pot (1994, Mariage Frères, France). Recalling the popular tin works of a bygone era in Osaka, these recent revivals are a living memorial which focus on themes of 'tea'. Tin, with its low melting point, is easily shaped and an excellent material for recycling.

'Multi-lingual Chair' (1992, Kotobuki, Japan). This chair can 'speak' in three languages. Specifically designed for the rotating theatre at Expo '92 in Seville, Spain, the head rest has two speakers installed which operate on three different channels from which you can select your preferred language. In 1997 it was selected for the permanent collection of the New York Museum of Modern Art.

unorthodox flexible form is emphasised by the brightly-coloured fabric covers: like animal ears or the ends of a finger puppet, they call you in, a soft furnishing siren from the rocks of a stressful world. Manufactured by Cesare Cassina, the father of modern Italian furniture design, it grew out of a chance encounter while Kita was in Italy on a self-styled sabbatical studying lifestyles. In fact he now divides his time between Italy and Japan. Although that might sound like the ultimate gap-year snooze, for Kita it was the overture to a rhythmic strand that has reverberated through his design work: how product design can improve the relationship between people and the environment. But first he realised that products are like flowers, they need the right medium to grow in, and lifestyle provides the context.

Drawn to Italy initially by an interest in Italian arts, he was shocked by both their philosophy towards living and their lifestyle. What surprised him most was that although both countries had found themselves at a similar level after the war, by the 1960s, Italian lifestyles had moved ahead. Italy now had 'lifestyle infrastructure' of parks and good housing, whereas in Japan, it was tiny cramped apartments, overcrowded trains and an urban fabric of amorphous architecture threaded together by overhead electric power lines.

This consciousness about lifestyle problems is now an important source driving the direction of his design work. Instead of just attraction or function, Kita's products are designed to induce affection and fraternity in the people who use them. One of Kita's recent designs that reflects this concern is Cha à la carte. Made from recycled pewter but using traditional craftsmanship from the Osaka-based company Suzuhan, the series of tea vessels exudes an aged ambience through its modern design. The vessel's forms are a curious amalgam: a kind of industrial finish meets portly village matron. Maybe it's their sonic form. Maybe it's their sheer balance that helps you relax. But for some inexplicable meaning, they just beg you to walk right up and give them a hug. Although Kita's philosophy of keeping old craft skills alive ensures that the wealth of knowledge accrued by years of experience is not lost, his products do look

incredibly stylish. You would be forgiven for mistaking form, styling and fashion as the key words to his work. Maybe that is his real talent – not just to spot the real 'function' of product design, but rather to do it in designs that seduce you through their forms first, their philosophy second. Kita has completely managed to avoid the nostalgia trap. He doesn't venerate the past but rather wants to make the positive points learnt through hundreds of years of cumulative experience part of Japan's present and future. It's probably important to do so to. Perhaps there has been no other culture that has so enthusiastically embraced technology, while refusing to stop hugging the past. Japan's love affair with technology isn't a revolution in the way that it is often portrayed. There are no heads on the castle ramparts or public spilling of 'traditional' blood. Rather they coexist. Or, perhaps it is better to say that like two boxers, they occupy the same ring, even if they are not on speaking terms.

But in spite of any uneasiness about the social losses he feels that are associated with industrialisation, he remains enthusiastic about good products

'Solar House' (1993, I.D.K. Design, Japan). 'One way of resolving this problem of the loss of balance between nature and human behaviour might be by adopting the idea of generating electricity from sunlight and wind. We could then generate power from these humble sources of energy for our everyday lives; we could drive cars during the day propelled by the power generated overnight from the wind. On the roof of this house there are solar battery panels as well as a windsail, which can both be used to generate electricity. When the wind is too strong, the sails will automatically fold away. It may be the arrival of a new vision, but perhaps, it is time to test our intelligence and our wisdom'.

making better lifestyles for the future. In 1992 he designed a single stem yellow plastic chair for Japan's pavilion at the Seville Expo that offers simultaneous translations in three languages. These are delivered through headphones that meld out of the top of the chair to wrap around your ears. More recently he has designed a solar house for the future. Still at the concept stage, the building's square plan is protected by wide eaves that take the traditional Japanese house style and, literally, extend it to reduce heat load. With a solar panel roof and windmill rising out of the roof, the two-storey structure's energy needs will be naturally met. Kita's energy independent house is perfect for Japan with its poor resources and helps to solve the question that the Industrial Revolution started, but never got around to answering. Namely, how will new technology improve lives without destroying the environment? It's a question that hasn't commanded too much attention in corporate Japan. His concern

for products to contribute to solving the problems of the rapidly expanding 'new age' doesn't seem to strike a chord with the audience in Japan which has grown economically powerful from a policy of looking towards other cultures for ideas and markets. It's either been a policy of looking to the past – retro products – or looking too far into the future – undersea cities.

Kita has more commissions from European companies than those in his native country, to design products that utilise new materials and create new functions. But with its exporting base moving to Asia, what will Japan's role be from now on? Dividing his time between Europe and Japan, and practising a kind of borderless design, has given Kita a unique insight into Japan's place in the world and where it needs to go from now on. As he says, 'one answer to Japan's problems is design, but that idea of the importance of design, its real meaning, is still not well understood here yet.' ∎

How do you see the present condition of urban Japan as a product designer?

Japan's problems now are related to the changes in lifestyle since the end of the Second World War. Industry and the economy have been the main focus and developments in people's lifestyles have been left behind. It's a huge problem for Japan. Of course the landscape isn't well designed, houses are tiny, trains crowded, there are electric lines everywhere you look. Progress in people's lifestyles stopped in around the 1960s. It's partially reflected in the streetscape of the towns and cities you see as you go around Japan, but actually the problems go much deeper. These lifestyle problems are intimately related to the needs and direction of my design work. The balance between lifestyles and the environment and earth is the key and my role is to improve this balance through the creative use of new technology. Houses without electrical wiring for example. Or products made from recycled materials. I am searching for the next step,

the new direction for products to take. Useful. Attractive. Economical. Products that only rely on these words or concepts will not be enough from now on, and what is needed – how should I phrase it? – are objects with soul, things with expression or imagination so people will value them and not just quickly tire of them and throw them away. After the Second World War, consumption became the main focus, but this has resulted in a poor relationship between people and products. We need to make things that people value. *Aichaku* in Japanese. For this, just form and function is no good, it's not enough, they need soul. That is the way I design. For example these aluminium pots I designed are made from melted down aluminium pots, just heat to 232 °C and you can form them into a completely new product, give them life again. Japan is not a Western country or a purely Asian country – it is a mixed society and is kind of a world first, an experimental society if you will. Now other Asian countries are looking at Japan to see what facets we are doing work well, and at those which don't. So in a sense Japan itself is kind of a sample, an ambiguous sample of East and West.

Why did you go to Italy?

I had an interest in Italian arts, and I first visited at the age of twenty-six. Their philosophy of living, of lifestyle, was a huge shock to me. It was during my stay that I was invited to work by Cassina and designed my first product for them. The 'Wink' Chair became quite a hit so I decided to stay longer.

What was it exactly that surprised you about their way of life?

Toshiyuki Kita and the author talking.

'Hop' (1989, Wittman, Austria). An organically-shaped sofa that looks ready to embrace people softly. Its name is derived from the form – it looks like it is ready to hop.

What came as a huge surprise to me about Italy was that after the war the level of Italy's and Japan's standard of living was the same. But by the 1960s, Italy had progressed a lot in terms of lifestyle, including housing of course. Why was Japan so behind? I was curious as to why, so I decided to stay there, instead of just a short trip and return home, as I felt that to live, to experience for yourself was vital to understanding how Japan had gone wrong. But working for Cassina, I enjoyed more and more success, so the research took a back seat! Japan's current problem is that people's lifestyles have changed, a house is just a place to sleep and eat before going back to work. Japan's main problem now is that since the beginning of modern industry something important has been lost. And as it's lost people increasingly forget what it was that had existed before. One facet of this is that

interpersonal communication has been lost, the environment has been degraded, and the old town-scapes have disappeared. Industry has moved abroad to Asia and China and so how will Japan 'make a living' in the future? What will we do to earn our keep? Japan's earlier products like cars and cameras had a higher quality than now and I believe that that was a reflection of the quality of its workers.

In what way?

Well in those days people understood and behaved differently, more sincerely, at festivals like the New Year's Day. They went to temples and shrines and embraced those traditional ceremonies. But recent

changes in lifestyle, as these customs have been lost, have reduced the quality of people. These small houses we live in now and poor lifestyles cannot produce the workers Japan needs. Italy and Germany also lost the war, of course, but what is different about their post-sixties societies? They both have what I call social infrastructure, or maybe 'lifestyle infrastructure' is the best expression. They have real cities with parks and good housing. Japan doesn't have these and so has lost its target for the future. Until the sixties, of course, the economy was the target, but now? What are we aiming for? Because I practice borderless design, travelling between Europe and Japan, I have my antennae out for possible changes. That's why I design these recycled products, and this is the message I would like to send out.

Looking over your products from the 'Wink' chair onward, I find all of them have an irrepressible humorous nature. Where do you get your design inspiration from?

Well I cannot explain clearly but it stems from my personality. I often find inspiration from nature, animals, plants and I guess my work reflects this playful side of my personality. Natural phenomena and nature are something I've always liked. Nature is always changing, flowers blooming, leaves changing colour in autumn. Well, anyway, I have definitely been influenced from somewhere or other. Curiosity has always been a key facet for me, for my designs and for life in general. And I've always liked making things too. Now is the computer age, so this chair design, 'Hop' [1989], for example, is for a home office. It's half office chair and half home chair and swivels in many directions so you can work here then swing around to do another task. From now on, the time spent on computers at home will increase dramatically. But there is no chair designed at present that fits this niche, is expressly designed for this new way of life. The flow of the new age is something we are now in and that is the designer's work. It's no good looking over your shoulder as we cannot go back to the past. You have to draft the route ahead. We as designers cannot look backwards. We have to move ahead, but there is no road leading us in the right direction. What we designers have to do is to

'Dodo' (1998, Adele C, Italy). With Dodo, design becomes a concept of mobility and diversity, for 'drawing-room gossip rather than frivolous chat, for studying or working, typing on a computer while sitting in an ergonomic position, and between one sentence and the next, pausing to stretch one's back; for having a beer, flicking through a newspaper and even taking a nap.'

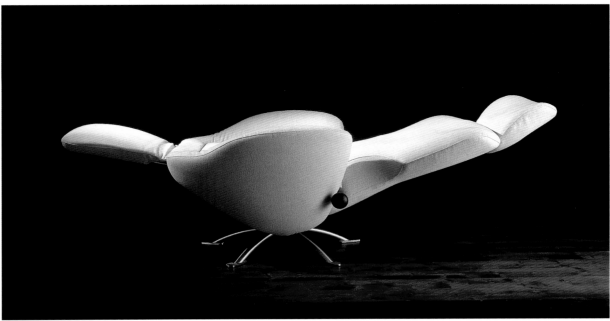

find the right balance and this is crucial for the world environment. We have to find an alternative to the petrol engine. We have to find the balance for recycling. To find solutions for the problems of the new computer age. We have to change our life-styles, not continue following the American consumer model of manufacture and throw away, manufacture and throw away. We have to put a brake on that.

What is product design?

Well if you make just one car then it will cost tens of thousands of pounds. But as the number manufactured increases then the cost comes down. So for these industrial products there are economies of scale. So there are two types really, products that are mass-manufactured and crafts. In the past if people wanted a chair then they would make it themselves. But now that is no longer possible, we work in different industries and buy the things we need that others have made and which are available in the marketplace. Without the availability of products we cannot live anymore. Towards products, society is now very complicated. So one thing that we can rely on to solve this is product design. Flowers don't grow up from nothing. Without land and sun and water and time they cannot grow. So to think of design from the stance of function or style is the wrong place to start. Products are like that too. You have to have the right base for good products. This is where my interest in lifestyle came from. It is the base for products. So this is Japan's biggest problem now. In the post-war hurry to industrialise and modernise, Japan's lifestyles have been left behind. So this is a problem from forty years ago which is now appearing in Japanese society. So from now on Japan will have a hard time of it.

For an exhibition called 'Ceremony' in 1986, you . . .

Yes. I constructed two types of space for the future: the virtual reality world and a tea ceremony space, an imaginary world, the world that inhabits our hearts. Our lives will of course be enriched by this new technological world. These together make the 'future'. The future will not just be technology but a spiritual world as well. I see the future as living half in the virtual world and half in the spiritual world. So at that time, if we are not careful, the distinction between reality and virtual reality will not be clear. So one's own identity will be crucial then. Children in Japan already spend half their time in the virtual world or with computer images.

In the exhibition you divided these two worlds into two different areas. Was that an expression of your concern to keep their identities separate?

They were split into two clear parts for the exhibition to clarify their roles, not as a symbol of their incompatibility. The balance between the two will be very important. But we will need both. Of course without new technology our lives will cease to be possible. But the problem will be how to distinguish between that which is reality and that which is not. How to control the balance between these two worlds is the key for the future, not just in Japan but world-wide. In our generation we understand the difference between the real world and the virtual world. The problems will arise for the next generation. How will they cope? People's personalities will change, I think, as the boundaries between the two become blurred. Technology is a wonderful thing. But wonderful things are the most dangerous.

What most fascinates you about the future of product design?

New materials and new functions. How to fuse the two into something real. For me the design process is important, meeting the client, understanding their problems. It is rare for me to work like an artist, as such, suggesting a finished product to the client; rather, I work with the client to help solve their problems. Later I make prototypes to check the three-dimensional forms. It's like being a doctor. I'm invited to help the sick companies, not the healthy ones!

As industrial techniques improve and products are refined further, won't the necessity for product design disappear?

No, the opposite will occur. When you look from one viewpoint the problems may be diminishing but as soon as you turn to look from another direction, another problem appears. For example, the case of cars in

Ceremony Space (1986, Omukai Koshudo, Japan). Designed to remind people of the culture of tatami and the culture of the spirit. A 1.8 m cube, made of only lacquered wooden columns and natural tatami mats, it contains the cosmos.

Japan: Mercedes does this, so we'll do it too. That kind of idea is now fatal for Japan. Japan has to make completely new products from now on. Also it is no good to look to the past. A nostalgic retro product may be a hit once but after that it won't be, and the company's effort and viewpoint will be looking in the wrong direction. It's so dangerous for Japan. The country's power will be diminished. What Japan has to do now is to make the next generation of products, for example, waterless washing machines. Now the Bullet-Train is a world leader, but what will follow it? If Japan doesn't do this then the economy will face problems and become weaker in the future. So instead of us product designers being asked to make something cheaper, we should be being asked to produce something new. One reason why I work less in Japan than in Europe is that Japanese companies don't often share my viewpoint. I am more often asked by Western firms to develop new products than by those in Japan.

How do you account for that?

Since the Meiji period [1868–1912] Japan has always sought inspiration from other cultures, but that time has passed and now it needs to be making new products before they appear elsewhere. Japan's economy grew strong from exporting and that was also one reason why it looked to the West, to see what markets there wanted. But now Japan's manufacturing is moving to Asian countries, what will the role of Japan be from now on? One solution to these problems is design, but that idea of the importance of design, the real meaning, is not really well understood yet. What we will need as Japan's population ages – it will be one of our biggest challenges – is something completely new to meet this. We may live in a different place, but as the times change we need new equipment, so what will that be? Also the use of traditional materials like *washi* (hand-made paper) and *urushi* (lacquer work) in a new and renovated way. These two threads will be

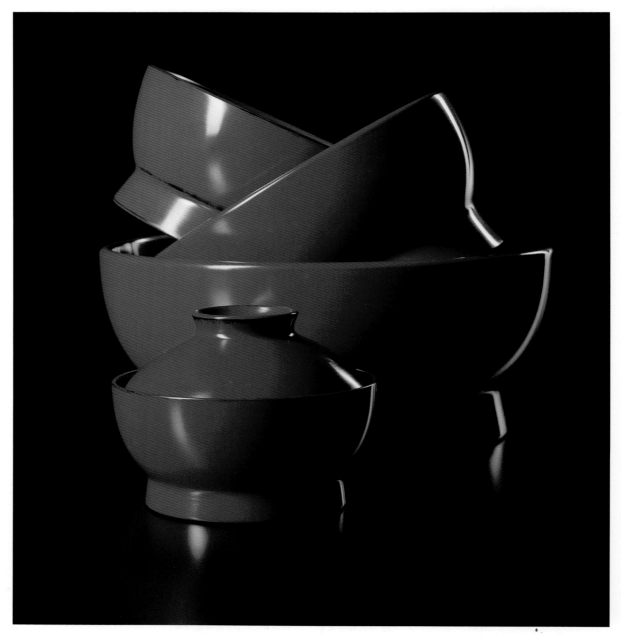

Yamanaka Urushi Bowls
(1997, I.D.K., Japan).

interlinked in future products. So the future will not be just high technology. It's a great mistake to think so.

Will these two strands be linked in individual products?

Well, I would like to create a combined product but what I mean is that both aspects will be necessary to ensure a balanced future. From now on, not just in Japan but world-wide, to take those old traditional ideas and the emerging technologies and harness them together will be the key to the future. So this is the type of product that I would like to be involved in designing.

Are you concerned that Japan's culture will be threatened by the increasing globalisation of technology?

Well it won't be lost but these types of products that revitalise traditional techniques of *washi* and *urushi* are something that I want to continue exploring. But it's vital that the chance is taken now as this is the last breath of Japanese traditional culture. In a sense we are in the middle, between the unknown horizons of the emerging technologies and the disappearing crafts of the past. That is why our role is so vital, for both directions. So to make new products that utilise both strands of our present existence is the key. I don't mean in the nationalist sense of the word, but pride or, maybe I should say, identity is being lost in the younger generations in Japan. This is something that is affecting not just lifestyles but the urban condition too. You see people walking around Osaka or Tokyo now with dyed blond hair. I don't want to sound out-dated but it seems to me that it is indicative of their desire to throw away, consciously or maybe unconsciously, their Japanese heritage and identity. That is such a dangerous route to choose. People don't stay in Japan for the New Year, they go to Hawaii. Japan in a sense is a reservoir of world culture. It was the final destination of Persian, or Middle Eastern culture, that was then fermented here to create 'Japanese culture'. So in a sense it is precious. So although the problems that Japan faces might seem to be purely internal ones, they are actually problems for the whole world.

Recently Japan has been the source of new technology that has then spread world-wide?

Well Japan has no energy sources or raw materials so the people have become the replacement raw material. And it just makes sense that if you have to export goods, then something compact for 2,000 dollars is much better than something large for the same price! It's been a question of necessity for Japan to choose this way. It's just pure pragmatism. But from now on the two key words will be technology and design. But in order to realise great design you have to have a base. And that base? It's lifestyle. So we have to design technology to make people happy. Let them realise happiness. So what distinguishes technological products from traditional ones? Well, traditions encapsulate time. So products that combine traditional materials like *washi* are able to traverse the divide between simple things and become objects that pocess a heart. So Japan's traditions are fermented from a combination of East and West. It's different from China, for example, that is really the centre of 'Asian' culture, so in that sense it is being a global culture which gives Japan a unique role. This diversity is most easily understood from our food. From just one glance you can see the variation, the richness.

So do you feel your Japanese identity when you work abroad? Even with your international lifestyle?

Oh yes, I'm always conscious of it.

But you cannot return to the past in Japan.

No definitely not. But through spirit or identity I believe it will be continued. The tea ceremony in Japan is one expression of our cultural identity. There is a relationship between objects and people, between individuals, and between them and the space. But what people see as a cultural relic, in the formalised movements of the tea ceremony, for example, is actually function perfected. It may seem natural but it is actually a perfect expression of function. There isn't a single wasted movement. It's perfect, and so connects to the heart.

So Japanese culture is an expression of function?

Well function and communication. In the two *tatami* mats of a tea ceremony room exists a complete and self-contained universe.

Do you see the influx of Western ideas and thoughts from the start of the Meiji Period as purely destructive for Japanese culture?

No. We learnt something from it too. I guess I am an extension of that with my borderless design.

Have you been influenced by design movements in other disciplines?

Basically speaking, no. At the time they each seemed to be quite impressive but looking back now they seem so distant. Even the recent ones! So traditional design in Japan, with its emphasis on simple expression, seems even now to be timeless. It's less a question of object than soul or emotion. If we don't acknowledge this then the earth will be destroyed.

Although product design is slightly distant from environmental issues per se, what are your feelings towards design's potential to solve them?

Well if we carry on with consumption then we will reach the point where we crash directly into environmental problems. How would we manage without paper or fabric? The balance between the environment and products and people will be destroyed when that happens. It was one of the strengths of Japanese traditional culture that it maintained the balance between people and the environment. In my work I want to harness new technology to help society return towards the direction of a balanced relationship with the environment. Gas-less car engines for example. Design isn't styling. Design is the key to realise this balance between the economy and environment, between people and products. It is the balance between all facets of life. Good design is good balance. So in that sense Japanese traditional design was sophisticated. Not just Japan but in Europe too. In earlier times people lived in balance with their environment. So it wasn't just a design balance but a social one. In the future the importance of this balance will be understood again. In twenty years time, if it is able to overcome present problems well, Japan will be mixing tradition and new technology, and will be a country empowered by design. If it cannot do that, then Japan will be finished. ■

Toshiyuki Kita was interviewed in his office in Osaka on 19 October 1996 and 26 December 1998

TOSHIYUKI KITA
1942 Born in Osaka

Education:
1961   Graduated in Industrial Design, Naniwa College, Osaka

Employment:
1967   Established design office in Osaka and started studying habitat, lifestyle, and traditional crafts in local areas

1969   Began working in Japan and Italy

Major Projects:
1970   'Kyo' Lamp
1971   'Tako' Bracket
1980   'Wink' Chair
1982   Digital Clock
1983   'Kick' Table
1983   I, II Chair for Rest
1986   'Cesa' Tableware
1986   'Luck' Sofa
1987   'Cyborg' Chair
1988   'Repro' Clock, Ash Tray, Stand and Pen Tray
1988   'Nice' Chair
1988   'Ara' Sofa
1989   'Hop' Sofa and Chair
1992   Chairs and Interior for the Rotating Theatre at the Japan Pavilion, Expo '92 Seville (including 'Multi-lingual Chair')
1994   Ibuki Monument, Wakayama

Awards:
1975   Japan Interior Designers Association Award
1981   9th Kitari Kunii Industrial Design Award
1981   'Wink' Chair

1983	Institute of Business Designers and Contract Magazine Product Design Award
1984	'Kick' Table, included in the Permanent Collection of the Museum of Modern Art, New York
1985	Mainichi Design Award
1990	Delta del' Oro Award
1997	'Multi-lingual Chair', included in the Permanent Collection of the Museum of Modern Art New York
1997	'Multi-lingual Chair', included in the Permanent Collection of the Pompidou Centre, Paris
1999	Fourteen pieces of work included in the Permanent Collection of the Museum of Modern Art, Saint-Etienne

Exhibitions:

1986	Ceremony Exhibition – The World of Toshiyuki Kita, Tokyo
1986	Silver and Urushi, Milan
1987	From the Twentieth Century to the New Century, Pompidou Centre Paris
1988	Toshiyuki Kita: Two Spaces, Barcelona
1989	Movement as Concept, Tokyo
1990	Arts Decoratif Museum, Helsinki
1991	Hiroshima Museum of Modern Art, Hiroshima

Publications:

Kita, T (1990) Movement as Concept, Tokyo: Rikuyo-sha

Paper Architecture

Shigeru Ban

⌈ Now the world really has become globalised, we don't need to have any pre-existing relationship with people in order to offer them help ⌋

Takatori Church (1995), Kobe.

Shigeru Ban's career has taken a lot of unexpected turns, but has never looked back. Unexcited by the potential for architectural study in Tokyo he went to the Southern California Institute of Architecture before graduating in 1984 from New York's Cooper Union School of Architecture. Working on an exhibition for the Axis Gallery in Tokyo, he discovered the potential of paper as an architectural material. He became the first Japanese member of disaster relief organisation Red R. In 1994 he became a consultant to the United Nations High Commission for Refugees and won five awards for his work in 1996 alone. But these achievements are incidental notes; the real rhapsody is in the work.

For the Takatori Church (1995) in Kobe's Nagata-Ward he created a simple, pared down community space that is simply astounding. Inspired by memories of other churches with layers of space, Ban's design for the church – to replace the original destroyed by the Hanshin Earthquake of 1995 – is structured from two superimposed forms. A 10 by 15 metre rectangle, fabricated from frames of steel scaffolding supporting thin walls of translucent polycarbonate sheeting, forms the exterior layer. Inside, a simple oval is composed

from paper tubes. Initially placed adjacent to each other, they fan out at gradually increasing intervals seemingly warped into an oval by a mysterious force to form a solid backdrop behind the altar. But a progressively more permeable front allows people access and lets light flood in. Designed to be built by volunteer labour, the church has a flat roof without drainage and simple wooden cross-shaped joints anchoring the paper tubes to the concrete floor. The internal ambience of the church, however, belies its

simple materials and construction. The filtered light and calm brown of the columns are a mysterious combination of the wooded approach to Ise Shrine, Japan's most sacred Shinto shrine, and the solemn volumes of a Western church. The translucent edge to the building filters out the surrounding city, the material a kind of impermeable membrane that sanctifies the space. It gives the interior the ambience of a misty forest edge – come here at sundown and you'd half expect to see deer.

Ban's design for the church is a continuation of the long architectural tradition of exploring the spiritual qualities of materials in churches. Milan has its marble *Duomo*, Le Corbusier used concrete for the Notre-Dame-du-Haut, Ronchamp, but the Takatori Church – the Paper Church – is a symbolic celebration of his use of paper as a building material. First discovering the material almost by chance while organising exhibitions of Emilio Ambasz's and Alvar Aalto's work for a gallery

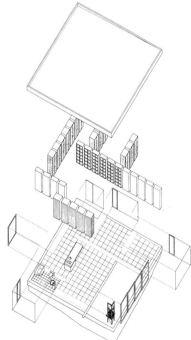

The Furniture House (1995), Yamanashi Prefecture.

Axonometric of the Furniture House.

in Tokyo, he later realised that it had potential for use as a structural element. Armed with this invention and inspired by the tradition of student volunteer work he saw while studying at the Cooper Union, Ban proposed paper 'log cabins' to the United Nations High Commission for Refugees (UNHCR) in response to the crisis in Rwanda in 1994. Although this idea was rejected as too expensive and structurally permanent, UNHCR did hire Ban as a consultant. His brief was to develop paper tube tent poles to alleviate the environmental damage from two million Rwandan refugees using local wood to support the plastic tent material relief agencies were providing. And it was while working on this project that the earthquake struck Kobe.

The exploration of unconventional materials and new methods of working is something that Ban has continued in other projects, including the Curtain Wall House (1995), and the Furniture House (1995) near Lake Yamanaka in Yamanashi Prefecture. While designing an earlier paper tube structure for a poet's library, Ban realised that he could make a building without the paper structural elements by putting a roof directly on top of bookcases. At the Furniture House, these 'bookcase walls', together with wardrobes and kitchen cupboards, were factory manufactured from orientated-strand-board (OSB) and simply screwed into the floor, each other, and later the roof, to form a series of structural active members that doubled as space dividers. By having them factory manufactured rather than made on site they could be finished to a higher quality and, weighing only 80 kilograms each, were easily moved and quickly assembled. In fact the structure can be built in a day, with just the roof to add, all saving time and construction costs.

In a country sometimes more associated with wild architectural styles and high-profile costly icons, Ban's low-cost, socially expansive architecture is unique in two important ways. It examines how recycled materials can be used to create contemporary spaces, and does

so in buildings that carry it off with such great style. Other attempts at green architecture, or environmental architecture, have often floundered on a rock of their own creation. They are fascinating intellectual studies of something we know is good for us, but finally the spaces they create are ones that we ourselves would never want to live in. Ban's architecture somehow crafts spaces of such inquisitiveness and hallowed reverence that we forget there is a clear message he is offering, not just for Japanese design, but for all of us. The final result of his designs is both visually delicious and a wonderful meal for the soul.

What makes Ban's spaces particularly remarkable is that he has been able to create entirely new spaces, spaces with a material quality that has never been experienced before. This is not through dependence on new technology to form or discover new materials, but by re-examining existing materials in recycled forms. There has always been something of a spiritual preference in Japan for 'natural' housing materials. And while wood was a sustainable resource, wooden residential architecture was a warm expression of this affinity to nature. But the environmental concerns of the next millennium coupled with a natural attraction to 'newness' in Japan – so housing is replaced on a endless short-term cycle – means Ban's work is now timely. By utilising the warm-brown lustre of paper tubes, by emphasising their 'natural' qualities, he manages to straddle both the rock, and the hard place. Paper architecture addresses both spiritual and environmental needs.

For me the best part of Ban's work is that he is moving Japanese architecture away from its recent role as the mouthpiece of developers and has started a new process. In addition to his projects for private and public bodies, his work for refugees, and society in a new expansive meaning of the word, illustrates in the most vivid way that architecture can be both spatial and social. ■

Paper seems at first glance a highly improbable material for architecture. When was your first encounter with paper tubes and how did you realise their architectural potential?

The exhibition I designed to display the work of Alvar Aalto in 1986 was the first time I ever used paper tubes in an interior space. Prior to that I had designed an installation at the Axis Gallery in Tokyo of Emilio Ambasz's projects where I used fabric screens to divide the space. When the screen that I designed for the exhibition arrived from the factory, it came in paper tubes. After we hung the fabric the paper tubes were just left over as waste. Usually people throw them away but I hate to dispose of anything and, in fact, I often collect things spontaneously and take them back to my office. I am very interested in raw materials and with a vague notion that I would like to think of some purpose for the material, I took some paper tubes back to my office. Louis Kahn is quoted as saying, 'materials are waiting to be used'. Paper tubes are manufactured simply to roll something on, but they are made of recycled paper, are inexpensive, and have a warm colour reminiscent of wood.

When I designed the Aalto exhibition I had only a very limited budget for installation. As the exhibition was to run for only a few weeks, after which we would throw the material away again, I decided to use the paper tubes that were still standing in a corner of my office. Although my budget was too small to use real wood, I wanted to make the gallery interior relate to what Aalto had done. He had used wood with a very organic feeling. Rather than replicate exactly what he had done, I wanted to express my own attitude too, so I replaced the wood with paper tubes. I inquired at factories about prices and dimensions, the possible thickness, the lengths, the diameters. The material is in fact free and flexible, with the capacity to be manufactured in endless lengths. So I used three different diameters for the ceiling, the free-standing partitions, and some pedestals, and still it was very inexpensive. That is how I first became acquainted with the paper tube. Later I discovered that the tubes were much stronger than I had expected and could be used for actual building, for structural elements too.

When did you first use paper for 'architecture'?

It was used for a small external structure at a Design Expo in Nagoya in 1989. It was about six metres in diameter and four metres high. My friend organised the landscape and he used a *suikinkutsu*, a musical instrument in the traditional Japanese garden. It makes a very nice but slightly eerie sound and was popular in the Edo period [1600-1868]. Usually the Expo is very noisy and crowded so I designed this small structure to allow people to concentrate on this sound. First we built it in Tokyo to check the details and also do a structural examination. In order to build a new structure we have to go through the national Architecture Centre, submit papers, go through examinations and hearings, all because this paper technology is not covered in Japan's Basic Architectural Law. It is a long, expensive process, particularly for such a small building, but with the help of a good structural engineer we tested it and got permission from the committee of the Expo as we were working.

And that was when you met Gengo Matsui, the structural engineer?

Yes. I was really lucky to meet him as he was one of the leading structural engineers and was always willing to challenge new methods. As he was so famous young architects usually didn't approach him, but I did not hesitate. He already had experience of many wooden structures, had worked with bamboo and was fascinated by the challenges of paper. It was due to his support that I could realise paper tube structures.

When the earthquake struck Kobe you were already working for UNHCR?

Yes. I had been working for UNHCR since 1994, the time of the Rwanda crisis. People there were suffering from cold in the rainy season in September so I proposed a better shelter made from paper, which has good insulation properties, is inexpensive and relatively warm. I sent my proposal and portfolio to UNHCR in 1994 and I went to Geneva to discuss it with the head of the Program and Technical Support Section. He was fascinated by the concept but told me they have a maximum of only 30 dollars per unit. They cannot

The Alvar Aalto exhibition at the Axis Gallery (1986), Tokyo.

Axonometric of the Odawara Festival Hall (1990), Kanagawa Prefecture.

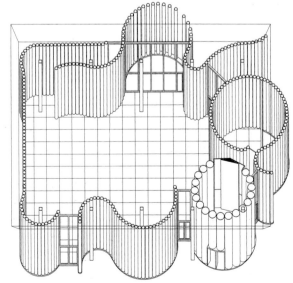

provide a better shelter to the refugees as they are not supposed to give them something which might encourage them to stay in what are supposed to be temporary shelters for a particular emergency situation. They can only give them the basics. He rejected my proposal but he was very interested in the paper tube structure as one of the biggest problems they face is environmental. UNHCR at that time provided only a plastic sheet for the refugees. They then cut down trees to make poles for a frame and with over two million refugees in Tanzania and Zaire, entire forests were being felled to make shelters and be used for cooking. UNHCR had tried providing aluminium tubes but the refugees sold them for the money and then started cutting trees again. Anyway, it was proposed that I work for UNHCR as a consultant to develop this paper tube idea further. That was at the end of 1994, and then on 17 January, 1995, the Kobe crisis happened.

Why did you go to the Takatori Church?

Many people wanted to work in Kobe as volunteers but they didn't know where to go and what to do. But through my involvement with UNHCR I knew there were Vietnamese refugees at Takatori Church and so that was the place for me to start. When I first met Father Kanda there, it was during a morning service that was being held outside by firelight. I had attended many other services and, although I'm not a Christian, this was the first time I felt the significance of what was taking place. I proposed rebuilding the church using paper but the idea was rejected. Father Kanda's reason was actually very convincing. While all the houses around the church had been destroyed by fire was it proper to rebuild the church before the neighbourhood? He himself felt that only after the original building was destroyed, had it became a real church. He had found that the building is less important than the space itself. Spiritual space could exist without architecture. That was a very convincing argument for an architect. However, he suggested I make a community space using volunteers. The area I was given was 10 by 15 metres.

I have visited many churches throughout the world and usually they make use of spatial layering. We don't enter the main space directly from outside so such layering is very important for the space. As rounded forms are structurally superior for paper tube structures because the forces are even, I took the rectangle and decided to make an oval form; in fact a Bernini oval, after the Italian architect who invented it and used it for many Baroque churches in Italy. I proposed to sort out the funding and the volunteers by myself, as promised. I needed about ten million yen. When I had acquired about 80 per cent I started construction and hoped the rest would arrive.

While the church design was progressing you became involved with housing for the Vietnamese refugees made homeless by the earthquake?

That's right. As the government was promising to build sufficient temporary housing quickly, I decided to work for the community rather than repair private residences. I knew the Vietnamese refugees from Takatori Church

and I was interested in what kind of conditions they lived in. I was shocked when I saw them. Their tents were very poorly constructed, it was now May so very hot, almost 40 °C, and on rainy days the floors were flooded. Many Japanese neighbours were complaining that their housing in the park was in danger of becoming a slum. They were pressurised to leave and I was very disappointed that the government failed to provide alternative housing. If they did so, it was very far from their existing location. The Vietnamese didn't want to move further away because they worked in shoe factories nearby that didn't pay transportation,

A finished 'Log Cabin' in Kobe (1995).

and with many other foreign children in their schools, they felt comfortable. They decided to stay in the park and I wanted to build better temporary housing for them. The church offered us a free dormitory for the volunteers and so we built about thirty houses, each 16 metres square at a cost of 250,000 yen.

An important design criteria was what would happen when the structures were dismantled. The government was building many steel, prefabricated, temporary houses for people made homeless by the earthquake without thinking of how to dispose of them. I thought it vital that they be cheap and easy to build, but equally, cheap and easy to take down. The government didn't realise how much cost would be incurred in dismantling them. I therefore used beer crates for the base. Paper tubes can be recycled or even burnt. Beer crates can be returned to the factory for recycling and are very lightweight. We calculated the wind pressure from typhoons and from this how many sandbags to put into the crates!

I would love to see that calculation!

The ceiling was made of double-skinned tent material and could be opened at the ends to let air circulate in summer. Located at two-metre intervals, the houses had the doors facing each other so people could extend the space in between them like a kind of semi-detached row house. It took only eight hours to assemble them once the parts were ready. While making the first six houses we were very worried that the city would stop us as it is illegal to build housing in that park, and it was right next to the city hall! In the morning the city hall staff even walked through it! So we assembled them very quickly. A plywood base on top of the beer cases connects to both the beer crates and floor and has slits cut into it to accommodate the ends of the pipes (an X in cross-section) which are nailed together. The paper tubes were also connected by the cross wires inside the tubes horizontally.

Did you consciously choose housing, and social housing in particular, as it is one area that Japanese post-war architecture seems to have been conspicuously uninterested in?

If you study the profile of architects you notice that it is crucial to realise some important projects before the age of forty. Most good architects built their own unique architecture when they were in their thirties and it is a very important period in which to establish one's own style. When I studied architectural history I consciously thought I should find my own direction. When I started working for UNHCR and working for Kobe I didn't consciously think that this would be what decided my next direction, in some kind of predetermined destiny. I think it is very important for architects to build social projects, not just monumental projects. At the beginning of this century, after the end of World War I and the Industrial Revolution, many towns were destroyed, creating a need for low-cost housing. Architects started creating projects for the general public rather than making monumental buildings for privileged people. After World War I, even Le Corbusier and other master architects of the twentieth century started work on housing projects and industrial buildings. Not just the number but the quality of that

architecture is one phenomena of architecture in the twentieth century.

Since the end of the Cold War there have been so many wars between nations or regional groups, for example, Bosnia, that refugees are increasing in number and natural disasters and crises force many people into homelessness. In the same way as the master architects who worked for the general public at the beginning of this century, we have to accommodate these minority people because after disasters, whether natural or man-made, housing always becomes the biggest problem. Be it Rwanda or Kobe, it's always housing. Of course I would like to design what is considered to be nice architecture but at the same time I believe that it is very important for us to face the real problems, especially housing problems. It is part of architecture, or it should be.

How does the design process work for you?

The site is the biggest influence when you start thinking about architecture. With the so-called International Style, the site was not so important, it could be anywhere. I try to rationalise some criteria of the requirements, the site situation, the budget, the owner's request – sometimes they are very negative – but I am very interested in producing a positive design, positive solution. So instead of just designing superficial ornament I am keen to solve the requirements of the existing problem and that determines the design solution. Of course I have my own methodology concerning the system or material used and sometimes I apply that, but the outcome is a synthesis of the two. For me, the details have to be as simple as possible. I never think about the details, I always try to erase them. In High-Tech design the structure becomes the ornament of the building but the client or the general public never understand or appreciate that over-designed structure. That is just self-satisfaction for the architect himself. My belief is that structure is important but not the structural design; not a structural solution that merely eases the superficial appearance of the structure.

You have now spread your work outside Japan. Do

you consider yourself to be an international architect or a Japanese one?

I would like to pocess my own style. Historically, Japanese people have been good at copying something, creating style by way of imitation. So many people now build in the style of Rem Koolhaas, and because of the strength of the economy and the skill of construction companies, they can build copies very quickly. Some buildings designed in Europe remain unbuilt projects or competition ideas that are not realised due to economic constraints, and Japanese architects just steal fragments of the work and reorganise it for their own design. They are very good at that! The big difference between many architects and artists in Japan and in the West is that their definition of influence and copying is so different. No-one can define the range of 'copying' or 'influence' but by studying the history of design we can define the limit, by ourselves. The same definition exists for good architects in any country, but second-level architects just copy. So the difference between the two can be perceived in terms of this definition. Second-class architects have a wider range of influences because they think that they are influences, but actually they are copies. Historically, of course, all of Japanese culture is copied from China and Korea but maybe I shouldn't continue . . .

Were you influenced by a particular person?

At school we had to study and analyse the history of architecture and all the masters influenced me. If you look at any of my work you can see the influence of Mies van der Rohe, Le Corbusier, even Frank Lloyd Wright. If you look at my early work you can see the influence of John Hejduk, or Richard Meier, but little by little I have established my own style.

Where do you think you will be in ten years time? Except for paper tubes, have you found another way to use paper or cardboard?

After I design something I get the impetus to develop an idea in a new direction. For example, this is a sample for the floor of the Millennium Dome, in London, where I'm working, and it is made from fine threads of paper, like string, used for packing. I asked

'The structure is important, but not the structural design.' Ban's own style, at the Paper House (1995), Yamanashi Prefecture.

Roof structure designed from LVL, engineered roof timber.

the manufacturer to make a mat out of it because I like the idea of reusing materials or recycling them after I have finished with them. In this way, both the structure of my pavilion and these other paper materials will themselves be recycled after the Expo has finished. I actually got this idea from the traditional Japanese ceiling called *anjiro tenjo* that is made from strips of wood or bamboo knitted together.

I am now designing a roof structure from LVL, engineered roof timber. The material seems similar to plywood but, unlike plywood which is glued in both X and Y directions, the thin sheets of LVL wood are glued in the same direction, making much stronger beams as a result. The site for this project is a very historical place and this new style timber roof will be hung in a three-dimensional curve. I was asked to use the traditional Japanese architectural style, including roof tiles, and this is the first time I have made use of the traditional-style pitched roof and roof tile. I didn't want to just design a traditional building but when I visited a local traditional Japanese temple I wondered why the roof had a concave curve. As its timber is in compression, the roof could be made flat or even convex. This temple curve was clearly made on purpose by master carpenters as an expression of their design. If I use a thin strip of timber I can make a tension curve that corresponds to this shape. It is more consistent structurally. So that is why I am now developing this building with, instead of an *anjiro tenjo*, an *anjiro* roof using LVL timber.

The Curtain Wall House (1995), Tokyo. This house was designed so that the client could enjoy the traditional openness of what is called the 'downtown culture' of Japanese city centres, but realised in contemporary materials. Views, light levels and ventilation are controlled through opening and closing this unique 'Japanese' curtain wall. Part sliding door, part shutter, this curtain is enclosed in winter by glass doors.

I'm interested to hear that you have been influenced by the traditions of Japanese architecture. Doesn't the notion of Paper Architecture have a Japanese connotation?
Consciously it is important but unconsciously it isn't important at all. As you know, I was educated in the United States so I haven't studied Japanese traditional architecture in any formal sense although of course I have seen many great examples. Every generation in Japan has different lifestyles. My grandparents can live only in a traditional-style Japanese house. My parents' generation need both Western and Japanese rooms, but for them a *tatami* room has become just a symbol – it's lucky if you have space for one some-where in your house – but they and of course now my generation cannot comfortably live in a traditional Japanese room anymore. I respect the Japanese style that projects require in order to fit into their site, and I respect the discrete history of Japanese architecture. But in order to design new Japanese architecture, I shouldn't just copy the style but should pick up some Japanese architectural concept and develop it further. Just keeping the style alone has no meaning anymore. If we have to make 'modern' Japanese architecture, but in concrete or steel, it is just a fake. It's not Japanese anymore. It's just the skin, just an ornament. People may think it is Japanese style, it may super-ficially look so, but the theory and ideas are not Japanese at all.

So where is the boundary that defines Japanese architecture? Is the essence of Japanese architecture connected with materials or spatial flexibility?
Materials. Flexibility of the space. And spirit of the space. Tadao Ando's work shows us that the style is not important in designing new Japanese architecture, it's the spirit.

When you look back now at your earlier projects can you see an influence, maybe a subconscious one, from Japanese traditions?
Well, when I designed the Curtain Wall House [1995] – it was recently selected for a MOMA exhibition called 'Un-Private Houses' – I was thinking consciously about

Japanese traditional architecture, at least the parts I felt familiar with; for example, the flexibility of the space, the connections between inside and outside, and when I developed the initial design idea I compared it with Mies's Farnsworth House. As you know, the Farnsworth House, where he invented the curtain wall of glass and metal cladding, is the first Western visually transparent house. Physically the glass is fixed so there is no actual connection between the interior and exterior. But in the traditional Japanese house with sliding screen partitions, the house is connected both visually and physically. So that is the fundamental difference between the traditional Japanese notion of transparency and Mies's definition of it. To return to the Curtain Wall House, the client's original house had been very traditional and I wanted to retain that kind of living style in their new house, using new materials, to show the Japanese concept of transparency, using the real curtain skin. Of course it was a kind of pun, but a practical solution too. We can draw the curtain

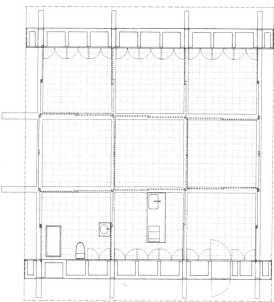

The Nine Square Grid House (1997), Kanagawa. The design incorporates a system of two walls and what Ban calls a 'Universal Floor', a unifying space into which the functional elements are placed. A 10.4 by 10.4 square-metre floor plane is subdivided by full-height sliding doors into nine squares. The spatial flexibility this provides allows for a wondrous permutations for seasonal or social moods.

Plan of the Nine Square Grid House.

closed for privacy or shade, and open it to expand the space and allow an interaction with nature. By naming it the Curtain Wall House I wanted to compare it with the Farnsworth House and so reveal the Japanese traditional notion of transparency.

And in the Nine Square Grid House (1997)?
Yes, in this project all the rooms can be divided by moving partitions or screens so you can manipulate them to make one huge space leaving even the bathroom and kitchen open and exposed to the rest of the house. I didn't need to name the individual rooms, like bedroom or living room, and you can divide the house any way you want. In summer you can use the north part of the space for cooler living. In the winter the reverse could be true. So this is my interpretation of the flexibility of Japanese traditional architecture. I am not planning this type of space because it is innately Japanese but rather because it is extremely practical and comfortable.

When you use this type of module is it based upon the Japanese traditional proportioning system of *shaku* and *sun*?
No, it is derived from function. I never use *tatami* modules, I design proportions carefully, following a geometrical analysis. Not Japanese proportions because I studied architecture through the analysis of Western buildings. It's important to remember that Japanese architecture wasn't purposely designed to have a particular geometry but because there are so many great proportions hidden among the rooms many beautiful geometries can be found.

When we first met you explained the impact of the students' volunteer work on your own development of a social consciousness in architecture. Do you feel that architecture in Japan is undergoing some wider change towards a more social context, or is it just you still fighting a lonely battle?
Not only because I did such projects, but because of the Kobe earthquake when many people volunteered, often for the first time in their lives, I get such a positive response from many young architects or students

in support of my activities. Many people would like to take part in such social activities but they cannot find an opportunity. But this pluralism isn't still widely expected or understood. For me there is no division or divide between Tokyo and Osaka, or Japan and China, even Tokyo and London. Now the world really has become globalised and we don't need to have any pre-existing relationship with people in order to offer help to them, in Kobe, or Rwanda, or other places that are suffering from famine or disasters. Before the Meiji Restoration [1868] in Japan everyone lived in a designated area called a *han* and they needed a passport to go out or move to another area. They had to live and die in the *han* to which they belonged. Some established architects are still living with that *han* mentality.

What would you like the legacy of your work to be?
Well it's not a legacy but I have just established my NGO [Non-Government Organisation] called VAN, Voluntary Architects Network, but because of my hectic schedule it is really impossible to devote time to this kind of activity in my office at the moment. I really hope to have the time to develop this organisation further, not only sending registered specialists abroad but organising our own projects as we did in Kobe, raising money ourselves to build specific projects in response to needs. No other NGO is doing that. So my legacy will not be architecture per se as architecture develops so slowly.

You said your idea of paper architecture was like your own child – difficult to give away for adoption – but no-one else has taken up the idea.
Actually many other designers have used this material for interiors but it is easy to use as an interior material because there is no need to obtain any official permission. But in order to use paper tubes as a structural material we need government permission and testing so that is the difficult part. In one sense I am pleased because I don't have to adapt my work for it to remain unique, but in order to move forward with the second stage of the development of paper tube architecture, many people will need to take up its use. I hope this

will happen because I have my own limitations. And I don't want to continue working on paper tubes my whole life. I don't want to be considered just a paper architect. Paper architecture has been a great way of introducing myself to the world but I don't want to be continually asked to design only paper-tube architecture.

You don't like High-Tech structures as an architectural fashion, but state that the structure should be simple to match the character of the material itself. But one facet of Japanese society is its love affair with technology.

One reason I am not interested in High-Tech is that in Europe and especially in the UK you have a great history of High-Tech buildings. Tower Bridge in London, for example, is such a High-Tech edifice, that steel and brick hybrid structure. Japan cannot beat this type of history. Many people copy High-Tech architecture in Japan but it is impossible to beat the original High-Tech, and since I have to compete with Western architects I should rule out areas where I cannot win. We don't have such a history and we don't have the history of working with consultants. In Japan there is no facade engineering and all facades are designed by sash manufacturers. There are no individual consultants for cladding, even for lighting too. When we consult such manufacturers then we have to use their products too. So there is no opportunity to develop new ideas. That is why I am enjoying working in Europe at the

moment because I can take advantage of your system. It is really difficult to break this Japanese system and that history cannot be recovered.

Both the name and appearance of paper architecture seems very low-tech, but is actually delivered through modern technology.

Manufacturing paper tubes is a High-Tech procedure. That is why I always say that paper is a High-Tech material. It can be made waterproof or fireproof. The tolerance of manufacturing paper tubes is very high, not just in Japan but all over the industrialised world. I always try to avoid the appearance of High-Tech. If you move closer towards other structural systems then you lose the unique characteristics of one structure and one idea. Maybe my role in the projects is to define the limit of the ideas and to keep the idea pure. At Hanover Expo, for example, one engineer proposed using a regular concrete foundation as it is easy to construct and stable. But I rejected it because the whole idea of the pavilion is recycling. A concrete foundation is really difficult to recycle. So I proposed using the pre-cast concrete slabs which are used in Europe to provide temporary vehicle or pedestrian access over rough ground on construction sites. It might be more expensive initially than using in-situ concrete but it is more important to keep the original idea pure. Once such a system is introduced and established it becomes more popular and consequently cheaper. However, because no-one uses it, it is so expensive to initiate. ■

SHIGERU BAN
1957 Born in Tokyo

Education:
1980   Southern California Institute of Architecture, Los
        Angeles
1984   Cooper Union School of Architecture, New York

Employment:
1983   Worked for Arata Isozaki
1985   Established private practice in Tokyo
1993-95 Tama Art University, Adjunct Professor of Architecture
1995-   Consultant to United Nations Commission for Refugees
1995   Established Non-Government Organisation VAN

Shigeru Ban was interviewed at the Kobe Plaza Hotel on 11 January 1997 and in his office in Tokyo on 7 January 1999

1995-	Yokohama National University, Adjunct Professor of Architecture
1996-	Nihon University, Adjunct Professor of Architecture

Major Projects:

1985	'Emilio Ambasz', exhibition design, Axis Gallery, Tokyo
1986	'Alvar Aalto', exhibition design, Axis Gallery, Tokyo
1986	'Judith Turner', exhibition design, Axis Gallery, Tokyo
1989	Paper Arbor Design Expo '89, Paper Tube Structure No. 1, Nagoya
1990	Odawara Pavilion – Paper Tube Structure No. 2, Kanagawa Prefecture
1990	East Gate – Paper Tube Structure No. 3, Kanagawa Prefecture
1991	Library of a Poet – Paper Tube Structure No. 4, Kanagawa Prefecture
1993	House of Double Roof, Tokyo Prefecture
1994	Issey Miyake Gallery – Paper Tube Structure No. 6, Tokyo
1995	Furniture House, Yamanashi Prefecture
1995	Curtain Wall House, Tokyo
1995	Paper House – Paper Tube Structure No. 5, Yamanashi Prefecture
1995	Paper Church – Paper Tube Structure No. 8, Hyogo Prefecture
1995	Paper Log House – Paper Tube Structure No. 7, Hyogo Prefecture
1995	2/5 House, Hyogo Prefecture
1997	JR Tazawako Station, Akita
1997	Walls-less-House, Karuizawa
1997	Square Grid House, Kanagawa
1998	Paper Dome, Gifu
1998	Ivy Structure House, Tokyo
1998	Furniture House No. 3, Kanagawa

Awards:

1985	SD Review
1986	Design Competition for the Redevelopment of Shinsaibashi, Osaka
1986	Display of the Year, Emilio Ambasz Exhibition
1988	Display of the Year, Alvar Aalto Exhibition
1988	Osaka Industrial Design Context L-Unit System
1988	SD Review
1989	Alflex Design Competition
1993	Tokyo Society of Architect's House Award
1995	Mainichi Design Prize
1996	Innovative Award Tokyo Journal
1996	Yoshioka Prize
1996	JIA Kansai Architects
1996	Mainichi Design Prize
1996	International Architects Academy Ecoplice House Competition
1997	The JIA Prize for the Best Young Architect of the Year
1998	Architectural Institute of Japan Tohoku Prize

Exhibitions:

1984	Japanese Designer in New York, New York
1985	Adam in the Future, Tokyo
1985	SD Review, Tokyo
1987	Tokyo Tower Project, '40 Architects Under 40's', Tokyo
1990	Last Decade 1990, Tokyo
1993	Chairs by Architects, Tokyo
1993	Hardware by Architects, Tokyo
1994	Architecture of the Year, Tokyo
1994	GA Japan League, Tokyo
1995	Paper Church and Volunteers, Osaka
1995	Paper Church, Tokyo
1997	Resurrection of Topos 3, Tokyo
1997	Stool Exhibition 3, Ozone
1998	Architecture of the Year, Tokyo
1998	GA House Project, Tokyo
1998	'97 JIA Prize for the Best Young Architect of the Year, Tokyo
1999	GA House Project, Tokyo
1999	Shigeru Ban: Projects in Progress, Tokyo
1999	Future Show, Bologna
1999	Archi Lab, Orleans
1999	Cities on the Move, London

Publications:

Ban, S. (1997) *Shigeru Ban GG Portfolio*, Barcelona: Gustavo Gili Publishing

Ban, S. (1998) 'Shigeru Ban', *The Japan Architect*, Vol. 30

Ban, S. (1998) *Paper Tube Architecture from Kobe to Rwanda – Shigeru Ban*, Tokyo: Chikuma Shobo Publishing Company

Quoting the Sacred in Modern Kyoto

Shin Takamatsu

⌈ The open-endedness of many spaces in Kyoto architecture and gardens, that are in themselves small but have a spatial expansiveness, is something that I can understand. Though they are small-scale and closed, their system is very open [...] even the cosmos is symbolised. For me this spirituality has recently been a strong hint, and is something I want to look at more deeply in Kyoto, although I don't have the desire to do tea ceremony or *ikebana*!⌋

In Kyoto, Japan's most artistically conservative city, we can find some of its most radical architecture that seems to draw no reference from the cultural life of the city, or from human life at all. The High-Tech finishes, manufactured forms and industrial allegory of the architecture of Shin Takamatsu is clearly a unique response to the experiences of life in urban Japan. Although the economic boom of the late 1980s, the 'Bubble' period now recounted with warm reverence by real estate barons throughout Japan, spawned an unprecedented diversity and interest in architecture, few designers took such a confrontational stance, let alone in the spiritual heart of Yamato culture.

Like many of Takamatsu's early projects, Ark, a dentist clinic and gallery, opened in Kyoto's Fushimi-ku in 1983, explored the relationship between a machine society and architectural space. Located adjacent to a railway station, the form of the building seemed like a giant locomotive. Was it beached by a tide of post-Industrial Revolution technology, or is it a portent of future transportation, poised to whisk passengers

Ark (1983), Kyoto.

to stellar destinations? The malevolent bulk of the structure, sheathed in concrete, topped with an aluminium painted vault and articulated by a series of ten metallic lights, used meticulous details in a coercive style that has been termed 'Dead-Tech'. With a total floor area of only 407.17 square metres, the impact of the building towered far above its simple volumetric space. Its unique form and mix of unorthodox functions was the precursor for a whole series of imitations as the 'Bubble' period economy exploded two years later.

But if his architecture is largely oblivious to any contextual or historical references, then where do these unusual forms come from? Surprisingly, he side-steps any logical affinities to Le Corbusier, the master of Modern architecture who said 'buildings were machines for living', and quotes instead the influence of Izumo Taisha, one of the most revered of Japan's shrines. Often visiting there in his youth, he was impressed with the sheer power of architecture. It was this spirituality, rather than any function or rationality of architecture, which he sought to realise in Ark and other early projects in Kyoto. But in spite of Takamatsu's spiritual empathy with elements of traditional architecture, he acknowledges his work was an attack on what he saw as the deep conservatism of Kyoto. Although his designs have been criticised as abetting the visual cacophony of the city, he sees any chaos apparent in the surface of his work not as a sign of confusion, but an ordered open system that serves as a receptor rather than instigator of chaos.

Since the early 1990s, however, in a series of projects including Kunibiki Messe (1993), Nagasaki Port Terminal Building (1995), and the Hamada Children's Museum of Art (1995), there has been a progression into the realm of more public works, accompanied by an increase in the scale of his projects. The severe detailing, almost brutal imagery, and underlying cynicism of his earlier work, has gradually been replaced by less aggressive surfaces and purer forms. The metallic details and detailed mechanics have given way to an irrepressible celebration of the power of form. Composed of assemblages of circles, ovals, square or rectangular plans, his buildings are frequently pierced by bold cones, sliced forms, or connected by wave-like sheets.

The Hamada Children's Museum of Art, located in Takamatsu's home prefecture of Shimane, was completed in January 1996. The brief for the five-storey museum and atelier called for the creation of a space for children to develop their own art works, and an exhibition space to display them, supplemented by management and storage facilities. Situated by the Sea of Japan, the solid white form of the building is divided by a transparent space. Like a fragment of a giant ark or an aeronautical wing, the upper museum areas seem to be held in levitational balance against the sky. The lower edge of this void is more ruptured and detailed, perhaps symbolic of a rocky return to earth. In common with earlier projects, however, is a lack of sense of scale. While Ark, or Syntax (1990), or Origin 1 (1981), used minute attention to detail to deprive the buildings of anthropomorphic, functional or even cultural scales, these new buildings pursue the same agenda through sheer faces of materials. The lack of any decoration – historically used to provide a sense of scale to society – gives the impression that his buildings still mean to challenge social norms.

Do these larger-scale buildings, with a greater physical and functional influence over public life, take a deliberately less confrontational approach? Although Takamatsu admits his early works ignored any concerns of context – a view he has now adapted to include the relationship between his architecture and its environment – even in this recent work there is still a uniqueness of composition, still a penchant for unorthodox forms.

For public clients in Japan, notoriously demanding a verbal rationale for the final visual forms, what is the process by which they come to accept Takamatsu's design proposals? He explains it this way: 'I work very closely with the client to draw up the programme which the final architectural forms completely satisfy. Other people may later try to attribute these forms in my work to images of boats, to Japanese fans, or bird wings, but for me they have no such connotation.'

It is somewhat ironic that only recently, with projects increasingly outside Kyoto and spread as far afield as Germany and Israel, has he come to feel the city's importance. The spirituality and symbolism of the city's gardens are an earlier expression of a uniqueness, almost an ordering of chaos, at least what that meant in seventeenth-century Japan. It's ironic that historic landscapes should elicit the greatest similarities with his work, given that his work seems superficially to be so hard and contemporary. But like a four-dimensional *kare-sansui* dry garden or a *sumi-e* ink landscape painting, his work suspends the true scale to create more ambiguous spaces. Spaces that in a sense are entered visually rather than physically; it's your mind that gets to go for a walk.

One perplexing aspect of the critical evaluation of his work is that he is so often spoken of in futurist terms. The metallic imagery of his work – Ark appeared in the movie *Batman* – seems superficially to have made it ripe for such for such allegory. But rather than being twenty-first century avant-garde, for me his work elucidates much more of a nineteenth-century Industrial Revolutionary zeal. The broad sweeps of the clean-cut forms remind me more of a Stalinist poster, stirring the masses to productivity, than the scale and complexity, the sheer frenetic animation, of the computer world. Much less High-Tech, I think of his work as a kind of industrial spiritualism. His buildings seem to know much more than they are actually willing to say, and therein lies his genius. He is able to communicate so much more by speaking in mixed tongues. When you see the beautiful pencil drawings of his projects' development it merely strengthens the conviction that craftsmanship plays more of a part than computation.

However his work may be judged in design terms in the future, it has at very least served as a potent marker for an era of great importance in Japanese architecture, and great interest to the rest of the world. Just as the first Chinese-influenced temples 'landed' as alien forms among the *machiya* landscape of Kyoto, and subsequently revolutionised Japanese design, the unique work of Shin Takamatsu is an evocative reminder of the power of architecture to agitate, reorientate – and not just passively reflect – the urban life and values of an age. ■

Nagasaki Port Terminal Building (1995).

Kunibiki Messe (1993), Shimane.

Hamada Children's Museum of Art (1995), Shimane.

What was it about architecture that attracted you?

I first thought I wanted to be an architect when I was about thirteen years old. I was born in Shimane Prefecture, the home of the Izumo Taisha Shrine, and even at that young age I was impressed by the power of architecture and thought I wanted to create something like that in the future. Izumo Taisha is of course religious architecture and so the first building I designed, a private home, was strongly coloured by the flavour of religious architecture. The attraction of religious architecture for me was that, unlike office buildings, these constructions were not functional or rational, but spiritual, and that was the first stage in the direction of my own architecture.

You didn't work at the beginning of your career for a major architect like many others do. Were you already sure of your direction?

One of the early influences on my career was the highly original architect Seiichi Shirai, and in terms of public architecture, Kunio Maekawa, with the former Waseda University Professor Takahisa Yoshizawa influential in terms of small vernacular architecture. But rather than the influence of other people, I felt even at the beginning of my career a desire to build my own work, to realise my own ideas as soon as possible. I studied at Kyoto University but was not particularly drawn there because of the architectural history of the city. Kawasaki Kiyoshi was my professor at Kyoto University. He had built many public works in Kansai, and was at that time still very young, only in his forties. However, I didn't receive any direct influence from Kawasaki who thought me too individualistic to teach.

How were you able to find your first commission as an architect and how do you feel about that first project, looking back now?

My first large project was called Origin although I had already built about ten private houses before that which the client for Origin had seen and was impressed by. It is usual in Japan to get work through connections but I got work from having my earlier projects seen so I was very lucky. Actually, the critic Tanemura said that this first project was very 'Izumo Taisha like',

and on hearing this I realised how greatly I had been influenced by Izumo Taisha. Although until then I had considered my architectural works to be very original, I realised that they were the result of my cumulative experiences. Origin was the head office of a kimono manufacturing company utilising traditional crafts and the client wanted a building that was ambivalent towards the modern versus traditional relationship, something which emerged from discussions with the client. The client's feeling indicated the need for a taste of traditional architecture. Origin as a building is very difficult to use, in the way Izumo Taisha is also difficult to 'use' as it is a spiritual building, and so function and rationale was not really considered in Origin's design: 'difficult to use' was in some ways a stimulus for my design. Without it being a conscious decision, I may have 'copied' or been overly influenced by Shirai's designs, which I saw as a student, and although I didn't work in his office, I met him on a number of occasions. Shirai's style also made use of ideas from the philosophy of traditional architecture, to find a new way of thinking, to build new works.

'How the building meets the water, meets the land and the sky, are the points of ultimate reference.' This is one architect's philosophy of the reference points of architecture. What are the reference points in your work?

Who said that? It sounds like something Tadao Ando would say!

No, it was Cesar Pelli.

From the beginning, I thought of the isolation of architecture. I didn't consider the surrounding environment. In earlier works of ten or twenty years ago, my style was of isolated and original works using self-referential values. I thought at that time that architecture was something that should pay no attention to the surroundings. However, recently I have come to believe that architecture is something that does relate to and can have a relationship with the environment. I have also started to think that it relates to water and the sky. Through architecture, the water, sky, earth surrounding the buildings can be recognised again.

Origin I (1981), Kyoto.

Syntax (1990), attacking the conservatism of Kyoto

These can assume a new value when developed in association with architecture. This is not in an abstract sense but in a practical one. Of course this may just be because I'm getting older!

'Dealing with chaos' seems to be the catchphrase to some degree of all Japanese architects. Is this how you see your work?

Recently, I have become more interested in chaos. But I don't think of chaos as confusion or to be thrown into disorder, but as an order, as an open system. This idea of chaos as an ordering system, an open system, has recently become a movement in architecture. I don't think of architecture as a way to realise chaos, but rather see the question as what is the possibility for architecture to receive or take up chaos? In my architecture the surface, the appearance, may seem chaotic, but actually there is an order to the work. Simple architecture, Mies-like architecture, is flexible to chaos I think. Such architecture becomes a receptor. As the city in Japan is so chaotic I don't think the appearance of architecture should be so. Architecture has the possibility to be open even in a closed system of order. I want to discover something within this type of order.

Carlo Scarpa's drawings reveal how he thought in all scales and dimensions when designing. How does the design process work for you?

Scarpa was the most complex architect I think, but he is one of the most important architects for me. He thought of architecture as a combination of body and object. If I had seen some of Scarpa's large works I may have changed my mind but he only built small projects with very closed relationships. The dimensions of the body were crucial to his work. I like drawing very much, architecture is born from the possibilities of drawing. Of course computers are tools which can be used to realise architecture, but I strongly believe that there is also an architecture that can only be realised through hand drawing, through movements of the body. I believe that there is some miracle power in hand drawing. Nowadays, there are no architects who can do hundreds of drawings for a project like him so in that way I like him very much.

Really? But you yourself do hundreds of drawings for one project.

Well yes.

Perhaps what is most surprising for me about your work is that it occurs in Kyoto, the cultural if not spiritual home of much traditional Japanese culture. How do you feel this has influenced your work? Do you feel the need to respond to the clear historical precedents of Kyoto?

It is only recently that I have felt that Kyoto is an important city for me, although recently I haven't had any chance to work in Kyoto! Kyoto is an unusual city, it has many traditional buildings and is in many ways a conservative place. In the past it was the birthplace of many talented artists but that is unlikely now. It is just conservative. I feel the desire to fight against this conservatism, and in order to make an attack on this conservatism in Kyoto, I considered objectively, the best and most-effective way. This was the objective of my analysis. This overlapped with the emergence of architects with a high degree of originality. The open-endedness of many spaces in Kyoto architecture and gardens, that are in themselves small but have a spatial expansiveness, is something that I can understand. Though they are small-scale and closed, their system is very open. Rock gardens are typical of this, incorporating symbolic references to the cosmos. For me this spirituality has recently been a strong hint, and is something I want to look at more deeply in Kyoto, although I don't have the desire to do tea ceremony or *ikebana*! This is the most important part of the history of Kyoto. But Kyoto's 'original' architecture doesn't actually exist, it was strongly influenced by the architecture of China and the engineers of Korea. The architecture of the city has more Buddhist than indigenous influences, an Asian colour. It exhibits an open-ended philosophy of space. Architecture with a spiritual existence, that is how I look at the history of Kyoto.

The idea that unique forms can be related to a particular place, the Eiffel Tower and Paris, for example, is an important concept for urban design, particularly in Japan where the cities are without

the layers of history of those in Europe. Do you see your work in this way?

In principle the architecture of Japan is wooden architecture. Seiji Inoue said that wood is a material that slowly ages, so through the process of rebuilding and copying a new architecture is made. The system contained in this is something very important and worth continuing I think; for example, a special scale and composition. I realised recently that the scale we use, the metre, is imported from Europe, but in Japan we have the *shuku-shaku*, which is larger than the metre. The sense of scale, regardless of whether the material is wood or steel, for Japanese people, has been changed. The *shuku-shaku* scale creates the most comfortable space for us Japanese and contains an inherent logic I wish to continue. It is not the forms of history but the system I wish to use. In Europe the situation is slightly different. That type of temporal material like wood wasn't used, so the point of view was different.

How did your design for the Myokenzan Worship Hall 'Seirei' (1998), Hyogo, develop?

Mount Myokenzan is a holy place for the Buddhist saint Myoken Bosatsu, who has been worshipped there for a few thousand years among the Myoken cedar and pine trees. The earlier Buddhist facility at the top of the mountain had become worn out so it was decided to replace it with a new one. To build new space for faith, we decided to use the wood cut down from the holy mountain. Having lived with wood for such a long period we could even say that our culture has been structured by it. However, ecological problems and difficulties of traditional and technological successions have made the situation for wood very severe and complicated, so much so that one could say that our historical and traditional structure is now in danger. Despite that, there is some hope that a retrospective view of wood is possible, decoding a new beauty to structure the culture in different form, a 'structure of the mind'. Japanese people from ancient times have continuously used wood to build their 'mind'. It is also often said that wood should be used in the place where it is cut. These simple reasons contribute to

the 'structure of the mind'. Hence our plan could not ignore this situation.

How do you find working in Germany, in a foreign culture?

Where I work in Germany and other countries, there are no other buildings surrounding the sites. There is just nothing there at all! As an architect I feel that I can embark on an adventure. I now work in Tel Aviv and other places, and I feel that there is the potential for new architecture to be accepted in a way that wouldn't be possible in the centre of Paris or Berlin.

Misumi Elementary School (1997), Shimane.

You opened your practice in 1980 and worked extensively during what was called the 'Bubble' period. Have the economic changes since its collapse influenced either your view of the role of architecture or the type of projects you are involved in?

I have an optimistic opinion about the 'Bubble' period. During that period people was conscious of the role of architecture in the city, in urban planning. Architecture brought activity to the city and consequently a wider recognition of its role. Of course there are many parts of the 'Bubble' period that we cannot positively appraise but I would still like to try.

Is there a precedent for your work and what is it?

A closed type of architecture cannot be maintained for long I think. Of course many architects develop a

Myokenzan Worship Hall
'Seirei' (1998), Hyogo.

design, see the work completed and use that as a
base for the next project. But I want to find a new
approach for each project, not use previous projects
as a base, even though of course it is difficult at times.
At present all designers have access to the same
level of construction technology so it is becoming
more difficult to realise different or unique projects.

Misumi Elementary School, Shimane (1997), has some very strong forms?

This is a small public elementary school for 412
students. The architectural composition is made of two
different sized circles, centred around a circular garden.
The corridors along the inner garden form an atrium,
admitting natural light into the classrooms. The walls
of the classrooms facing the corridor are removable
so that the children can enjoy the natural scenery
integrated into their rooms. It is a simple geometric
composition producing a flexible and self-emerging
space. Specific rooms such as workshops, a library,

music rooms, are placed at random around water
features in the inner garden, just like lambs playing on
the hillside. What I tried to achieve in this architecture
was to weave the water element and children's lives
into the space, protecting the children from strong
seasonal wind and yet letting them still breathe the
richness of the wind into their bodies.

Some say you cannot divorce architecture from the life and history of the city – how much of a role does context play in your design process?

Wherever you go in Japan now there is the same
scenery and situation. Wherever you go there is the
same Tokyo, same Osaka, we have to deal with this
similarity. There is not much difference now as to
whether the project is in Tokyo or in the centre of
the countryside, but within this framework I do still
consider the site and surroundings when designing
my architecture. ■

SHIN TAKAMATSU
1948 Born in Shimane Prefecture

Education:
1971	Bachelor of Architecture, Kyoto University
1974	Master of Architecture, Kyoto University
1980	Doctor of Architecture, Kyoto University
1997	Ph.D. Engineering, Kyoto University

Employment:
1980	Established Shin Takamatsu Architect & Associates, Kyoto
1993	Established Takamatsu & Lahyani Architects Associates GmbH, Berlin
1996	Established Shin Takamatsu Architect and Associates Co Ltd
1997	Professor of Kyoto University School of Architecture

Major Projects:
1981	Origin I, Kyoto
1986	Origin III, Kyoto
1987	Kirin Plaza Osaka
1990	Nima Sand Museum, Shimane
1990	Solaris, Hyogo
1990	Syntax, Kyoto
1991	Earthtecture Sub-1, Tokyo
1993	YKK, Okayama
1993	Kunibiki Messe, Shimane
1993	Nima Museum of Bohemian Art, Shimane
1994	Quasar, Berlin
1994	Symphony Garden Tottori
1995	Hamada Children's Museum of Art, Shimane
1995	Shoji Ueda Museum of Photography, Tottori
1995	Port Terminal Building, Nagasaki
1996	Meteor Plaza, Shimane
1996	Tamayu Health Spa, Shimane
1997	Misumi Elementary School, Shimane
1998	Myokenzan Worship hall 'Seirei', Hyogo
1999	Babelsberg fx. Centre, Potsdam
1999	Gamagori Network Research Centre, Aichi
1999	Wacoal Headquarters, Kyoto

Awards:
1984	Japan Association of Architects Prize for Young Architects for Origin I
1985	Venice Biennale Award
1987	International Interior Design Award
1989	Annual Prize of the Architectural Institute of Japan for Kirin Plaza, Osaka
1989	Osaka Prefecture Architects Presidential Award for Kirin Plaza, Osaka
1994	Kyoto Prefecture Meritorious Cultural Service Award
1995	American Institute of Architects Honorary Fellow
1996	Education Minister's Art Encouragement Award
1996	Bund Deutscher Architekten Honorary Member

Exhibitions:
1982	Paris Biennale International Architectural Exhibition
1982	Venice Biennale International Architectural Exhibition
1985	Paris Biennale International Architectural Exhibition
1985	Venice Biennale International Architectural Exhibition

Shin Takamatsu was interviewed in his office in Kyoto on 18 January 1997

1987	The Tracks of Form: Architecture of Shin Takamatsu, Tokyo
1988	Shin Takamatsu Exhibition, Paris
1988	Shin Takamatsu Exhibition, London
1988	Shin Takamatsu, Kirin Plaza Exhibition, Paris
1989	Europalia '89 Japan, 'Transfiguration', Brussels
1991	Shin Takamatsu: Drei Projekte, Berlin
1991	Venice Biennale International Architectural Exhibition
1993	Shin Takamatsu Exhibition, San Francisco
1994	Shin Takamatsu + Gabriel E. Lahyani, Germany
1995	Shin Takamatsu Architect, Tokyo–Kyoto
1996	Architecture as Scenery, Tottori
1996	Architecture to the Future, Osaka
1998	Shin Takamatsu Exhibition, Kobe

Publications:
Takamatsu, S. (1984) *Works Takamatsu Shin*, Tokyo: Graphic Company

Takamatsu, S. (1986) *Modern Architecture – Space and Method*, Tokyo: Doho-sha Company

Takamatsu, S. (1987) *Like a Master Watch-Maker*, Tokyo: Sumai Library Publishing Company

Takamatsu, S. (1988) *The Killing Moon and Other Projects*, London: Architectural Association

Takamatsu, S. (1989) *Contemporary Architects Collection: Shin Takamatsu*, Tokyo: Kajima Publishing Company

Takamatsu, S. (1989) *Shin Takamatsu*, Paris: Electa Moniteur

Takamatsu, S. (1989) *Shin Takamatsu*, Tokyo: Kajima Publishing Company

Takamatsu, S. (1990) *GA Architect 9 – Shin Takamatsu*, Tokyo: ADA Edita

Takamatsu, S. (1991) *Shin Takamatsu: Drei Projekte*, Germany: Aedes Galerie und Architekturforum

Takamatsu, S. (1993) *Shin Takamatsu Exhibition Catalogue*, New York: Rizzoli

Takamatsu, S. (1993) *JA Library 1 – Takamatsu Shin*, Tokyo: Shinkenchiku-sha

Takamatsu, S. (1994) *Shin Takamatsu + Gabriel E. Lahyani*, Zurich: Artemis

Takamatsu, S. (1995) *Shin Takamatsu: Architect*, Tokyo: Nihon Keizai Shinbun Company

Takamatsu, S. (1995) *Shape of the Sun*, Tokyo: Chikuma Shobo

Takamatsu, S. (1996) *Shin Takamatsu: Architecture and Nothingness*, Milan: l'Arca Edizioni

Takamatsu, S. (1998) *To the Poetic Space*, Tokyo: Shinkenchiku-sha Company

Order

If New York is frenetic and London coolly fashionable, Tokyo is three-dimensional stream of consciousness meets urban psychobabble, New Modernism next to Post-Modern, Latin-Greco historicism next to classical-meets-mis-quoted-bastardised-Post-Modern. If Tokyo were human it would be institutionalised for life. Instead it somehow manages to meld these diverse voices into a strangely harmonious symphony. First time visitors may marvel at the incredible urban congestion and notice the bizarre built forms, but like an oil slick in a storm, there is undoubtedly a broad, calmer order to what at first glance might seem complete chaos. The following four chapters introduce diverse yet compelling answers to the question of how to design with this chaotic phenomena. Takefumi Aida uses fluctuation to co-ordinate with the amplitude of the city and its landscape. Hiromi Fujii has taken a cognitive approach to create space that, stripped of any inherent meaning, means as much as you want it to. Yoji Sasaki creates boundless urban landscapes with nature the order of the city, not architecture or engineering. Kazuhiro Ishii's marvellous structures rotate in harmony with the cosmos. And Tadao Ando's concrete forms harmonise with the natural order of the site. But maybe this whole order versus chaos question isn't really relevant? Well, it all depends on whom you ask. Some economically-driven – or dependent? – planners say that the market laissez-faire means cities are fair game for all. Or if you are a fan of that particular brand of Japanese historicism that means that everything – good and bad – is 'uniquely' Japanese, then even chaos, if it's native, may be no bad thing. In a sense, any search for an appropriate order can never be anything other than a search for the Holy Grail itself. Any search for stability or structure is like the search to dress in fashion, no sooner have you got there than being in style itself becomes out. But the question of an ordering system for design is perhaps – even more than tradition – the one facet that ties a designer's work into the stream of consciousness, past, present and future. The work of these designers reveals an incredible diversity of thought, not calm, clear thought, but a deep cerebral longing that answers a basic human need for order, for structure, for knowing how the parts relate to a whole. A whole history of civilisation, even, and what contemporary design understands the present, philosophical as well as aesthetic, condition to be. These designers' work is a bit like Stephen Hawkin's Theory of Everything. It is so fundamental to an understanding of where we are that it is both intellectually challenging and intensely fascinating. These projects may be, or possible may not be, the greatest ever design, but in many senses they are clearly definitive ones. Order? Probably. Disorder? Maybe. Deeply provocative design? Oh yes. ■

Letting Nature Speak

Tadao Ando

「 Architecture carries the role of raising people's awareness towards their city 」

The Oyamazaki Villa (1996), overlooks the confluence of two rivers that flow out from the south of Kyoto City.

Since its 'modern' discovery in 1908, when Frank Lloyd Wright used it for Chicago's Unity Temple (the Romans are thought to have used it first), concrete has been a material associated in the popular imagination with industrial buildings, road subgrade, rough architecture at best. Tadao Ando has become one of Japan's most influential architects by using its unclad surface to meld history, context, and geometry, into a dialogue with nature. Since he launched his career twenty-one years ago at the Row House, his hallmark concrete walls have been so widely imitated that they have become a new vernacular, recycled and reapplied in housing, public institutions and recreational facilities from Hokkaido to Okinawa. Perhaps only the SRC beam, the elevator and the curtain wall have had such a powerful influence on the architecture of twentieth-century Japan.

The Oyamazaki Villa in southern Kyoto Prefecture, completed in 1996, is like many of his projects since the mid-eighties, a cultural institution in a semi-rural setting. To visit this art museum, a gallery extension to an old villa, is to travel – through straggling suburbs, tree covered approaches, and lush rolling gardens – to the heart of Ando's architecture. Out of respect for

the 1920s villa, a rare architectural survivor from the Taisho period (1912–26), and in order to preserve the existing grounds, he declined the temptation to make a cultural 'monument' and instead set the building mostly below ground. The cylindrical concrete gallery is accessed from a 35-metre-long linear space, its thirty-nine steps accommodating the 6-metre change in ground level. With the gallery roof covered in white-flowering gardenia and the linear circulation space incised between existing trees, the physical bulk of the annex is so skilfully melded into the landscape it seems to pre-date the villa.

But is his recent work, including this project,

The Row House (1976), Sumiyoshi, Osaka, replaced a pre-war wooden row house with a concrete box that redefined the relationship between Japanese housing and nature and brought attention to Tadao Ando's architecture.

really what it is often said to be, an extension of the Japanese traditional aesthetic where building and nature exist in a state of ambiguous fusion? It's probably not easy to accurately compare Ando's contemporary work with the building–nature relationship epitomised by Katsura Imperial Palace, Kyoto, because there have been such huge changes in the nature of building and landscape – in both directions. He says of this aspect of his work: 'I don't think that architecture should speak too much, but should remain silent, and let nature – in the form of sun and wind – speak'. With particular eloquence, Oyamazaki Villa speaks to both history and nature. But what about geometry, the other key to his work?

Although in plan his buildings are frequently composed of overlaid squares, axes, and circles, he somehow manages to make them invisible in the three-dimensional spaces he creates, so as at Oyamazaki, his buildings are experienced as spatial labyrinths rather than clashing geometry. Passage, progress, time, place, experience and performance: the stepped approach and the mysterious luminosity of the gallery interior are not just evocative but multi-coded metaphors. This ability to load his buildings with visual metaphors is what transforms what could so easily be the intrinsic harshness of the concrete into spaces that people can relate to. But when his career took off in 1976, with his design for the Row House in Sumiyoshi, south Osaka, it was with a site only 1 per cent the size of the Oyamazaki Villa. A 57-square-metre plot situated in dense housing into which he inserted his concrete sliver of a building, the two-storey residence providing a bathroom, two bedrooms, a living room, a dining kitchen and a courtyard.

It was the courtyard, a 16-square-metre central rectangular space, open to the sky, that was fundamental to this design and to his early philosophy towards nature in the city. Renouncing any attempt at a more conciliatory approach, he sealed the site with concrete walls rejecting the chaos of the site's context in favour of nature. By arranging the rooms around the central courtyard, he enclosed an outdoor space where one would usually find the indoors, an unexpected reversal which allowed nature into the house: fragments

of light, sky, wind, and rain. The Row House became a place where people and nature confronted each other under a sustained sense of tension. In an age before environmental pollution, global warming and green architecture became part of the everyday vocabulary, it must have been nice to see nature not just survive, but get some tacit respect.

The lessons he learnt from this project guided his subsequent career and led to the establishment of his position as Japan's leading voice on all subjects and scales of design. From nature in the city, to the landscape's importance in Kobe's earthquake recovery, to the theme-park developments that characterise Japan's cities, even raising people's awareness of what a city could be, it all intrigues him. To meet Ando in person is to find a man, now in mellow middle age, who belies the images associated with his lack of formal education and pugilist past, someone completely accessible, remarkably un-egotistical. He radiates incredible energy and has an indefinable 'aura'. He was constantly punctuating the interview to add notes and sketches to a notebook, as though ideas were pouring through his mind like a cosmic stream that he didn't want to lose. That's not to say he lets things hang in the air unsaid. Ask him a question he doesn't find interesting and he tells you so. Ask him a question about a current project being explored through models lining his office walls and he's off gesticulating. He talks passionately for twenty minutes without a pause.

These days design fashions come and go, but Ando's is one that just won't go quietly. He has managed to keep reinventing his work so that his predominant use of a single material can still create new projects that are identifiable as his, but unique to the actual site. The seductive simplicity of his designs have, not surprisingly, made them ripe for imitation. Most 'imitators' have seen only the visuals, not the vision. While their work is mute, or at best hums, his composes. Perhaps he gave the best summary of his work recently when he said 'I don't think of "architecture" or "parks", I think of designing places'. What he should have said is evocative, intriguing, enigmatic, powerful, spiritual, places. ■

You are now possibly Japan's best known architect. Have you been surprised by your success and how do you deal with the pressure that fame has brought?

I don't really care so much about success, nor am I really surprised by any successes as an architect, but of course sometimes, I myself am surprised by the building that actually comes into existence. In other words, I don't start out knowing exactly how my buildings will ultimately turn out once they have been completed. Many architects say they have an idea of what what the building will look like but in my case I only know for sure about 70 per cent of the project; 30 per cent are surprises I get on the site. I think if I knew that everything that was on the drawing could be realised, then I don't think it has to be constructed. In other words, for me architecture should be something that ultimately will turn out to be more than what I expected in the drawing. Regarding the pressure that you mentioned, I don't really care about that nor about failure.

In your writing you talk about sun, light, water, wind, but I don't often hear you mention the word greenery?

Well first of all I'm trying to build architecture in nature, in other words architecture is building something in the natural surroundings, and in doing that I would have to first destroy that natural landscape. The question then is how to reinstate this, even with the addition of architecture, and that makes me think about the original nature that existed there. Of course whether it is green nature or sunlight or water, I think all these elements are life themselves and something that has life is bound to change and so I try to reach these changes that are taking place in the lives of these elements.

You are presently designing a park in Nishinomiya connected with the 'Umi no Shugoujutaku' project. In a park such as this where there is no built element as such, do you approach the design process differently?

Well, I will give you an example. We could sit in a building that is perceived to be architecture. But what if we think of architecture as the work to produce a certain place for people to gather. Just imagine that there is a cherry tree in the middle of a space. If this was in blossom then people would naturally gather around the tree, have a hanami, a cherry blossom viewing party, sitting around the tree to eat and drink. That I think is another form of architecture in a sense: that architecture is a work to produce a place and doesn't have to have a roof. It could be just a certain place that people enjoy in the same way as the park.

Japanese people often say they have a very close relationship with nature, but if we look at the Japanese city we find few parks and even fewer open spaces. You have travelled widely; do you agree with this assertion, or is that a kind of cultural misconception?

Well I think the Japanese climate is quite mild, it provides a comfortable environment in which to live. The winter is fairly mild and during the summer, although it's hot, the maximum temperature is 36 to 37 °C. Therefore we are able to enjoy our natural environment. Moreover, with the four seasons, we have quite high humidity with enough warmth to facilitate the growth of trees. However, in the post-war era, in which we had full-scale industrialisation, I think it was necessary for the Japanese economy to concentrate the urbanisation and the population heavily in the cities. This has led us to experience overcrowding in the city where we do not have much flat land. If you go to the mountainous areas there is much nature that you can enjoy but there is not much opportunity left in the cities. So that probably led to the inevitable situation where the Japanese people, in such a period of urbanisation, were not able to take advantage of the Japanese sense of closeness towards nature. They didn't have the room to accommodate such nature in the cities.

When travelling in Europe, which landscapes most strongly influenced you?

Of course, when I travel around I don't just go to look at the landscape but there are some impressive examples such as the Parthenon on the Acropolis in Greece. I was interested in why that particular location

The Church of the Light (1987–89), Osaka.
Located in a quiet residential suburb, the triple cube of the church's rectangular void is violated by a wall that slices through at 15 degrees and defines the entrance. A ceiling-to-floor cross is cut out of the concrete walls providing the only lighting piercing the sombre gloom of the interior. Blue-black, brown-black, rabbit-warren graduated black, toe-curling Stephen King black, you end up with the feeling that where there is religion there is no such thing as perfect darkness but wish to thank Ando for having tried so hard.

was selected for the Parthenon. You go through the gate in the direction of the Acropolis and on the other side of the hill you find the theatre; that sort of a setting is quite attractive. I was also impressed by the Tivoli Gardens and Hadrian's Villa – these are also excellent landscape ideas and of course I was influenced by all of these as well as the Renaissance landscape and British gardens. But in our case I would say Japanese landscaping is characterised by the lack of form; in other words, it melts into the surrounding nature. Despite the intention to design landscape, when it is realised or achieved, the effect may not directly appeal to people in the way that has been intended. There is an annex to my office on the other side of the street and right in front of the entrance there is a big tree. People wonder where the entrance is, and it just so happens that you have to go under the tree to find it. So it is not a directly appealing landscape but it is something that is almost hidden and melts into the surroundings. I tend to consider these Japanese types of landscaping and I'm also conscious of the Western type of landscaping and try to work with both sides.

What do you think of the role of architects and architecture in modern Japan?

Well, you can think of various roles that architects might have in this society and I believe it depends on the individual architect as to what they think their role is. In my case I am always conscious of the particular architectural or life spaces I would like to create.

How do you feel about the city in Asia? With satellite communication and 'borderless economies' some people are again predicting it has outlived its usefulness.

Architects have been playing a very important role in creating cities and I have taken the view, at least initially, that there were specific types of city in Asia just as there were characteristic cities in Japan. But with the emergence of Disneyland many of these cities have become more like theme parks. And theme parks are temporary in nature. So what you see in Asia today are cities that have become more like theme parks and since they are temporary will need some refreshing after twenty or thirty years. So there is a dichotomy of those types of theme-park cities, as opposed to the more classical type of city we find in the UK or in France for example. I think the decision regarding which direction to take is difficult, but in view of the economic impact I think it is inevitable that the Asian cities will continue to develop this way. On the other hand, there are cities that have developed with local features in a more classical style and in their transformation from the classical period to the modern age they have incorporated new discoveries. I would like to proceed in a different direction to the theme-park-oriented development as the city, for me, is more than just entertainment.

Technology has always been architecture's twin, playing a crucial role in its progress. At the end of the second millennium, technological progress seems to be evolving even faster than architecture itself. Do you see any potential danger in that technology could become divisive and a factor pushing boundaries in the wrong direction?

Along with the instantaneous propagation of information world-wide, this digital information has given birth to an illusionary network of our world. The tendency towards slowly but surely losing both the sense of belonging to a particular region and obstacles posed by the world's physical boundaries is clearly evident. This trend of 'globalisation' carries the danger of losing the characteristic and intrinsic culture and traditions each nation or people has inherited; the sense of association with a specific region and the moral and spiritual character found in its roots, as well as the race of people itself. This is especially the case in the Asian region that has only recently begun to 'modernise' and where the economy has been given a major emphasis in both political and social policy. The material aspects of civilisation have been unduly glorified and the indigenous culture, traditions and history of each region have come to be ignored or even scorned. Architects – in the conception and creation of their architecture – must remain aware of the growing amount of excessive and unnecessary information and the trend towards homogenisation, and must reflect on what their real responsibility is.

Hiromi Fujii explains his use of the grid in his projects as an organising system that has no cultural references or character, as simply a way of structuring space but having nothing to say about it. Does your use of the grid have a similar meaning or is it derived from some Japanese cultural notion of ordering space?
By using the grid I'm trying to create order, in other words going back to the Greek age. In architecture what we will continue to inherit is probably the sense of order, and a grid is used as a means to express that order, although I think it is better not to make it visible with the space that is actually created. When I use a grid it is a means of expressing order. In the Greek age, order was expressed through form in a manner that could be confirmed visually. The order was expressed from the top to the bottom. I was not really convinced with that type of order.

Many architects in Japan express exasperation that the Japanese city is chaotic. Do you feel chaos should be excluded or do you take a more positive view of it as an intrinsic aspect of Japanese urban culture and society?
Well I consider chaos as being something which possesses dynamic life. And I think that Japanese architects should think more seriously about the relationship of cities to their own lives. Are cities just there for people to enjoy or just for people to work – is it just a working environment? In Japan I think cities just exist as places for people to work, and their homes are merely a place for them to sleep. There is no true life in these places. And I think that people should work in order to live their lives more fully. But that is not the assumption that is made in Japanese cities at the moment. I think that what is lacking in Japan is the richness, the enrichment of lives, in the working environment or the home setting. And that enrichment is what creates the culture, but that is not found in Japanese cities at the moment.

You have won the 1997 RIBA Gold Medal and you are going to speak in London. What do you plan to talk about?
In the lecture, I plan to discuss the architect's responsibility. I think the responsibility for the architect is to consider the functional aspect of the building as well as the aesthetic and the safety aspects. The same can be said for cities, they should be cultural, allow for economic development and, at the same time, should be safe. Although this might appear a simple concept, few Japanese architects have thought hard about this in the past twenty years. Not many people questioned their own roles in society or in the city. In Japan, especially during the past twenty years, cities have been much more economically driven by business people who have built a lot of theme parks in order to make a profit. Again, also for profit's sake, they have built a lot of manufacturing plants and produced automobiles and other products, and architects have just had to follow this trend. But I don't think that is the ideal state. Architects themselves need to think more seriously about what they would like to achieve, what kind of dreams they have and how to realise them.

Has there been a specific event that has made you more conscious of architecture's unique role?
Architecture can be said to be the profession whose task directly involves accepting the rapid changes in the world in which we live. I myself have lived in bewilderment of it all, but over these last few years I have received a very intense mental shock, the Great Hanshin Earthquake in 1995. It has made me reflect on a great many things. The earthquake that befell us generated in me a feeling of utter despair and helplessness at a level that I have never experienced. A major part of the work I've accomplished over the thirty years since I first established my own office has been in the Osaka and Kobe area, as well as the Hanshin area that occupies the space between the two cities. Even though my buildings did not suffer any damage, I was truly stunned at the level of devastation that occurred in these cities. The absolute necessity of protecting people's lives in terms of their physical safety is already an acknowledged condition of architecture, but I am aware that the fulfilment of safety and

functionality alone does not bring about architecture in its most authentic sense. What I have been attempting to reaffirm is that the most important aspect of architecture is its ability to move people with its poetic and creative power; to reappraise once again the question of whether architecture can be a true culture in and of itself.

How would you define architecture then?

I like to believe that if we assume that what makes 'real' architecture is not merely its specific plan or design, its relation to the technique or even the cost involved, but the aesthetic expression of an architect's awareness of the issues involved. The problem then lies not in architecture, as a completed structure per se, but is encompassed within the process that is involved in its creation and in the manner in which that architecture acquires life. It is during the process of transition from the poetic inspiration to the realisation of form that the depth of the architect's ideas and thoughts is brought into question. It is through repeated internal deliberation and contemplation and by trial and error that the intensity that supports the formulation of architectural expression will become more profound.

What have you proposed for the reconstruction of Kobe?

You might know that I am advocating the so-called green network in Kobe, after the earthquake, which plans to plant 250,000 trees altogether, 50,000 of which will be trees with white flowers like magnolia.

White because it is the Buddhist colour of remembrance?

In the spring when these flowers bloom we want to remind people of the Great Hanshin-Awaji Earthquake and to think about the victims and remember the occasion. I think that raising the awareness of the city residents as to what a city really is becomes another type of urban development. Architecture's role is to provide that sort of mechanism, or that sort of device, to raise people's awareness towards their city or towards the urban environment. We have already planted 100,000 trees of which 25,000 are the white

flowering trees I mentioned earlier and this spring many of them were in bloom. And so we can expect many more to bloom next spring. We distribute about 20,000 trees per year to the citizens and we have also planted many tall trees of about three metres. I'm busy going to many tree-planting ceremonies in elementary schools! And so I think that by the year 2000 this will become the monument for the earthquake. It's not a building but the trees that will serve the role of monument.

The Naoshima Contemporary Art Museum (1992), Kagawa Prefecture, is a perfect example of Ando's oeuvre – pure geometric forms so skilfully incised into the landscape it seems as though nature had designed itself in anticipation.

Do you have a social message in your work you'd like to communicate?

It becomes more important as we live in the Cyber Age, or the Virtual Reality Age, that children growing up in the city are able to learn the reality of the city by planting trees, By taking care of the trees they learn that plants need water in order to grow and that they bloom and wither. That sort of reality is lacking, I think, from the lives of children these days as they watch TV, or play video games, so I would like to create a city where these young people can truly learn the reality of life. It's a big project. It is very difficult for Japanese architects these days, particularly for a small office like ours. Because the Japanese people are not particularly outspoken they don't really say what they want to do. And I think it's characteristic of the Japanese people that if you say too much you are resented.

Naoshima Contemporary Art Museum Annex.

An oval plan sitting inside a rectangular wall, the annex contains four twin rooms, two suite rooms and a café and is accessed by a cable car from the museum below. The centre is an oval water garden with a 20 metre long axis and 10 metre short axis. Through the surface tension of the water and the effect of the space reflected on the blue walls surrounding it, it appears almost as a three-dimensional water sculpture surrounded by a colonnade which can be used as a semi-outdoor gallery.

Are you optimistic about the future of Japanese architecture?

History is a very important factor for architects; for example, the reason why some British architects are so good at the high-tech type of architecture is that they have inherited a tradition, starting from Crystal Palace, of working with metals and mechanical types of material. In a similar way, the Japanese people have been living together with nature for so many years and that sensibility may be in their architecture. We should be able to come up with something that is unique, that no-one else can realise. I think this is a very critical issue, the fact that the Japanese have forgotten what it means to be Japanese. There should be a certain way of expressing the Japanese mentality and thought that is somewhat different from other types of self-expression. That is my view. When we are deeply moved or impressed by the Katsura Palace, I think that is also related to the emotion that we might feel when we go to Naoshima Museum of Contemporary Art; for instance, there is a connection. That is the basis from where we should work towards the architecture of the future.

Recently I visited Oyamazaki Villa in Kyoto. Perhaps you could tell me a little about that project and how you came to be involved in it?

The initial plan was to replace the building with a mansion. It was bought by Asahi Beer and Kyoto Prefecture, and I was commissioned by Asahi Beer. There are many examples of the Tudor style in England, but few in Japan. It was a Taisho period villa so I wanted to preserve it and add on new structures. People come there to enjoy the old Tudor-style building, the landscape of that particular place, or the new extension that we have made. If you look at Japanese cities you can rarely find buildings from the Meiji or Taisho or the early Showa periods (post 1926). But actually cities should have 'survivors', in the sense that if you look at London, for example, you will find different buildings surviving from different periods. In this respect, Kyoto is quite rare and unique in that there are buildings surviving in the city from several hundred years ago in conjunction with modern architecture. In that sense I think that culturally speaking it should be more interesting than the ordinary theme parks which have emerged world-wide. Theme parks like Disneyland are made so people can visually enjoy the various attractions they offer but, culturally speaking, a city like Kyoto should be more interesting. If you are not culturally oriented you might find nothing of interest in such an old city but if you truly want to enjoy the multi-layered culture of the city then Kyoto offers one of the best locations. If you look at Rome by way of comparison, the city has stopped at a certain time point so there is no modern, or rather current day, development so to speak.

Is some of your success attributed to the way your office is organised?

We have about twenty-five people in the office and we split them up into teams of two or three. The structural engineering and the building systems are outsourced so we only take care of the architectural side. I am involved in all our projects. First of all I come up with the concept, the design idea and then I hand this over to the staff who do the drawings, make the models. I initially throw the project open to everyone and we conduct a competition of ideas and we try to find out if there is anything interesting that we might be able to use. I also participate in the competition, but I'm the jury so I decide my way! But as the staff are all engineers themselves, they would not be convinced, even if my idea were selected, if they were not confident that my idea was best. So my total efforts are needed in order to convince them. That is how I proceed with the process.

What are your early recollections of architecture?

When I first set my sights on becoming an architect, in my early twenties, the strong impressions left on me by such fine works as the Peace Centre, Hiroshima, by Kenzo Tange, L'Unité d'Habitation, Marseilles, and Notre-Dame-du-Haut, Ronchamp, both by Le Corbusier, are even now repeatedly called to mind. They give me courage in pondering aesthetic considerations along with the universality of the public aspects of architecture.

What is architecture's greatest gift to twentieth-century cultural life?

Well twentieth-century architecture has come to be created from techniques and materials such as steel, glass, concrete and aluminium, common the world over. These tend to make buildings around the globe essentially the same, and in the same way as living a dull and repetitive lifestyle, they have become mundane and boring. It is important for us to use the resources of the earth in a more diverse and disparate manner without disregarding the unique lifestyles that are born from the differences in our cultures. I would like, even deliberately, to resist the tendency towards a 'shrinking' earth. In truth, however, there is really no reason to expect that – despite the use of common materials and techniques – modern architecture in Asian countries, the United Kingdom and the United States, as well as in European countries, will be 'exactly' the same. Architects must contemplate their responsibility in regard to a number of things, the most important of which I believe to be the value we place on culture. It can be said that culture is based on the moral and spiritual characteristics and sensibilities which people have inherited through the ages, in addition to their characteristic language and sense of association as a nation or region. I myself have a new consciousness of the importance of utilising architecture to carry into the twenty-first century the covenant of culture that has been passed down to us through so much adversity. ∎

Tadao Ando was interviewed in his office in Osaka on 26 April 1997 and by correspondence 29 June 1999

TADAO ANDO
1941 Born in Osaka

Education:
1962–69 Self-educated in architecture, travelled in USA, Europe and Africa

Employment:
1969 Established Tadao Ando Architect and Associates
1997- Professor at Tokyo University

Major Projects:
1976 Row House, Osaka
1984 Time's Kyoto
1989 Church of the Light, Osaka
1991 Museum of Literature, Himeji
1991 Water Temple, Hyogo
1992 Japan Pavilion Expo '92, Seville, Spain
1992 Naoshima Contemporary Art Museum, Okayama
1992 'Fabrica' (Benetton Research Centre), Treviso, Italy
1993 Rokko Housing II, Kobe
1994 Chikatsu-Asaka Historical Museum, Osaka
1994 Suntory Museum, Osaka
1995 Meditation Space, UNESCO, Paris
1998 Toto Seminar House, Hyogo
1998 Daylight Museum, Shiga
1999 Shell Museum of Nishinomiya City, Hyogo

Awards:
1979 Architectural Institute of Japan Annual Prize (for Row House)
1985 The Finnish Association of Architects Alvar Aalto Medal
1989 French Academy of Architecture Gold Medal of Architecture
1991 American Academy and Institute of Arts and Letters Arnold W. Brunner Memorial Prize
1992 Carlsberg Architectural Prize
1993 The Award of Prizes of the Japan Art Academy
1995 The Pritzker Architecture Prize
1995 Chevalier de l'Ordre des Arts et des Lettres France
1996 The 8th Praemium Imperiale
1996 First 'Frate Sole' Award
1997 Royal Institute of British Architects Royal Gold Medal
1997 Officier de l'Ordre des Arts et des Lettres France
1998 The 6th Public Buildings Awards for Chikatsu-Asaka Historical Museum

Exhibitions:
1991 The Museum of Modern Art, New York
1993 'Tokyo', Centre Georges Pompidou, Paris
1993 The Royal Institute of British Architects, London
1995 The Basilica Palladiana, Vicenza
1996 6th Venice Biennale, Venice
1998 National Museum of Contemporary Art, Seoul
1998 Royal Academy of Arts, London

Publications:
Ando, T. (1987) GA Architect 8: Tadao Ando, Tokyo: A.D.A. Edita Tokyo

Ando, T. (1989) Tadao Ando: Yale Studio and Current Works, New York: Rizzoli

Ando, T. (1990) Architectural Monograph 14 : Tadao Ando, London: Academy Editions

Ando, T. (1991) Tadao Ando – Details, Tokyo: A.D.A. Edita Tokyo

Ando, T. (1993) GA Architect 14: Tadao Ando, Tokyo: A.D.A. Edita Tokyo

Ando, T. (1995) Complete Works – Tadao Ando, London: Phaidon Press

Ando, T. and Drew, P. (1996) Church on the Water/Church of the Light, London: Phaidon Press

Ando, T. and Pare, R. (1996) The Colours of Light/Tadao Ando, London: Phaidon Press

Ando, T. and Jodidio, P. (1997) Tadao Ando, Cologne: Benedikt Taschen

Rotation in Harmony with Nature

Kazuhiro Ishii

「 Between power minus thirty-two in our bodies and power plus thirty-two in the universe, is us, the city, and our architecture 」

The architecture of Kazuhiro Ishii has seemed to court controversy since his career took off in 1975 with the completion of the first of a series of three gloriously unique buildings that utilised the number fifty-four as their defining motif. His design for the intriguingly named 54 Windows wasn't any new structural or ordering paradigm but merely the axiom of 'form follows function'. The windows' variations were the outer expression of the range of room functions, from waiting room to X-ray room, from office to client meeting room, all the way up to fifty-four. It was only later when quizzed for a critical explanation that he discovered the prevalence of the unit of fifty-four which he saw as an unspoken evocation of Asian diversity.

Followed over the next decade by 54 Columns (1986), a wedding hall, and 54 Roofs (1979), a nursery school, Ishii explains these works as an exploration of Japanese cultural identity, offering a stimulating alternative to what he sees as the Western aesthetic values of Modern and Post-Modern architecture. Although he studied abroad – obtaining a Master's Degree from Yale University and working in the offices of British architect James Stirling – Ishii's work has been defined by a search for identity, a 'Japaneseness',

that respects the historical built traditions of Japan. He felt that Japanese architecture at that time was overly represented by the regular geometry and pure forms of Modernism, buildings that expressed a Western reductivist notion of beauty concerned with purifying the basic concept, denying and even removing the minor elements of the design to achieve it. Whereas Western architects liked to stay within a fixed number of variations in a building, his '54' projects boldly refused to remain limited by that aesthetic notion and instead celebrated diversity, a character which Ishii says 'brings them closer to the character of the innumerable variation of the earth itself'. The response from the architectural establishment, however, was 'one of anger and anxiety' says Ishii, provoked in part by his decision to use bright colours for the window frames that further emphasised their prominence, individuality and diversity.

His thoughts, from musing in the '54' projects upon the endless variation in life, then moved to something more structured: the search for a new system of architectural ordering. Dissatisfied with the grid of Western architecture, whose influence had permeated design from Greek Temples to Modern high-rise architecture,

54 Windows (1975), Nara, has a kind of irrepressible vitality that humanises the building's geometry.

Extruded, curved, sloped or upright, the structural diversity of the 54 Columns (1986), Saitama, is emphasised through bright colour strips that bound the column edges.

The collection of structures that form the Seiwa Bunraku Puppet Theatre (1992), Kumamoto, is nestled against the surrounding mountain slopes.

The Seiwa Bunraku Puppet Theatre's spiral roof.

he found his answer in a natural structuring system – rotation of the Milky Way.

Ishii took this concept and applied it to two highly original residential projects, the Spinning House (1985) and Gyro Roof (1987), and most recently, the Seiwa Bunraku Puppet Theatre (1992) in Kyushu's Kumamoto Prefecture. Designed for a *bunraku* troop whose skills were slipping away from lack of a practice venue, the twelve-metre-high building, in plan a T-shaped stage and seating block connected by a linear corridor

to a circular exhibition space, at first glance appears like a small cluster of agricultural buildings. But while the exterior's wooden construction and grey-tiled roof evokes images of Japanese vernacular traditions, a glance inside reveals something quite out of the ordinary. Very different from a traditional post-and-beam-style construction, the roofs' structural system is a three-dimensional rotating composition of wooden elements that intertwine and mutate as they spiral upwards to form a circle at the apex. The interplay between the hewn serenity of the wooden beams and certainly natural, but slightly curious, quality of their arrangement make for a powerful alchemy – as though the Milky Way had landed in a forest and rearranged the trees for its own amusement. What makes this project particularly remarkable is that he has achieved this revolutionary idea using the traditional craft skills of Japan. Where others rely on computers to deliver their future vision, Ishii has achieved his with locally grown timber and a few centuries of accumulated carpentry skills. The rock crowd of 'contemporary' Japanese architecture – all weird facades but empty rooms, all dry ice but no song – might do well to look at Ishii's work. These are uniquely compelling, fascinating spaces, seemingly created from, at their simplest, a few old bits of lumber and some glass.

With its emphasis on contemporary collages of traditional Japanese materials and forms, Ishii's work has received a varied response. Panned by one critic as simply imitating old buildings it has also been termed 'Japanese Post-Modern'. But this is a category he firmly – and quite rightly – rejects, explaining with an oxymoron of his own creation that what Japan needs is not Modern or Post-Modern architecture, but Pre-Modern. Although the image of Japan in the West may be of a High-Tech Shangri-La, Ishii sees his own culture as belonging to an earlier age, and to keep it alive in architecture, that means wood. Perhaps it's an implicit acknowledgement of latent strength. Perhaps it's karma. But for someone fleeing the clutches of Modern architecture you cannot help but think it would be an act of smart Darwinism to use a moniker that avoids the term Modern at all.

However his search for a Japanese solution for the problems at the city scale may simply be overtaken by economic change, something neither Western, nor Japanese but universal. This may render the need for any city, let alone a 'uniquely Japanese' one, obsolete. With satellite communications, borderless economies and expanding travel, the economy is now a world-wide one. Even Ishii admits that the 'urban areas are losing their rationale, with modern communications the vibrant city and the quiet mountain-top are the same'. So what of his predictions for the future? It's true of course that historically cities have grown and expanded, been vibrant and exciting, from a kind of internal pressure from growing economic and social advancement. Ishii's prediction for the twenty-first century – Non-City in the City – sees a future, not of discrete national cities, but an economic cosmic stream that flows over national borders, terrain and ideology. So in a sense hasn't he talked himself out of a 'Japanese culture' or at least one that architecture needs to help sustain?

There may be no obviously identifiable association between the '54' projects and the 'diversity' of an Asian city, or relationship between the Milky Way and the Seiwa Theatre's rotating roof. But Ishii's stellar work is a provocative, yet convincing, attempt to provide an answer to the search for a 'Japaneseness' in an architectural culture that has seemed recently to fall between the rock of a pastiche Japanesque and the hard place of a *Blade Runner* High-Tech. Ishii's original and creative work – and his carefully argued and unique rationale for it – has the power to trade fours with the rhythm of Western design and not lose a beat. ■

When you look back over your earlier works, is there a strong element, or idea, that ties those projects together?
Well my architecture is targeted towards reality rather than beauty. Beauty in Japan and in Europe too has always been concerned with purifying a basic concept, on denying and removing the minor things.

What kind of reaction did you receive from critics when these '54' projects were first realised?

In the 54 Windows project I think the best criticism I received was from Reyner Banham. He said that in that building I was using the same techniques and architectural vocabulary that European architecture used, yet it was also different. Whereas European architects like to stay within a limited number of variations in one building, I didn't stop and remain within that I imitation of modus intellectual aesthetics. 54 Windows possessed an attitude that he said was Japanese or at least Asian. Japanese aesthetics at that time were

architecture or Greek temples admired. That structural beauty, the grid beauty, is also in our heads rather than in reality. In the great cities like Paris, Washington, or Beijing, the grid system they use is simply an image, like our idea of beauty. A wiped-off clean table. I realised there is no grid in the universe but instead there is rotation. Rotation is the important structural system in our Milky Way where we have 100 billion stars all connected by a thin rotating plate. So next I designed the Spinning House, the Gyro Roof, and the

Gyro Roof (1987), Saitama. The roofs themselves spiral up and outwards as though during launch. Half traditional icon, half lunar module, they are a unique expression of the Kazuhiro Ishii's architectural philosophy of rotation.

Gyro Roof as seen from the street.

expressed or represented by the Modern architecture of Kenzo Tange and, more recently, Fumihiko Maki. But with that project I made people angry and anxious! Why does this guy use so many elements – and not just that – but elements that can be changed? If the elements are changeable then so is the totality. Usually the chair, the desk, the floor should all be wiped off, cleaned up, even for architects like Le Corbusier. But that is characteristic of Western culture and we have our Eastern culture. Actually I have discovered recently that that is the character of the earth itself, not simple and not clean. So the pure, clean beauty lives only in our mind, not in reality.

Seiwa Bunraku Theatre where each ceiling is rotating right and left.

To skip back slightly, why did the number fifty-four, in particular, come to be used in your early projects?
The first project was 54 Windows, and I simply followed the axiom of 'form follows function'. It was a doctor's house so a lot of different functions were required; an office to meet patients, his office, the patient's waiting room, the X-ray room, and six rooms which didn't need a special character. The doctor said 'why not make dice'? So when I named the building I simply counted the total number of windows and it was fifty-four. But it became a target of criticism, and I was asked constantly to explain the significance of fifty-four. The most famous example of the 54/108 series is the number of gongs temples strike on New Year's Eve.

After completing the 54 Windows, 54 Roofs and 54 Columns, your architecture seemed to take a quite different direction. Was it also an expression of your dissatisfaction with the aesthetics of Western architecture?
After those three projects I jumped from the endless variety we have in our life here to a composition or system, but not the grid system that Modern

Buddha said we make 108 sins a year, so one sin per 3.5 days, or two sins a week! We erase these sins with 108 gongs, and fifty-four is half of that. Western people consider this to be an Asian or Japanese unintellectual, unscientific person's dogma. But they are wrong. Do you know the number of baseball ball stitches? It's 108. The worst golf handicap is thirty-six; thirty-six means eighteen holes and the par is seventy-two, so seventy-two plus thirty-six is 108. Do you know Shikibu Murasaki's *The Tale of Genji*? [Murasaki was a lady of the Heian court in around 1000 AD and author of Japan's most famous love novel.] Well the *The Tale of Genji* has fifty-four scrolls; fifty-four scrolls to express a man and his love for life. And do you know the World Trade Center in New York, the one that King Kong climbed? That is the 107th storey and so the floor that King Kong jumped from is the 108th storey. I think that Yamasaki was unconsciously led that way by history. Rather than the digital 1-2-3, perhaps the 54/108 series is representative of the character of the earth or human beings. In this respect, I'm proud to use 54: 54 Windows. 54 Roofs. 54 Columns.

These projects were controversial when you designed them in the 1980s and are still unorthodox today. How have they been received by the general public?

I have been accepted quite well by the general public. I'm not the type of architect who designs beautiful, clean, dream-type buildings that express the spirit of high-class people. But I'm loved by ordinary people. The clients don't know if what I am doing is good or not but my approach is contrary to that of Modern architecture, whose clean beauty is a beauty people should accept and then they can be bourgeois: high-class people living in high-class houses. In Japan everyone is middle class so we don't need that kind of high-class building like a Greek temple. A character I think is cultural. Some people say I'm doing a kind of crazy architecture: and why? I think simply because that matches Japan.

Your work, and particularly your recent emphasis on vernacular motifs, has sometimes been termed

Japanese Post-Modern. How do you feel about this description of your architecture?

That's wrong. Why is wood Post-Modern? Wood is more the material of the earth. The problem of Post-Modernism is actually only half a problem for us because Modern architecture is the product of Western, not Asian, culture. Everything that existed until 150 years ago is not Modern architecture, so we live in a modern age and in a pre-modern age, not a post-modern one. So first we have to solve the problems of before-Modernism, the age we are still living in now, so we have to pick up much older culture. Until 150 years ago the buildings in Japan were completely of wood. When I did projects on Naoshima Island [1983 and 1995] I used the traditional architectural vocabulary in order to maintain the character of the old village. In Europe, buildings are made of stone, so even if you put a steel and glass building in the town, it cannot invade it: you have a kind of shiny diamond in a tough town. I don't like to be called, and I'm not, a Post-Modern person. I don't believe that is the way. When we see Tokyo Station or a Post-Modern building, it's the same: an import of history and import of change. Wood means forests. Wood is a fixer of CO_2 today. So when we think of wood there are two topics to consider, one is the history of the material in old buildings in Japan, and the other is of a CO_2 fixer for the twenty-first century.

If you feel the past holds important lessons for present Japan then do you feel optimistic about the future, and the city in the future?

From now on in my work I think I will go back to the city. My catchphrase is: Non-City in the City! The city historically has been characteristic, achieving, exciting for people, because it had the pressure of growing from the inside. But today the economy is a world-wide organism, it has no limit. We may need limits for political reasons but not for economic ones. In Tokyo, New York, Paris, lots of people may still go into big cities but that economic pressure is no longer necessary. So the city will become scattered, and with a kind of minus pressure, will change and may collapse.

The other reason is to do with satellite communication. With satellite communication, the city loses its rationale; now a city and a mountain are the same. The other problem concerns modern materials. Many of today's modern cities need maintenance. Industrial products like steel need maintaining, which we have to pay for. When we can no longer pay for maintenance then the city will collapse. Like the movie *Alien* (1979), it will be dark without electricity, with collapsed pipes, and a strange alien will appear at the end. Like New York today! So the city is in danger. I think that after 2010 or 2020 we cannot afford to build any new highways because we will have to pay for the existing ones. The modern city is really a huge garbage dump. So the future is no longer the age of the city, and the twenty-first century will be the age of the non-city. We should live more closely to the capital of the earth and universe. Variation, rotation, history and garbage!

What was the starting point of your interest in rotation and the cosmology of architecture?
Well, when I started I wasn't even aware that they were the essential character of the earth and universe itself. I really hadn't known that. I was just a little frustrated by the confines of the square, circle, planes, beautiful buildings and so I tried rotation. At that time I formed a discussion group with some friends who I had known in my junior high school fencing club, and who were now scholars in fields of geocosmology, economics or weather specialists. Usually such scientists aren't so responsive to a very human field such as architecture but when we all got together each person was asked to talk about their speciality and its relationship to the earth; not just our own field, our special world, but its relationship to the earth and universe. Well my image at that time was of a distant universe, but they explained that the structure or pattern of the whole universe is all around us.

In what way?
Today, with modern telescopes we can see a distance of a metre to the power of thirty-two. We can see into our own body almost to the power of a metre to minus

thirty-two, a scale where we are looking at DNA. What do we find? That the spiral of DNA is almost the same as the pattern of the universe. This means that instead of the universe being out there, past heaven, as we might unconsciously envisage it, it exists right here in our bodies, at the power of minus thirty-two. I was so excited by this, that between power minus thirty-two in our bodies and power plus thirty-two in the universe is us, the city and our architecture. We and our architecture are both part of this wider stream and so we don't have to worry so much about architectural form and city patterns. It's already decided, here in the universe. All our designs, our tables, furniture and everything should be – well not just should be, but as a reality is – part of this whole stream from smallness to bigness.

What about fractals – they are another system that exists at all scales. Are you interested in that as well?
I think so, but as I am not a specialist I am not so sure. In fractal patterns everything is continuous but in addition to the spread of scale, differentiation and diversification are also the very essential character of our universe. So beauty, or the simple thing that looks beautiful, the architecture, or furniture made from only one material, simply makes our brain restful and relaxed. But the reality is this – differentiation and diversification. Do you know the Lion dance? All those bright colours, all those practised movements – but it's just an image. Images can make differentiation and diversification easier, not science. Maybe Asian architecture is more in tune with that kind of image world. It's very different from the Western world, from high-class icons. Perhaps the 54/108 configuration is the Asian races' understanding of differentiation and diversification. But today the reality has changed and a thousand thousand million is one unit of this differentiation and diversification. The number of stars in the galaxy is around that number. Every galaxy. And the Milky Way too. And the number of galaxies is the same.

My friends told me lots of exciting things. The earth is the only star to posess granite, so our land is moving. We are living in water-continent earth. Plate tectonics. Granite, influenced by water, is changed to sedimentary rocks, and one result is today's cement that we use in architecture. That sedimentary stone made our air pressure at the surface of the earth. One pressure unit, and that made life including us possible. But at the beginning it was seventy units here on earth. Nothing could live. So what was once seventy is now one, and we are using the result of that modifier as architectural material.

After life appeared, the sea was polluted by oxygen and consequently the air of the earth too. We are the result of pollution! So at the beginning, in the sea, green plankton appeared, they took in CO_2 and gave out O_2. As the earth has a tendency towards making things stable, iron caught O_2 and changed itself into $Fe\ O_2$ or O_3. Water is gradually changing but one day the amount of iron necessary to catch oxygen was present. Iron oxides fell on the ocean bed and over a long time, and due to plate tectonics, pushed up the ocean floor to land-level. We use these oxides inexpensively as steel. That's the result of the prevention of the earth's pollution by oxygen. I have heard that today the most important element on earth is plankton and that they are changing the direction of the earth in a negative way for us. Already the time to keep creatures on the surface of the earth is ending – we are not welcome creatures! The change of the earth's surface temperature makes this percentage change at an amazing speed.

On the continents, the important things are grass and trees. I haven't had the opportunity to use grass in architecture yet, but what I can use is wood – it's a kind of small sphere, small world, material to use. Some architects like to use steel or concrete but these materials are the result of modifiers of the earth's surface long ago. That's my story of the role of wood in architecture. Wood is like dry ice which is CO_2. Wood is the same as that – gathered CO_2, frozen CO_2. But wood has power too. Young trees to just mature trees – they catch CO_2. After that we should cut them down and plant new trees. We have to retain this frozen CO_2 in houses, in architecture. If we burn it

or make paper, then the CO_2 returns to the earth. That is why I use wooden architecture.

Rotation as the natural structuring system that is then applied to architecture is a fascinating concept, but . . .

There are no squares in the universe, no plane in the universe, everything is in rotation.

When I look at the rotating roofs of your designs for the Seiwa Bunraku Theatre and other projects, I feel such a clear representation of the idea of rotation may ultimately be one of its weaknesses. Isn't the most fascinating aspect of the universe in rotation that it is invisible, that the structuring system is secret?

Yes, you are right. Maybe I have to be more clever. But I love weakness too. Rotation is a huge phenomenon, not just at the architectural scale. Today we could say that the square and plane are also in rotation, everything – like the Pope in Rome – is in rotation!

Rotation in these projects was at the scale of individual buildings, but how about at the urban scale. Have you tried to imagine a rotating city?

Well a castle maze, like the approach to Himeji Castle, is a type of rotation. I would like to create a rotating city but I haven't had the chance. But I would like to tell you my best idea. The rotation pattern came from the river overflow. Do you know Ryoanji, the most famous Kyoto garden with thirteen stones arranged on a 'sea' of gravel? The priests say the pattern is derived from the ocean or is a motif of tigers and their offspring, crazy things like that, but the truth is that in those days that was their daily scene after the river flooded. It is similar to those first pictures from Mars that showed oceans of untouched stones all arranged in the same direction as if a flood had flowed over them, pushing them in that one direction. I guess this image is the same as that of the earth before humans, or monkeys, or animals arrived, and moved stones around. So maybe we should memorise that picture and when we make a city we should make it return to

The internal view of the Spinning House's rotating roof. When you look up at night it appears like a black hole.

The exterior of the Spinning House (1985), Tokyo.

the original landscape of the earth, before agriculture, before man moved stones.

Is rotation a search for order as such? What are you searching for in your work?

For order, we have from power minus thirty-two to positive thirty-two so we have a long horizon to look over; not just order here in front of us. Even ordinary people know information, the news from TV, very quickly, so we don't have to worry about not knowing the future but rather the past. The past is made today – and arrives today. The great past arrives today. The future is the same. Past and future are now mixed, so that's another order. So the human order or the machine-age order may have gone. I mean Apollo's landing on the moon was thirty years ago, but Le Corbusier's *Towards A New Architecture* [1923] was nearly eighty years ago. So this was more than twice as recent as his book. If Apollo happened thirty years ago then surely the machine age must be over. But architects are still discussing whether architecture should be influenced by machines, whether machine theory or beauty is good or not? Whether machines should be more local, or more human? But actually this is already quite a dated topic. And also time. The history of the earth is 460 million years old. And the universe is 1,500 million years old. Some stars were recently discovered, which means the time needed for the light to reach us was 1,500 million years. So we can tell – without being Einstein! – that space and time are very different from the space and time of Sigfried Giedion's *Space, Time and Architecture* [1941]. I have therefore started to rethink what I have done and so I was happy to make this kind of building associated, like Gyra Roof House, with rotation.

One attraction of rotation is that it is universal, not related just to one culture, to Japanese culture. But your work is often said to be an interpretation of Japanese history. Do you see rotation as having some connection with Japan?

In that sense my understanding, or maybe misunderstanding, of the rotation idea or differentiation idea is Japanese. But I feel strongly that Modernism evolved from the Industrial Revolution. To counteract that, I have used in several of my recent public buildings, rather strongly perhaps, the four-hundred or eight-hundred-year-old architectural image; buildings which clearly have the form of historical architecture. This was born out of the hope that we can maybe find a better way than the present basis, which is American democracy in Japan. But what if we make a public building, a town hall, for example, that looks like the one I designed in Naoshima? The people there asked me if the design was ok – to use an image that was not associated with 'our' democracy. We are architects so we can provide only architectural forms to give our island people their image of democracy. We can go back a few hundred years to help them understand.

How do you see architecture in Japan in ten years time?

Maybe we can find three or four important trends, cultural maybe, political or economic, in geocosmology. In Central Europe you kicked out Communism but here, in Asia the central largest country is Communist. So Asia is moving in a different direction from the West: how to live with Communism? How to live with poverty? How to live with the endless growth in economics? We have to think about the Asian way to solve today's situation, which I believe will guide us in a new architectural direction of architecture. ■

Kazuhiro Ishii was interviewed in his office in Tokyo on 21 March 1997 and on 7 January 1999

KAZUHIRO ISHII
1941 Born in Tokyo

Education:
1967   Bachelor of Architecture Tokyo University
1974   M.E.D. Yale University
1975   Ph.D. Tokyo University

Employment:
1976   Established Kazuhiro Ishii + Architects, Tokyo

Major Projects:
1971   Cyclotron House, Saitama
1975   54 Windows, Nara
1978   Black Buttress House, Tokyo
1979   54 Roofs, Okayama
1983   Naoshima Town Hall, Kagawa
1984   Tanabe Agency Building, Tokyo
1985   Spinning House, Tokyo
1986   54 Columns, Saitama
1986   A Bridge for Our Generation, Nara
1987   Gyro Roof, Saitama
1989   Sukiya Village, Okayama
1992   Seiwa Bunraku Puppet Theatre, Kumamoto
1994   Seiwa Product Pavilion, Kumamoto
1995   Naoshima Welfare Centre, Kagawa
1996   Log-Column House, Tokyo
1996   Sant Juan Bautista Museum, Miyagi
1997   Geo-PAO, Hiroshima
1998   Health Welfare Centre, Hitachiota City

Awards:
1989   Architectural Institute of Japan Award for 'Sukiya-yu'

Exhibitions:
1991   'Cosmos, Visions of Japan', Japan Festival, Victoria & Albert Museum, London

Publications:
Ishii, K. (1985) *Thoughts on Sukiya*, Tokyo: Kajima Publishing
Ishii, K. (1997) *The Geocosmology of Architecture*, Tokyo: Toto Publishing

Within Fluctuation one finds Order

Takefumi Aida

「 It's impossible to make architecture move, although I'd like to 」

The big idea has always been important to architects: from Frank Lloyd Wright's vision of a Mile High Skyscraper to Le Corbusier's 'Machines for Living'. But Takefumi Aida, a Tokyo architect and Shibaura Institute of Technology Professor may have got closer than most to realising his dream with an architectural system that links bamboo to traffic jams, to post-war pop idol Hibari Misola, then melds into Japan's urban landscape.

After starting his career with 'silence' – the Nirvana House (1972) and Annihilation House (1972) – and then toying with the metaphor of 'playfulness' for a series of residential projects structured from images of child's building blocks, from the mid-eighties onwards, Aida has been making waves with his new method of architectural ordering – fluctuation.

Inspired, but, as he admits, slightly confused, by physicist Ilya Prigogine's book, *Chaos–Fluctuation–Order*, Aida says he was less interested in applying the notion of fluctuation in terms of physics, than in its metaphorical usage. He discovered that there was a kind of interference between the physical appearance of the movement of many natural and man-made phenomena and their actual activity. Cars in traffic jams appear unordered but there is an imperceptible structure to

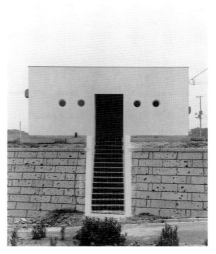

A square plan, symmetrical composition and white walls formed the basis of the Annihilation House (1972), Fujisawa. Aida said the design imprisoned function within inherent forms in order to liberate architecture from function.

The west facade of the Toy Block House I (1979), Hofu. The dental clinic and residence was the first of a series of ten houses and projects that used the basic 'building blocks' of architecture – the cube, cylinders, triangular prisms – to create full-sized houses. A three-dimensional double entendre, it skilfully plays with scale to sit like a toy among the 'playthings' of the surrounding city carpet.

The entrance to the Kawasato-Mura Furusato Hall (1993), Saitama.

Fluctuation drawing of the crypt at Tokyo Memorial Park.

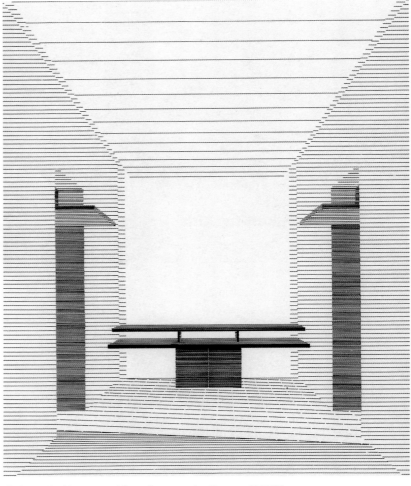

the breaks and bunching inherent in the congestion. The cars' aggregations have a certain order or amplitude to them that Aida sees as a double-sided possibility – that it could be an order with a slight variation, or conversely that there is almost no order but to a certain extent there is. He believes the fluctuation phenomena isn't just limited to science but also explains subtle differences in the movement of, for example, bamboo when the wind passes through a stand.

But how does he move from the theory of fluctuation to fluctuating architecture when the buildings refuse to move? It's all to do with the perception of movement created by people's passage through his work. So although in a strict physical sense there is no motion from the architectural space-forming elements, changing views first creates, and then destroys, the appearance of order. It's an idea that makes his architecture–landscape relationship close to the concept of the Japanese stroll garden which contains elements whose spatial relationships are revealed by a carefully controlled sequence of unfolding views that the visitors themselves generate as they move.

He has applied 'fluctuation' to civic spaces –

Saitama's Kawasato-Mura Community Centre (1993); the mixed commercial–residential architecture of the GKD Building (1987) by Hiroshima's JR Station; and to one of the capital's modern sacred sites, the Tokyo Memorial Park (1988). Located in Bunkyo-ku, the 6,290 square metre site, adjacent to Rekisen Park, honours the 160,000 residents of the capital who died in war. A pair of axes, one defined by the park boundary and the other perpendicular to the main traffic artery of Kasuga Street are realised by layers of fragmented walls. Rising up from the paving as towering pillars or squatting among the planting like vertically-challenged *torii* (the gate to a Shinto shrine), they slice through the site – an alluring gateway that draws people in from the road and delivers them to the open plaza facing the crypt. It's here that they reveal their bipolar nature: if during the approach they seemed ordered by their axial arrangement, they now produce a complex layering of framed scenes of the park and urban surroundings. It's an emotional journey not unlike a magic house where you seem to be entering a peaceful box which suddenly reveals a fantasy of fragmented views. Shadows cast by the walls only increase the sense of fragmentation – and sense of solitude in front of the crypt. Aida says the purpose of abstracted *torii* images was to circumvent the difficulty of using specific religious motifs in a Tokyo metropolitan institution and yet they create the sequentiality of *torii* at a shrine – where passing through an increasing order corresponds to raising the spirit as you move from the real to the hyper-real state.

Which brings us to the singer Hibari Misola. Misola, whose voice may not have taken them to a higher plane but at least seduced a generation of salary-men in the 1950s, produced what Aida calls comfortable music. When the music's pulse is first analysed it appears to have a fixed focal point but actually has a resonance of points. It's the lack of a fixed focal point or, as he says 'absence of centre' together with the trait of resonance that is similar to the traditional Japanese aesthetic of a vacant centre surrounded by amplitude. It is amplitude, together with fragmentation, that links his work to the wider city. But this also reveals one of his work's weaknesses: fluctuation just doesn't work when urban sites aren't big enough for both architecture and landscape. In a way, there is a sense that his work – from the early 'silence' projects, through the Toy Block Houses, to fluctuation – has suffered from a curious dichotomy. It is under-pinned by unique and powerful, intellectually driven concepts, but the physical realisation is such a lucid fulfilment of the ideas, that the external appearance of the works finally outweighs them. You almost wish the constructed spaces – architecture alone is too narrow a term to describe what he creates – were somehow less vivid a realisation. Your curiosity is finally almost extinguished by a design wind.

Recently, his work has been to expand the concept of fluctuation from using planes to using points. The Furuse House in Shimane Prefecture on the western side of the main island of Honshu is a curious looking

beast. Part layers of fused columns, part free-standing pillars, the one-storey wooden building looks as though a tornado with a military background has passed through and ordered the elements for its self-satisfaction. Created to form a dining room, kitchen, living room, bedroom, study and bathroom, the spaces are animated by a single line of green painted posts that runs diagonally through the site. This one linear element, forced through the geometry of the building, completely changes the nature of the site's order. The posts and walls that form the rooms are not solid or continuous but rather create a series of flowing spaces that ooze outside and provoke a dialogue with the surrounding landscape. Perhaps this project, more than the earlier Tokyo Memorial Park, is able to reach out and communicate with the landscape. Maybe it's because the order is finer grained and so more easily able to merge into the landscape – it's more of a heat-hazed image than a hard-baked form. Maybe it's because the building's 'points' seem morphologically closer to a stand of trees and elucidate primordial flashbacks. But this house is certainly another fascinating realisation of an architectural theory that is so much more than a just a cute idea.

Aida has achieved a very difficult thing – to take a method of structuring space, a theory of order that is in essence unrelated to architecture – and realise it in built forms. The fragmented appearance of his

The aerial view of Tokyo Memorial Park (1988), as seen from the west.

Fluctuation drawing of the Furuse House.

The Furuse House (1992), Shimane.

The entrances to each of the buildings of the Kawasato-Mura Furusato Hall, including this one to the Community Centre on the left, are all marked by a line of painted H-beams whose graduated colours heighten the sense of perspective.

The view of Kawasato-Mura Furusato Hall from the south. The lines of parallel white walls, some off vertical, that lead up to the 'architectural' forms are like cemetery gravestones come to life, animating the space with a cool serenity.

projects actually seems to sit fairly comfortably in their sites in Japan. Could this be because the rest of the built environment is so fractured, because Aida's own brand of chaos actually occupies its own space in the city, fluctuating between the two poles of chaotic urban structure and banal individual buildings? Perhaps the notion of fluctuation actually does fit a unique subconscious structure in all of us, is recognisable in all of us? Fragments provide links. Fluctuation provides order. Resonance provides serenity. Aida's fluctuation offers a vibrant method to embrace the dichotomies that contemporary Japanese architects face. His best encouragement? It came from a fellow architect who likened his layered structures to the Great Wall of China that stretches out to the world. 'I want to do that', says Aida. ■

Could I start by asking you about the Kawasato-Mura Hall project?

This building won first prize in a competition and is located an hour from Tokyo city in Saitama Prefecture. The site is quite large, 15,500 square metres, with the actual architecture occupying only 3,400 square metres, mostly as two-storey ferro-concrete buildings. If you look at the plan you can see that there is a series of layered walls parallel to each other, arranged across the site. Some of them are strongly expressed as architectural elements, others are fragmented walls, metal columns, or walls with openings like linear Japanese *torii* gates. It was my intention to integrate this 'building' with the green landscape to create a concept of community that takes into account the traditional landscape character of the area. The landscape introduces the main elements of a river bank, river bed, trees and a bridge, paths, fields of flowers and meadows. In other words, all the components of a traditional community landscape, but layered among the built elements so as to suggest streetscapes.

What is the function of this project?

There are only eight thousand people in this village and it is a community centre for them, with a library, a conference room, and a room for bathing with a Japanese-style bath. This is also a pond and parking, with the site entrance located across a small bridge

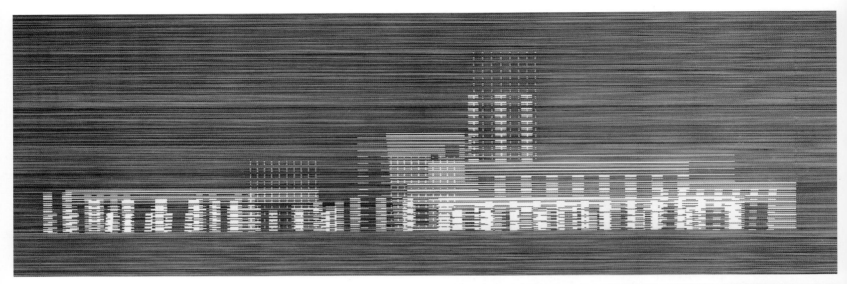

Fluctuation drawing of Kawasato-Mura Furusato Hall.

Layered walls of the Tokyo Memorial Park's Rest House are suddenly fragmented and juxtaposed across incoming lines of paving and greenery.

at right angles to the arranged elements. The water has a special meaning. Do you know the Japanese word *kekkai* – it means the boundary or the division between two worlds? In traditional Japanese landscape stones tied with string were laid on a path to indicate that we could not enter and go beyond that space. That was the symbolism behind this bridge. There are five different kinds of facilities in this building: baths where old people meet and talk, an area for children and housewives, an office for the building, a library, a cooking school and somewhere for health checks. Nowadays, in the Japanese countryside people live together with their enlarged family and there are often relationship difficulties with so many people in just one small house. When families visit this building they can go their own way. Although this building looks like the contemporary architecture we might see in Tokyo, actually when I designed this building I was inspired by the Edo period [1600-1868] *machiya* or row houses where there is a layering of several buildings as you look along a street. In my design I intended to represent this type of layering of buildings as a metaphor of *machiya*, a combination of streets and roofs, all integrated with the landscape of rice fields. The layers

of the design are arranged in a parallel manner and there are five entrances, all marked with a sign and colours that vary from white to grey; white marking the main entrance.

Was this reinterpretation of traditional communities the reason you won the competition?

Perhaps it's an unusual aspect of competitions in Japan, but the Mayor of the town chose the winning design almost by himself. He felt that this design was quite contemporary and the other designs were more traditional and emphasised the rural character of the site. But I think the main reason for its selection was that the other proposals used two- or three-storey buildings in a kind of condensed plan that left open space, whereas my design used a lower building profile that is more suited to the Japanese landscape.

You said the overall concept was from the layering of traditional *machiya*. But are these entrances or other elements of the design also from Japanese traditional architecture or are they your own method of design?

Well to go back to an earlier project, the Tokyo Memorial Park, I used a series of fragmented walls arranged on two main axes that related to the key parameters of the site. Kasuga Street runs along one side and so one axis is defined by running perpendicular from Kasuga Street into the site and layers are arranged parallel to this. The other axis was defined by the direction of the park boundary, the two intersecting in the prayer area in front of the crypt. In Japanese traditional architecture, landscape and the building, in spite of a certain openness, were physically divided. Well I wanted to integrate the landscape with the architecture and so I utilised fragments of these walls, ordered by a system I called fluctuation. When you look at buildings in Greece and Rome there are numerous fragments around the ruin. I utilised these images in this building to emphasise the notion of monumentality while making connections with the past, but in a contemporary way. The use of fluctuation is similar to the traditional Japanese aesthetic of the absence of the centre. In Japan the centre is absent or very weak, but surrounding it is amplitude. In the West you have a certain centre focused on a strong image like a church tower, but to me this is so strict and formal. I wanted to make this park area more informal so I didn't feel entirely comfortable using such a formal image. Instead, I decided to convey this through resonance around the centre of the park space. In order to create such a space I made only the area around the crypt a more formal space by way of symmetry – sometimes a formal image arises from symmetry, other times informal – but again through the fragmentation there is some ambiguity.

How did you first come upon the theory of fluctuation, and how has your work developed from the basic conceptual level to that of creating architectural spaces?

Ilya Prigogine wrote a book entitled *Chaos–Fluctuation–Order* that greatly affected me. But as it was a physics text I only understood one-third of the book! It wasn't my intention to use the notion of fluctuation in terms of physics, but rather to use it as a kind of metaphor of a plane that is actually still but appears to be moving continuously. It was this kind of metaphorical use for fluctuation that most interested me and was what I wanted to explore in my work. There are many forms of fluctuation, of course, occupying different areas of science and nature. For example, when the wind blows through a stand of bamboo, the bamboo shakes and sways with a certain order. Although all the strands appear to move uniformly, they actually exhibit a slight differentiation, and that imperceptible difference in movement is the phenomena of fluctuation. It is a certain rule of this kind of condition of riding on the same order, but not having exactly the same movement. That is what I mean by fluctuation. Another example is traffic in a highway jam. There are a lot of cars and there appears to be no order to the car's alignment, but if we record these traffic jams a certain order is perceptible. For some reason groups of vehicles evolve or places where the cars group up and form a jam and places where they don't. If we look closely at this phenomena we can find a certain order or amplitude.

Another example is music. When we listen to pleasant music, like that of Mozart, or the music of *enka* singer Hibari Misola, and investigate its structure in terms of pulse, we see that what initially appears to be a fixed focal point, is not actually that stable and that there is a resonance to the points. It's related to the human pulse or breath, and music that appeal to both Japanese and Westerners has this quality. Both the pulse and breath seem to have the same pitch or amplitude but are in fact quite different. If you look just a short time they seem to be completely ordered but actually there is a slight degree of irregularity. The other way of seeing this is that there is no order, but to a certain extent there is order underlying the phenomena.

The overall view of the Tokyo Memorial Park from the north shows the two slightly dislocated grids that form the basic geometric structure of the fluctuating design for the park.

But how do you move from this theory of fluctuation to the design of an actual immobile building?

In fluctuation there seems to be order but actually it doesn't exist. It seems to have a fixed focal point but actually it doesn't. There is an absence of centre and instead there is a resonance around that point. That is the notion of fluctuation that I used. At the Tokyo Memorial Park there are two main axes. Elements are arranged parallel to it and so correspond to each other in planes – that is a kind of order. Despite the existence of a structural order, a person entering this space will see a number of different kinds of view, or perspective, which break the order and which depend on that individual person's movement and the angle at which they look at the layered scenes. It's impossible to move architecture – although I would like to – but people's movement creates the changing phenomena. When you move through the space you will see a different kind of perspective, or view, of the building and elements in the park. Even if the elements are arranged on the same axis and although in a sense the order is the same, as people move through the space, approach the building or move away from it, the way of viewing is changeable. It is this, rather than a notion of conflicting spaces between the two differing axes on the site, that is significant when I use fluctuation.

How is your work related to Japanese traditional

architecture? The structures appear to be like *torii* or to have a layered approach like a Japanese traditional entrance?

When you move between these *torii*-like gates you experience a sequence of events as you pass through them. And after passing through this series of gates one will arrive at a hyper-real state, similar to that experienced in a Japanese shrine, that also utilises these kinds of sequences through the experience of continuously passing through *torii* gates. These continuous gates – at a shrine, *torii*, at this park, with these gate-like elements – represent the transition from the real world to the spiritual world. The increasing sense of order corresponds to the raising of the spirit as you approach the hyper-real world. However, this institution was designed for the Tokyo metropolitan government so it wasn't possible to use a specific religious motif. In its place I introduced a metaphor of the gates by using these walls, as a kind of neutral motif. Of course if one could use a direct quotation that association would be reinforced more clearly.

Hiromi Fujii, the Deconstructivist architect, says he used the grid in his work in order to remove all traces of culture and all cultural meanings. When you say that you would like to use more direct cultural quotations, does that imply that you see the relationship between architecture, society and culture as being a prime role of architecture?

That's a very difficult question! In Japan, people in general don't have any interest in architecture. In comparison to Europe, we hardly see any articles on architecture in Japanese newspapers, and as a designer I only have contact with government officials – it's quite a rare case to have direct contact with the citizens as such. When I was a student, only one tenth of students even knew of 'architects' and wished to choose architecture as a profession. Most people thought architects and builders were the same, until about twenty years ago when Tadao Ando, 'architect', could be found in the newspaper for example. Even my wife didn't know the word 'architect' – it was still 'builder'. In Japan even now we barely recognise 'architects' as a certain profession. Traditionally, it was gardener or builder; it still hasn't changed that much.

How do you feel about your work? Is it a monument of 1990s architecture or a modern interpretation of the old architectural traditions?

My works are mostly an integration with landscape in terms of metaphors, rather than monuments of 1990s architecture or a modern interpretation of the architectural tradition. My works extract the atmosphere of the Japanese traditional landscape from some images in our memories and then integrate that atmosphere on the project's site by superimposing iconic layers. In Tokyo, or a chaotic urban situation, the most interesting and important thing for me is how to place the architecture in the urban landscape without 'attacking' or using some other aggressive stance. The project at Kawasato-Mura was in the countryside, whereas the Tokyo Memorial Park was in the city, and so although

the situation was different, the method was the same. Both use a method that is open to the landscape with no enclosure. It's a key point of my architecture.

How does the design process work for you – how does the design develop?

First I do a small sketch and discuss it with my staff. A couple of weeks later we talk again and they show me their ideas – and if they are good I incorporate them in my design! My designs are like that. I discuss them with my staff and then mix them. These projects are presented to the client using a mixture of models and computer graphics.

Is your architecture part of the wider diversification of approaches which has taken place in Japan recently?

The history of architecture shows that there is never just one solution to a problem. Yet today, for all the

Fluctuation drawing of Tokyo Memorial Park.

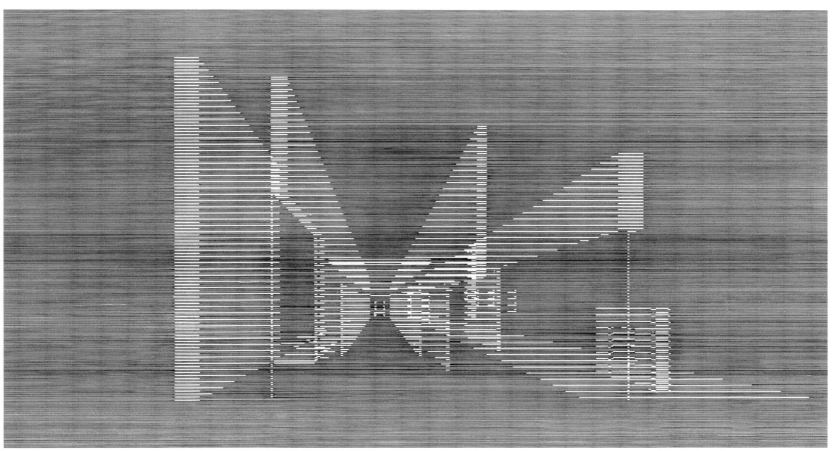

diversity that Japan encompasses, I believe it is at a turning point. This diversity should be regarded only as a multiplicity of approaches, but each with its own fixed focal point. The key word here is 'fluctuation'. We must shake up architectural preconceptions, impose upon them slight fluctuations. I see fluctuation as an architectural metaphor that might help solve some problems, and can help to gauge the amplitude of change that is needed. The present 'diversity' in architecture is really only limited to superficial manipulations of form, and an overview shows architecture to be pretty much stabilising. I see fluctuation as a concept that can be used in a real sense to apply slight tremors to this stasis and so induce the formation of a new order that has a certain amplitude.

As the focal point of architecture becomes increasingly blurred, the loss of centre is an idea that has relevance to contemporary architecture. This condition of a weak centre is something that Japanese architectural space possessed traditionally. Paddies, farmhouses, woods and mountains, Japanese traditional landscapes have long been characterised by juxtapositions. At Tokyo Memorial Park, the juxtaposition of elements arranged on the axes means that neighbouring buildings, trees and the sky become part of the landscape. The fragmented walls that interpenetrate and conflict result in an exterior that is both more architectural and makes the architecture more outdoor in character. This is an attempt to change the fixed relationship between exterior and interior into a fluctuating one, and at the same time to effect a union of inside and outside. In the back of my mind when I was designing this project were pairs of words which I felt that if they were united, then we could free ourselves of fixed notions of architecture. Life and death. Regeneration and preservation. Invisible context and clear geometry. Architecture and nature. Even consciousness of the West and things Japanese. An architecture of fluctuation I believe can help achieve such a unification.

When you look back on the architecture you designed in your 'fluctuation' period how do you evaluate it now?
This is quite a difficult question to answer and at the

moment I haven't reached my own final answer. The reason for this is that the thought processes of contemporary people are coming closer to fluctuation itself. The architectural concept is able to stand by itself but when it comes to being expressed in actual architecture, both I and the buildings themselves have trouble coming to terms with it. If present architectural skill progresses slightly more so that movable structural elements become possible, then it will definitely become possible to realise architectural fluctuation.

You have moved from 'silence' to a stronger dialogue with nature and the urban situation. How has your view of Japan's urban condition and relationship with architecture changed?
I think that from now on the quality and individuality of Japanese cites will become uniform. So I feel strongly that I want to build things that have a distinct individuality.

Due to commercialisation and the uniformity of today's life, the main differences between modern cities have started to blur. Their identities are not so clearly visible as they used to be. How do you see the future of the urban landscape in Japan in another ten to twenty years. Isn't the development of a generic city really inevitable?
The differences between the Third World and the Developed World will gradually be reduced from now on. We will increasingly travel along the road towards shared quality. In Japan we have large-scale cities dominated by tall buildings with clean, large open spaces, but in twenty years time, even though it is contrary to my hope, they will not become cities that we can show to the world with pride.

In the next ten years what would you like to achieve? Is there a particular building type or project you would like to realise?
My architecture has had three stages of development. The first stage was silence. The second stage was playfulness, where for example I used Mondrian's pattern or dice, and from there I moved to the Toy Block House (1979). The next stage was fluctuation – as I

explained – and purveys a particular Japanese atmosphere. During the first age, of silence, the starting point of architecture for me was cubic, symmetrical and white. Toy blocks are really the genesis of architecture and the houses I designed during the next stage were three-dimensional explorations. In contrast, the layers of fluctuation are two dimensional, and recently I designed using the line, which is one dimension. Next is an individual point, and then death! That is my image of the future.

What would you like your architectural legacy to be?
In general, architects cannot survive unless they remain in the main flow of their generational time. In my case, which is slightly different from the surrounding scene, I have continued to make things according to first silence, then playfulness, then fluctuation, with one more concept to follow.

What was the concept behind the Furuse House's (1992) sequence of points defining space?
In olden times, when people made new buildings they started by erecting columns. Especially in Japan it was usual to use wooden structures. So for the Furuse House, which was on a site of white sand, my first impression was of wooden columns. The columns were to realise the notion of a separate interior and exterior but one which was weakly connected. Next to define the interior space I added the walls. Parallel walls were connected on the X axis while those on the Y axis created openness and free space. Columns could be partially arranged parallel to the walls or could be arranged to cross on a sloping axis.

Why did you move away from Fluctuation to Lines in the Furuse House?
When I started thinking about the concept of fluctuation, a series of my works was based upon line drawings. This was the best expression I felt of the idea of architectural fluctuation.

Was the design of the Furuse House and its connection with the landscape through the series of lines that seemed to extend symbolically, if not physically, from the site's boundaries an expression of your wish for architecture to extend beyond the physical building itself and occupy a wider territory in Japan?
In Japan, as I'm sure you know yourself, usually the environment around the site is in a terribly bad condition. For this reason it is very difficult to harmonise architecture as landscape. In the case of urban situations the landscape isn't made at all. So I use line drawings as a way to break down the boundaries.

Your last architectural phase will be points. Have you started this phase, and if so, what do you hope to express with it?
At the moment, I am still thinking about it so I cannot give a good answer. Perhaps when Point Architecture is achieved, the ideology of twentieth-century architecture up until now will be erased. It should be expressed by a new word rather than the present term 'architecture'

How did you make the move from architectural layers to a line? Was there some intrinsic problem with the layer that limited its application?
For large sites where we can be concerned with the landscape and with views, there are no fundamental difficulties with layers. But with small sites, this style of layering is quite problematic. One architect came to my office and suggested I design these layers out to the world, like the Great Wall of China! I want to do that.

What would be an ideal architecture for you?
Contemporary people are surrounded by so much that they have lost their sense of emotion. I would like to create architecture that allows people to call back those lost emotions.

Do you still believe that 'order' is the essence of architecture? If not what is it?
I believe in order. What differentiates humans from the animal world is that we share an intellectual legacy. And that is what we call history. History is the common property of the human race. And because we share this history we can have creativity. I believe that a hidden order exists among this creativity. ■

Takefumi Aida was interviewed in his office in Tokyo on 9 August 1997 and by correspondence on 6 August 1999

TAKEFUMI AIDA
1937 Born in Tokyo

Education:
1960   Bachelor of Architecture, Waseda University, Tokyo
1962   Master of Architecture, Waseda University, Tokyo

Employment:
1967   Established Takefumi Aida Architects
1976-   Professor at Shibaura Institute of Technology Tokyo

Major Projects:
1971   Anti-Avant-Garde House, Fujisawa
1972   Nirvana House, Fujisawa
1972   Annihilation House, Fujisawa
1974   House Like a Die, Izu Shizuoka
1974   Persona House, Tokyo
1976   Stepped Platform House, Kawasaki
1979   Toy Block House I, Hofu
1979   Toy Block House II, Kawasaki
1980   House of Mondrian Pattern, Tokyo
1981   Toy Block House III, Tokyo
1982   Toy Block House IV, Tokyo
1983   Toy Block House VII, Tokyo
1983   Memorial at Iwo-jima Island, Tokyo
1984   Toy Block House X, Tokyo
1984   S House in Karuizawa, Gunma
1987   GKD Building, Hiroshima
1988   Tokyo War Dead Memorial Park, Tokyo
1990   Shibaura Institute of Technology, Saito Memorial Hall, Saitama
1992   Furuse House, Shimane
1993   Community Centre of Kawasato Village, Saitama
1998   Mizuno Funeral Hall, Saitama

Awards:
1982   The Japan Institute for Architects Annual Prize for Newcomers
1983   Second Prize in the International Competition for Doll's Houses
1986   The 10th Award for Landscape Architecture by Kanazawa City
1991   The 5th Award for Landscape Architecture by Saitama Prefecture
1991   First Prize in the Kawasato-Mura Furusato Hall Competition
1994   The 8th Award for Landscape Architecture by Saitama Prefecture, for Kawasato-Mura Furusato Hall
1998   The 12th Award for Landscape Architecture by Saitama Prefecture, for Mizuno Funeral Hall

Exhibitions:
1973   Triennale, Milan
1977   Works of Takefumi Aida, Tokyo
1978   New Wave in Japanese Architecture, Touring Exhibition in the United States
1981   An Exhibition on Post-Modern Architecture, Louisiana Art Gallery, Humlebaek, Denmark
1982   Exhibition of Seven Architects, Kobe
1983   Drawings of Japanese Architects, Seoul
1984   Architect's Drawings, Sagacho Exhibition Space, Tokyo
1986   The Works of Takefumi Aida, John Nichols Gallery, New York
1986   Exhibition of Contemporary Japanese Architects, GA Gallery, Tokyo
1987   The Works of Takefumi Aida, MA Gallery, Tokyo
1988   Exhibition of Contemporary Japanese Architects, GA Gallery, Tokyo
1990   GA Japan '90, GA Gallery, Tokyo
1995   The 53 Origins, Gallery MA, Tokyo
1997   The Fifth Belgrade Triennial of World Architecture, Yugoslavia

Publications:
Aida, T. (1967) 'Approach to the Urban Residence, Symbol of the Urban Residence', *Shinkenchiku,* January
Aida, T. (1967) 'Design Vocabulary, Sky Light', *Shinkenchiku,* April
Aida, T. (1967) 'Urban Design Note: City and Factory', *Shinkenchiku,* October
Aida, T. (1967) 'Possibilities of the Assembly of Factories', *Kindaikenchiku,* October
Aida, T. (1967) 'Saikai Hyoryuki', *Kindaikenchiku,* November/December
Aida, T. (1968) 'Review of Landscape Architecture', *Kindaikenchiku,* May
Aida, T. (1968) 'A Space of Encounters', *The Japan Architect,* June
Aida, T. (1968) 'Review of Tabiji. Works of Imai Konji', *Kindaikenchiku,* September
Aida, T. (1968) 'Wall House: The Concept of Encampment', *Toshijutaku,* November
Aida, T. (1969) 'Go to See the Sky of Europe', *Geijutsushincho,* February
Aida, T. (1969) 'Can the House Serve as a Point of Origin?', *Toshijutaku,* September
Aida, T. (1969) 'Image of the House', *Kindaikenchiku* September
Aida, T. (1970) 'From a Polluted City to a Revitalised City', *Kindaikenchiku,* August-September
Aida, T. (1971) 'Architecture as a Regard', *Kenchikubunka,* February
Aida, T. (1971) 'What are the Techniques in Architecture', *Toshijutaku,* April
Aida, T. (1971) 'Is it Possible to Establish Rules in a City?', *Toshijutaku,* June
Aida, T. (1971) 'Image of the House and a Model', *Kenchikuchishiki,* July
Aida, T. (1971) 'Revitalised Architecture', *The Japan Architect,* July
Aida, T. (1971) 'Movement Towards the Primary', *Toshijutaku,* September
Aida, T. (1971) 'Plan for Box Houses', *Toshijutaku,* September
Aida, T. (1971) 'Box-shaped Concrete Houses', *Atarashi-Jutaku,* September
Aida, T. (1971) 'An Open Environment', *Kindaikenchiku,* September
Aida, T. (1971) 'Robert Venturi from Our Point of View', *Architecture and Urbanism,* October
Aida, T. and Kijima, Y. (1971) *Peter Cook – Action and Plan,* Tokyo: Bijutsu Shuppansha (co-translators)

Aida, T. (1972) 'Anti-Avant-Garde House', *Kenchikubunka*, February

Aida, T. (1972) 'From a Vertical City to a Horizontal City', *Kankyobunka*, April

Aida, T. (1972) 'Lightness Intellectuality', *Shinkenchiku*, August

Aida, T. (1972) 'Speculation in the Dark', *The Japan Architect*, November

Aida, T. (1973) 'Leisure Theory of Territory', *Shinkenchiku*, September

Aida, T. (1974) 'Takefumi Aida 1964-74', *Kindaikenchiku*, March

Aida, T. (1974) 'Twelve Memoranda on the House Like a Die', *The Japan Architect*, July

Aida, T. (1974) 'When the Architecture Disappears', *The Japan Architect*, July

Aida, T. (1974) 'Scenery – Even at That, Can the Architecture Continue Relating Something?', *Space Design*, November

Aida, T. (1974) 'Forest Lawn Memorial Park and Mortuaries', *Architecture and Urbanism*, November

Aida, T. (1974) 'From the Awe-inspiring World of Sensuality', *Shinkenchiku*, November

Aida, T. (1974) 'Function of Individual Housing: An Architect's View', *Kenchikuzasshi*, December

Aida, T. (1975) *Roy Mann Rivers in the City*, Tokyo: Kajima Shuppansha (translator)

Aida, T. (1975) *The Theory of Architectural Forms*, Tokyo: Meigensha

Aida, T. (1975) 'From the Awe-inspiring World of Sensuality', *The Japan Architect*, February

Aida, T. (1975) 'Eliminating as a Method for Architectural Form', *Shokenchiku*, October

Aida, T. (1975) 'Forms, Spaces of Silence and Calm', *Architecture and Urbanism*, December

Aida, T. (1976) 'From Silence', *Architecture and Urbanism*, May

Aida, T. (1976) 'About Silence', *Shinkenchiku*, June

Aida, T. (1976) 'Concealment', *The Japan Architect*, June

Aida, T. (1976) 'Form and Geometry', *Shinkenchiku*, October

Aida, T. (1976) 'About Silence', *The Japan Architect*, December

Aida, T. (1977) 'Forms and Drawings', *The Japan Architect*, March

Aida, T. (1977) 'Between Silence and Loquacity', *The Japan Architect*, June

Aida, T. (1977) 'My Esquisse', *Kenchikuchishiki*, November

Aida, T. (1977) 'Silence', *The Japan Architect*, November/December

Aida, T. (1978) 'A Good Architect is Born from a Good Client', *Nikkei Architecture*, 20 February

Aida, T. (1978) 'Silence: In the Culture of Sympathy', *Architecture and Urbanism*, March

Aida, T. (1978) 'Silence', *Catalogue 10. A New Wave of Japanese Architecture*, September. The Institute for Architecture and Urban Studies, New York

Aida, T. (1979) 'A Book I was Inspired By', *Kenchikuzasshi*, February

Aida, T. (1979) 'A New Wave of Japanese Architecture Waving Back to the USA', *Architecture and Urbanism*, March

Aida, T. (1981) 'A Die Named Architecture', *Kenchikubunka*, July

Aida, T. (1981) 'On Playfulness', *Shinkenchiku*, August

Aida, T. (1981) 'From the Lecture of Kenneth Frampton', *Kenchikubunka*, September

Aida, T. (1981) 'To Unite Architecture With the Five Senses of a Man', *Nikkei Architecture*, September

Aida, T. (1981) 'House of Mondrian Pattern', *Kenchikuchishiki*, December

Aida, T. et al. (1982) *Towards the Horizon of Architectural Forms*, Tokyo: Shoukokusha

Aida, T. (1984) 'Toy Blocks: The Concept of Coexistency of Construction and Destruction', *Architecture and Urbanism*, February

Aida, T. (1984) Architecture Note, Takefumi Aida, Tokyo: Maruzen

Aida, T. (1985) 'Tabino Tegami', *Shinkenchiku*, June-September

Aida, T. (1985) 'On Playfulness and Toy Blocks', *The Japan Architect*, September

Aida, T. (1986) 'Something Hard', *Architecture and Urbanism*, September

Aida, T. (1986) 'Architecture of Arquitectonica', *Process Architecture*, February

Aida, T. (1986) 'S House in Kitakaruizawa', *Architectural Digest*, December

Aida, T. (1987) 'Works of Takefumi Aida', *The Japan Architect*, May

Aida, T. (1987) 'Kazama House', *The Architectural Review* Japan, November

Aida, T. et al. (1989) *What Kind of House Do You Feel Comfortable?*, Tokyo: Shoukokusha

Aida, T. (1989) 'Architecture Fluctuation and Monument', *The Japan Architect*, February

Aida, T. and Watanabe, T. (1994) *Martin Pawley, Buckminster Fuller*, Tokyo: Kajima Shuppansha (co-translators)

Aida, T. (1996) *The Genealogy of Urban Design*, Tokyo: Kajima Shuppansha

Aida, T. (1998) *The Works of Takefumi Aida*, Tokyo: Shinkenchikusha

Continuous Space in the Urban Landscape

Yoji Sasaki

「 Nature is the order of the city, not the structure of architecture or the structure of civil engineering 」

In the world of Japanese landscapes, three stones can mean a lot. With three stones you can symbolise the sacred island of Hohraijima, or imply a flotilla of turtles doing backstroke. If you pulverise them you can rake them out to create the whole cosmos. While the rest of us might struggle to do more than arrange them in a forlorn grouping at one end of a timidly themed 'alpine bed', historically Japan has made a cultural art form of infusing not just individual elements, but their designed landscapes, with meaning. So why then does the profession of landscape architecture make such heavy mowing of implying meaning to their contemporary projects? It cannot be lack of context, as every town in Japan has its own temple or shrine landscapes of which it is proud. It cannot be lack of requests as every client seems to want a piece of tradition, combined with a type of Jon Jerde Horton Plaza. It's more a question of adjusting these historic precedents to the new functions and scales required of designed landscapes.

Yoji Sasaki is an Osaka landscape architect who has built a unique set of projects that explore traditional motifs but in contemporary arrangements and locales. He created the NTT Plaza (1994), a large space in Hiroshima, using the 'feelings from Japanese garden technology to make it a memorable space'. Situated at the base of an office tower, the plaza was a raised platform accessed from the street by a linear bank of steps. As you start to see the plaza floor you are confronted by washes of black-and-white paving that lap at your feet and welcome you in. Incised into this organic base is a series of linear paths. Concrete with fragmented slabs, in-situ concrete, rectilinear sawn stone, these movement lines imply the vocabulary of the traditional garden but storm through the site. Up and over level changes, searing past trees, crashing into the building's walls, their motion gives flight to fairly staid materials, their energy trapped, as if through a mysterious process of sedimentation, into the paving. Dotted around the space are wavy stone benches, their fluid forms a metaphor of the city's location on the Inland Sea, creating focus points for the eyes. Sasaki used traditional notions of space to create the landscape for this urban site. *Utsuroi* is a dramatic changing scenery of landscape, light and the plaza's paving with bands of reflective, polished granite contrasting with the absorption of the adjacent pebbles. Trees were sited at crossing points to show the space

NTT Plaza (1994), Hiroshima

Following the Kobe Earthquake (1995), this house was only saved from the fire that swept through the area by the boundary trees that screened it.

as crowded, even if there is only one person there. A bridge joined the plaza to the street – a symbol of passage like the route to a tea house, part anticipation, part preparation.

Yet for the modern discipline of landscape architecture in Japan, is the traditional garden aesthetic, its 'nature', really one and the same with its contemporary designed open spaces? I think Sasaki's use of traditional spatial metaphors is really just an internal conceptual device. Can you remove the materials and concepts from their context and still communicate something? I guess not. What is more significant is that he uses these to create a new ordering system for modern urban landscapes. Instead of the traditional Japanese gardens that were enclosed and complete within their boundaries, Sasaki sees landscape architecture as 'like the painting of Jackson Pollock. That even if you remove the frame the space is still continuous'. It's this contemporary strand to his work that has the greatest significance for urban landscapes. Instead of contained self-referential 'gardens' he is designing broad sweeps of space that flow past the architectural structures and sweep them along in

the flow of his landscape concept. It's the fact that they don't actually do that, that makes them seem so powerful. The sites for Sasaki's projects are as constrained as everyone else's, they just refuse to believe so.

The earthquake that hit Kobe in 1995 provided him with the opportunity to create a new order for the emerging city that was being rebuilt. Within days of the earthquake and in spite of the city still being rattled by aftershocks over a hundred times a day, Sasaki was one of a group of landscape architects who set out to assess the damage. In addition to the human loss which was rapidly rising – 1,590 dead the first day, 5,051 within the first week – the damage to the city's spaces was almost beyond comprehension with 390,000 buildings destroyed, 67 hectares of the city burned and 336 parks damaged. But behind these figures was the fascinating story of the resilience of Kobe's natural fabric. Trees were often the only vertical elements left standing; trees and hedges the only breaks in the fire's path; the open spaces growing up as the heart of new communities. It was the reality of the green fabric still tying the city together that convinced Sasaki that the quality of the land, the character of the spaces, was the real structure of the city. To forget any notions of an 'ideal city' and, as he says, 'to design to support people's lives', he proposed that the traditional neighbourhood scales and motifs be used, with streets rather than Western-style parks the system that would order the reconstructed city. In a way Sasaki's approach was pure pragmatism, but just over the border from pure idealism. He both realised, and has been able to implement, a fundamental truth that has evaded Japanese cities for so long. They are not Western cities but have their own identity, and that this identity, based on traditional values in a sense, is still valid for creating the spaces for future cities. By incorporating elements from the city's history yet providing spaces with the scale and suitability for modern urban life, his designs become a powerful alchemy of recognition and *déja vu*. In a way it's all so incredibly simple. You don't need a masterplan at all, in fact it's the last thing you need. Cities, quite simply, are about the people who live in them, and the spaces they use.

Sandwiched between the two more established disciplines of civil engineering and architecture, landscape architecture has probably realised this basic truth but struggled to broaden its role beyond painting green on their leftover spaces. With 70 per cent of the population sandwiched into 4 per cent of the land, the reality of urban Japan means that there will probably never be the space for a Hyde Park, a Central Park,

or even a Campo dei Fiori. Like this project in Hiroshima, there will probably be narrow strips along transport arteries, rivers, or thin slivers between buildings. Small spaces certainly, but no less important for that.

Maybe the only doubt about Sasaki's work is his reliance on metaphors. Without the benefit of having met him or an explanatory text in hand, will the people visiting his landscapes have time to notice alternative hidden meanings, let alone read them? In a sense, he is giving up the power, possibly even the right, to guide people through his understanding of the traditions in contemporary landscapes. They may well take the opportunity he is offering to choose alternative readings of the city, or to not bother at all. Democracy in landscape may turn to bite the hand that set it free.

It seems to me that in order to survive as a cultural art form in Japan, designed landscapes have to do what the traditional gardens did – engage people in the reality of their actual lifestyles. A modern landscape in Japan will never be anything but at best a cultural relic – at worst a complete irrelevancy – if they cannot compete with Play Stations, and Cinemax movies. Landscape reality has to be more interesting than virtual reality to survive in Japan. But it would be wrong to see this as a contemporary Internet issue, when in fact it is the most recent manifestation of a long cultural rear-guard action. Historically it was *kabuki* plays: the black clothes of the puppet handlers are visible to the audience but people are not supposed to see them – and don't. In present urban Japan too, there are things people shouldn't see, and don't. Call it a convenient landscape equivalent of 'see no evil'.

But Sasaki may still be right to be less interested in landscape as a process or place than as a metaphor. It might be about spiritual purity at Ise Shrine, about predicting change at Stonehenge, or religious beliefs at the Nazca lines, but at least one person in Japan also understands that the most memorable designed landscapes are, finally, about something else. ■

Many people can probably readily identify with the garden history of Japan. But how close is this to the modern discipline of Landscape Architecture?

Our generation is the first generation of modern landscape architects in Japan and we constantly have to emphasise the division between the meaning of the Japanese word for landscape, *zoen*, and landscape architecture. In the United States, after F.L. Olmsted, landscape architects had to solve urban problems and the environmental deterioration from spreading industrialisation through the ancient garden technology of Europe. American landscape architects fought each other to define both the nature of the problems and their response. In Japan, we have never had a period of this kind in modern times. Japan, too, has a long history of garden design and garden technology and so a deep influence from ancient gardeners, but the only way to find the vocabulary of modern landscape architecture was through looking at the ideas, philosophy and techniques from the USA, which had diverse and open approaches towards public design ideas. We have to solve urban and environmental problems not only using garden technology but by thinking about environmental art, new materials such as glass or metal, media, technology and computers. Such a kind of liberation in materials will teach us the next steps of landscape architecture and will invite us to a new world of landscape architecture for the future. So the approach between architecture and landscape is quite different I think. Architecture is much more integrated with technology than landscape, which uses the materials of living nature: water, trees, light. I think we can learn from materials or an environmental approach but we cannot find the design philosophy from an engineering approach. Why? Simply because design is a sensibility, not a system.

I wanted to ask you about the NTT Plaza in Hiroshima. You designed a ground-floor plaza and a sixth-floor roof garden in what was essentially a very constricted site.

That's right. This project is typical of many spaces in Japan's urban areas. In the centre of Japanese cities we don't have any large open land, or plazas, or parks like in London or even New York. What we have instead is a kind of *sukima*, a narrow sliver of space between buildings that leads people in. In a sense, it is a kind of miscellaneous open space. How to make such small open spaces wonderful and memorable is one of the key questions of landscape design. In Japan we have a lot of modern architecture made of concrete and glass, buildings covered in shades of grey tiles – harsh materials often at an inhuman scale. So my design approach is to transform such spaces into a human scale and a much softer texture, much 'wetter'. I guess these feelings come from Japanese garden philosophy and we can use some part of garden technology to investigate the space, and to make it memorable.

You said that this type of space needs to feel crowded even with one person but wasn't the traditional garden based on the idea of landscape as a place you enter visually, but not physically?

Do you know the Chinese proverb *garyu tensei*? The artist drew a dragon and when he finished showed it to the audience, but one person said it was not complete as he had forgotten the black eyes. The proverb means when drawing the dragon one has to draw the eyes, and for landscape architects the dragon's eyes represent people. When people enter the space, only then is it complete. Our designs are not gardens as much as they are activity spaces. Not places to look at, but places to see inside yourself. So the space should invite people – of course we also have to answer for their activities – so this is quite different from garden design philosophy. To use traditional philosophy but express it in much more modern design is very important in contemporary Japan.

Could you tell me about the Enko River Art Promenade (1996) in Hiroshima?

This riverside project is a significant space in Hiroshima because it is one of the few open spaces that has sufficient size to link various parts of the city. It is 900 metres long on both sides of the river and extends from JR Hiroshima Station to a new housing area. This is the first stage of an art promenade along

The sweeps of material give a broad urban scale to the Enko River Art Promenade (1996), Hiroshima.

and so the space becomes very isolated from the adjacent areas. There were a lot of shops along the river bank but there was no connection between them and the river because the greenery was like a wall blocking views to the surface of the water.

My concept was to create a cherry tree terrace – like the Japanese house *engawa* terrace. It is a kind of gate to the city, like a long corridor leading to its heart. I covered the earth with a wooden deck 120 millimetres above the ground level that keeps the tree roots covered and allows rain water to pass through the spaces between the boards. This wooden deck 'floats' above the trees' roots and makes it possible to walk along the space. I also wanted to introduce the notion of *shokkaku*, or sense of touch. I was very anxious about the floor texture, and wanted to make some variation in the sensations we can feel through our shoes with rough and smooth surfaces. I used three kinds of surfaces, white concrete, grass and the boardwalk, each of which shows the shadows from the trees in a different quality.

Your use of materials seems to have been forcefully influenced by traditional methods, and particularly how you define spaces, not through changes in level, but through emphasising the quality of the materials. But the forms you use – I'm thinking of the half-moon paving design – are not from Japanese history?
That's right. I always think the floor should be continuous. It shouldn't stop at the edge of the site,

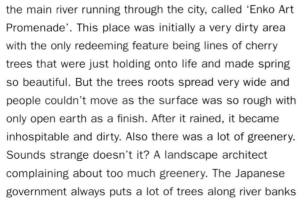

the main river running through the city, called 'Enko Art Promenade'. This place was initially a very dirty area with the only redeeming feature being lines of cherry trees that were just holding onto life and made spring so beautiful. But the trees roots spread very wide and people couldn't move as the surface was so rough with only open earth as a finish. After it rained, it became inhospitable and dirty. Also there was a lot of greenery. Sounds strange doesn't it? A landscape architect complaining about too much greenery. The Japanese government always puts a lot of trees along river banks but continue to flow outside the site boundary to other areas, the road sides, building's atriums, underground parking. Let's remove the edges, eradicate those limitations of the boundary. Japanese residential gardens are always complete inside their boundaries but when I design I think about the drawings of Jackson Pollock. His drawing isn't framed or defined by the frame itself, so even if you remove the frame, the space is still continuous. So for urban design the floor should be continuous, including the buildings, including the plazas, to make one space and then architecture will be much more potent. Trees will be much more potent. So the question of floor design is very important for landscape architecture. It should be more simple, more powerful; even with humble materials we should let people's eyes make these connections.

In this project, the light poles continue until the end of the riverside but are pointed to the top of the mountain so all the vertical elements lead peoples' eyes to the far-away landscape. In this way, people discover nature and the surrounding mountains, the huge scale of the natural landscape, which people never usually find when they are inside the city. So the floor should be kept powerful, every element should have a meaning in the city's order or relate to the continuing landscape's order so people can discover the expansive feeling and exhilaration of the urban-scale landscape. This is the kind of hidden order I'm using in the city. The connection between the area inside and outside the boundary is very important. Then, from the relationship between the inside and outside, people can find out not just about their environment but their own circumstances in it. It's my philosophy. Capturing the change. Incorporating living nature. A structural concept of openness. We can define space not just by the physical elements of walls or buildings but through materials or textures. This is very important for urban landscape design, especially in Japan where we have a noisy building structure, a lot of non-order, so we should make the landscape very simple. In these cases, an interpretation of Japanese garden technology or form may work and hold the key.

Hiroshima as a city is so closely associated with images of the atomic bomb. Did this influence the design?
Hiroshima has many memories associated with the atomic bomb and there are still memorial stones everywhere, with people's names on, that relatives have placed for victims of the atomic bomb. In this area alone, more than ten thousand people died and fell into the river, so the river still has an important image connected with the bomb, and has an important memory for the citizens of Hiroshima. I retained the stone monuments that existed on the site as I felt they shouldn't be touched. I was actually a little worried during the design as I thought that people may be a little conservative and my modern design might be rejected. But someone told me about Isamu Noguchi's famous Peace Bridge in Hiroshima. Built after World War II, the unusual organic design inspired Issey Miyake, the fashion designer, growing up in Hiroshima, to become a designer. Urban design is so important as it has the power to change people's lives. Design makes people. I was very inspired and actually a little worried when I heard that.

The government in Japan always wants to make people act with 'one spirit', but actually the people themselves are extremely international with very open minds. They might have suffered a lot of damage from the atomic bomb but they hope for peace. Noguchi's design fused this expression of peace together with the relaxed feeling from American culture, quite different from that of traditional Japan. Through Noguchi's design, people found this feeling of freedom and peace. This made me realise that design should be memorable, design should be powerful and urban landscape architecture should provide a kind of spiritual space or opportunity. Design can help forge communication with the deepest point of people's spirit.

The 'Bubble' period was a great time for architecture in Japan in many ways. It allowed many younger designers to emerge and establish their own voice. Was it also a good time for landscape architecture?
Frankly speaking, no. Developers used images from other countries, clients requested that this space

should be Italian, this should be French, this should be English style – so in that sense Japanese urban design was very international! But it was all a fake. There was no time for thinking deeply, it was very shallow.

Seventy years after it first appeared, is Modernism still relevant to landscape architecture?
The nature of Modernism was a big question for me before I went to the States to study at Berkeley and Harvard. There I met two people who greatly inspired me: Peter Walker and Dan Kiley. From them I learnt that Modernism is not complete, not over. Landscape architecture is still in the Modern period. We still have to keep Modernism, have to learn history, have to learn classic design philosophy, and only then can we make design more powerful. We should strive to express more powerful designs, not keep or copy the ancient or classic styles. How can we develop or find out the vital questions from our cities or circumstances, and then answer them through design? Before I went to the States, I always developed my designs to obtain a solution, to answer a question, but afterwards I decided my designs should defer the question to the user. Why is this space here? Why is this tree here? There are no solutions in urban design, there are only questions. Such design is more important now for contemporary landscapes and for contemporary cities as there is always such a volume of information that people tend to think their ideas through the filter of the media. I feel they should think for themselves and discover their own spaces in the landscape, f ind out space for themselves. Why are they living in this city? Why are they using this bench? Landscape design needs to always keep questioning. And even through their answers, to show them another question.

Regarding the health of the city, some pessimists say the city is like a patient, that we can cure some points through applying landscape like an anaesthetic. Probably they mean only a local anaesthetic that improves the feeling in one small area but doesn't cure the disease. Do you think landscape in the city is limited in its effect, or is there the potential for a much wider and more important role?
Edmund Bacon made the open space system in Philadelphia and his drawing of the urban design for the city shows a very important concept. He drew the city using only open space, tree lines, green areas and parks, the type of network that really makes the city's urban design. Before that, urban designs were characterised by architecture or roads. I like to think that the scale of landscape architecture is both bigger and smaller than architecture or civil engineering: with details, textures, micro spaces, broad strokes of space flowing across the city. I believe landscape in the next century will be the saviour of the city and even of the earth itself.

From Ando's courtyards in the 1970s onwards, architects in Japan have frequently claimed to be 'dealing with chaos'. Is chaos a kind of 'natural' ordering system in Japan?
Chaos is an important feeling, especially in Asia. The space between buildings and edges between the building and outside is very important, it is Japan's typical spatial feeling or atmosphere. Chaos is one part of our culture, of Asian culture. So chaos is a very useful vocabulary. But when we think about chaos we have to find the chaos with a Japanese identity. The Japanese government always tries to kick out chaos by saying that the country should be a paradise. But in modern times, ideal spaces are reserved for the wealthy. A few people, even now, maintain this attitude towards design, creating beauty for the wealthy. But such types of approach don't solve any problems at all in Japan.

In the late twentieth century we have to find a new form of paradise for urban areas. One is chaos. Another one is space, not for many people, but for one individual person. We need spaces that are both private and public. Paradise in urban areas, in landscape architecture, evolves from the creation of such space. People want a private space in the city but many spaces are not designed for that – they are always too open and busy. People want to find their own space in the urban area or their own bench in the urban space.

Once we find such spaces, people will love the city again. Modern cities isolate people and create a sense of loneliness. Landscape architecture cannot solve every problem but it can show the benefits of private space as a forum for people to find out about themselves. Landscape spaces can show people how to purify themselves through touching nature, can show people that they are not alone. I think this should be our approach in the next century. We don't need to make huge megalomaniac spaces of some idealised vision of the world, we need to make small spaces for the individual. Maybe we should think of chaos as the gathering of these small spaces.

You were intimately involved in proposing a planning strategy for Kobe after the earthquake in 1995. What did you discover about the role of the landscape?
From our research we found that healthy trees – and especially evergreen trees – contain so much water that they are like a water wall. Trees together with open space make a secure fire line. Just behind Okuni Park in Nada Ward, Kobe, over sixty people died as fire swept through the housing, but in front of the park the fire storm was stopped by a 6 metre road and a single row of tall evergreen trees. In other locations, trees physically protected houses from falling down. After the earthquake, a lot of vehicles needed access to the damaged areas, but in places where there were no trees lining the streets to prevent the total collapse of the buildings, this was not possible. Just after the earthquake, trees were the only vertical elements left standing in the city. Suddenly people could see Mt Rokko behind the city. It was so close. People were surprised as they had forgotten it, screened out by layers of high rises.

Why did people use even very small parks as gathering places after the earthquake had struck?
After the earthquake, people gathered at several places, which provided a means of escape and alternative habitation. Many people went to schools and congregated in the playgrounds but there were various problems. The lights were kept on twenty-four hours a day, there was no privacy, and people wanted to live

near their pets or to continue to look for missing friends during daylight. Such people left and returned to the parks. Many of the government-designated large parks were up to two kilometres away, but the physical reality of the city was against moving such distances. Train lines and highways ran east to west, and north–south routes were blocked by falling houses. So people gathered in the small parks near their houses, each only about 1,500 square metres in area, accommodating more than a hundred people. Within two days of the earthquake, people were settling in the parks, surviving under awnings, getting futons and other essentials from their houses. They were cooking here and in

In some parts of Kobe, trees physically protected houses from falling down.

photos you can even see them smiling, in spite of the severe conditions. They were still optimistic that the government would come and help them but after many days passed, no officials came. Volunteers arrived quickly but the government was in great confusion. We found that 200 metres was the distance that people travelled to come to this park, not the government's 2 kilometres.

How were conditions changing over time?

HAT Kobe Nadanohama. The project is a symbol of the rebirth of Kobe and produces court-type open spaces and street-like open spaces connected by a system of alleys and pedestrian streets that wind through the blocks of housing. The design was based on a six-point strategy of natural framework, transparency, intersection, permeation of greenery, association and participation.

built. From three months to three years the government should be constructing real permanent housing. Three is also an important mental unit. For the first three hours people's only priority is to survive with their life and families; in three months they hope to recover their lifestyles, recover their lives; after three months it is time to recover the city. This is the time schedule for recovering a city after an earthquake and it forms a manual for urban design, one based less on spatial qualities then on human ones.

You have been working on a master plan for Ashiya City, also devastated by the earthquake. What are you proposing?

The first plan the city government showed people was arranged on a grid pattern, ignoring the new reality of the city; some parts totally devastated, others a rippled mix of standing buildings and collapsed ones. People were enraged that their still-standing houses were going to be demolished to make way for this grand new plan. It was all for the name of efficiency and commerce. People wanted to retain the feeling of small tree-lined roads. They had lived and grown up in areas with that atmosphere and they didn't want to lose it now, after already having lost so much.

What we proposed instead were city blocks, or *gaiku* defined by 6-metre-wide roads, crossed by 4 metre roads that formed an internal crossing space, an open space, in the centre of the block. These could be amenity areas in non-emergency times, gathering spaces in case of earthquakes. Then we added hedges and trees to the sides of these secondary roads as a kind of fire-proof linear park. At the crossing points we also proposed a 'park centre', a small building that in emergencies people could live in, store food, and gain protection from fire. So this basic module of a city block could be repeated across the city, modified as local ground conditions changed, with stations, plazas

Actually, three was a very significant number. For the first three hours people were gathering information about their friends, or family, and helping neighbours. Between three hours and three days, they had to survive themselves and restart their lives, finding places to live and sleep. After three days the temporary toilets were full, corpses had to be removed, and any stored food that people had was now eaten up. Then from three days to three weeks, a new community had to be made from among the unfamiliar people who were gathering in one location by chance. After three weeks and until three months, temporary housing had to be and public facilities. This is landscape planning, just trees and open space.

Do Western cities, with what is generally perceived to be their larger percentage of open space, offer any relevant clues to how the open space might be arranged?

Looking at the European or American city, they are like watermelons: you cut them open and they have a big delicious space, I mean a park, with major facilities dotted around them. But in Japan, the city is very complicated. Historically we didn't have any parks until the modern era, only roadsides or crossing points, temples or shrines, but even they were enclosed by high walls. So open space, yes. Public space, no. Compared with a watermelon, Japan is a grape, with each grape a small park or passage or *roji* and, like real grapes, they should be tasty. In time, the grapes

should fill the space as wine! This is my vision of Japanese urban landscapes.

In the new areas of Kobe we are designing, people were starting not from a zero base point but from a minus point. We need to help this city recover its memory, recover its culture, recover its lifestyle, and recover its activities. It is also important to forget any concept of the ideal city. At first, after the earthquake, many people thought, wow, this is a great chance to realise the ideal city! But really we should forget that objective and instead, design to support the victims. Modern city planning is very dangerous. Nature is the order of a city, not the structure of architecture or the structure of civil engineering. Let us progress from the minus condition to the zero condition and then, in the future, to the plus condition. That is our design attitude. ■

YOJI SASAKI
1947 Born in Nara Prefecture

Education:
1971   Bachelor of Agriculture, Kobe University
1973   Master of Landscape Architecture, University of Osaka Prefecture
1988   Visiting Scholar, University of California, Berkeley
1989   Visiting Scholar, Harvard University Graduate School of Design

Employment:
1972   Joined Konoike Construction Company
1989   Office of Peter Walker and Martha Schwartz
1989-   Managing Principal of Ohtori Consultants Environmental Design Institute
1995-   Lecturer at Kobe University
1996-   Lecturer at Kyoto University of Art & Design
1997-   Lecturer at Kinki University

Major Projects:
1986   Maoi Auto Land, Hyogo Prefecture
1992   Naganuma Community Park, Hokkaido
1994   NTT Motomachi Plaza, Hiroshima
1996   Enko River Art Promenade, Hiroshima
1997   Station Plaza, Suita City
1997   Kita Asaka Station Square
1999   NTT Musashino Research Centre, Tokyo

Awards:
1990   First Prize, Community Park Design Competition, Naganuma Town

Yoji Sasaki was interviewed in his office in Osaka on 5 July 1996, on 17 March 1997 and on 16 September 1997

1990   First Prize, Housing Design Award
1996   The JILA Prize Honours of Design
1997   Grand Prize Design Competition of Japan Public Design Foundation

Publications:
Sasaki, Y. (1993) *Natural Man, Dan Kiley*, Tokyo: Process Architecture
Sasaki, Y. and Narumi, K. (1995) *Urban Environmental Design*, Kyoto: Gakugei Publishing Company
Sasaki, Y. et al. (1996) *The History of Modern Landscape Design*, Tokyo: Process Architecture
Sasaki, Y. et al. (1998) *Basic Study: Landscape Design*, Kyoto: Syowado Publishing Company
Sasaki, Y. et al. (1998) *Landscape Design Today: The Challenges for Landscape Architects*, Tokyo: Kajima Publishing Company

Stripping Away any Inherent Meaning

Hiromi Fujii

「 We haven't complete chaos in the world, so we must co-ordinate with disharmony, with chaos, through human behaviour 」

'Dealing with Chaos' has been the clarion call for a whole generation of Japanese architects. But instead of just 'dealing' with chaos, how much more powerful it is to actually create it.

Fragmentation, transposition, disconnection, inclination, inversion, contravention – Tokyo architect Hiromi Fujii's response to the disorder of the world is co-ordinated chaos. Where others might see urban Japan as a complete disharmony of built and unbuilt elements, Fujii believes that there isn't any complete chaos in the world at all, and what there is we should synchronise with human behaviour. Although his most recent projects have adopted a more dysfunctional appearance, his early projects from the seventies have a fine-grained ordered appearance, an almost clinical sterility inserted into the rough-hewn hysteria of the surrounding fragmented housing. Utilising an ordering system that aggressively responded to the surrounding disorder – the grid – it was a system that he has increasingly used, combined into overlain fractured forms, to create works that seem chaotic themselves.

But for the Miyajima House in Tokyo's Shinjuku in 1973, Fujii encased a three-bedroomed house and music studio in a gridded facade of light-coloured tiles that flowed out to the site boundary. Rising up out of the tabula rasa of the vegetation-devoid site, the facade's grid removes all morphological references to housing, and all anthropomorphic sense of scale. Incised into the symmetrical volume is a narrow entrance channel. Seemingly drawing air into the building and deterring the city from entering it is part ventricle, part thorn. The grid's module is not just a superficial device, it also structures the internal spaces. Passing through from dining room to kitchen, bedroom to bathroom, and lounge to balcony, the grid seems to be formed less from the solid squares of materials than from the thin joints between them. It's this facet of the project that illustrates Fujii's early concerns: that by removing any assumptions that materials or forms might provide he could negate the subconscious assumptions that architecture typically induces. Sometimes false practicality, more often custom derivative ones, he believed that the removal of these implied connotations would enable people to reach a new Nirvana of genuine meaning. It's a tremendously appealing notion, intellectually, but one you cannot help but sense might turn to bite the hand that feeds it. If you are free of all implied or learnt

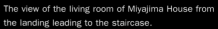

The view of the living room of Miyajima House from the landing leading to the staircase.

Miyajima House (1973), Tokyo. The view opening up over the garage on the East side.

meanings then why not feel free – to feel nothing? If one were to 'negate' any meaning from the form of a dog, and deconstruct it into a fur rug with an arbitrarily placed wet nose – it might free you up from historical meanings, but finally would you still want it in your house. I'm not sure whether or not the logical outpost of Fujii's search isn't a head long rush into oblivion.

But although Fujii, a Shibaura Institute of Technology professor, may actively embrace the theory of chaos, the aim of his architecture is not to confuse but to challenge established mechanisms of perception. By stripping away any inherent meaning in architecture, by setting people free from acquired meanings and

functionless folly to a place that would use the ambiguity of its location to create a passage space offering a view. The architectural space itself is composed of four types of cubes that overlap, contort, intersect and converge. Both the individual grey cubic forms and their inter-relationships are emphasised by gridded walls, differentiated by thin lines of colour. Their deconstructed forms traverse the boundary like a discarded horizontal concertina, disjointedly snaking its way across the site.

Fujii describes the red and green lines traversing the spaces and the grey gridded joints forming the background structure they relate to as a method to enable observers to decode the spatial organisation.

The Passage (1994), Matto, Kanazawa Prefecture. A three-dimensional semiotic study known to the locals as 'the undulating road'.

associations, Fujii believes the self has no choice but eventually to enter the world where sense is the only effective guide.

At first appearances though, his most recent buildings still seem more chaotic than co-ordinated. Devoid of the usual references of horizontal and vertical planes, the dislocated geometry makes for unsettling architecture: have his buildings been shaken by a recent earthquake? Fallen victim to lax building codes? Did someone break the scale model by mistake on the way to the drawing office? For a recent project, The Passage in Matto City, Kanazawa Prefecture (1994), Fujii took his metamorphological architecture and applied it to a folly-cum-passage. Located close to the site boundary between commercial facilities and a parking area, the project developed from an initial

The tilting and overlapping of floor, wall, and ceiling surfaces aren't just a media for decoding the organisation of the spaces but they also serve to generate a sense of ambiguity. As you pass through the space, the floor and wall surfaces seem to generate waves of undulating stimuli – Fujii likens it to sonic stimuli – which are both unsettling and yet evocative. It's not just the layers of the building that seem to overlap but previous experiences and landscape scenes. By the time you have walked through, you feel a curious dichotomy: temporary twentieth-century sensory overload meets primordial flashback. I'm not too surprised the locals simply call it the undulating road.

Fujii's work is a challenge, not so much visually as intellectually. He is attempting to change an existing system, where due to the prevalence of everyday meanings we automatically attach to all things, not just architecture; people look at things but without being conscious of them. To challenge this complacency, Fujii attempts in his work to make an interplay between 'acquired meanings' in architecture – for example, when people see a column it connotes a structural support – and his new 'designed meaning'. The friction and interplay between the two produces a new meaning or perception. Fujii's work can be seen to be extremely timely for the country as a whole. If Japan continues to pursue its technological path with the same vigour as it has done for the last three decades, then the line between what we see and sense in reality, and what we think we see and sense in virtual reality, can only become further blurred. Usually, one would then look at established meanings from real objects to sort out which is the 'true' one. Maybe Fujii's architecture is a timely opportunity to sort out meanings in 'real' objects while there is still time. In twenty years time there may not still be enough objectivity left to compare with, even if you wanted to.

In his search for an architectural paradigm to realise this new insight, he has used the grid; not just for the project in Matto, but repeatedly in his work. It's a methodology that Fujii believes serves to create space, but has nothing to say about it. A grid has no cultural connections and so therefore no meaning. But it's interesting that he uses the grid as the source for non-identity, given its association with the architectural traditions of Japan. The *tatami*, the *shoji* screen, raked gravel patterns in the garden, the grid was the basic module at the heart of Japanese spatial flexibility and traditional aesthetics. Fujii's use of it for its visual and existential plasticity may be less of a departure from cultural references than he is willing to acknowledge.

Although Fujii is not alone in Japan in his search for a new architectural perception, his work has been compared most frequently to that of American Peter Eisenman, the most prominent of the 'deconstructivist' architects. Fujii sees the comparison as an attempt to hard-boil an egg that doesn't really belong in the same nest. It was only when Eisenman called one of his projects 'deconstruction' and collected a group of similar projects together that Fujii's work was labelled as such. With the starting point and intention of his work fundamentally different from Eisenman's, it's only in the movement away from static space towards transformed spaces that their work really overlaps.

Few Japanese architects of his generation have developed such a strong theoretical base to accompany their work. Fujii's marvellously thoughtful and thought-provoking work has brought a new sensory perception to architecture in Japan. So much more than just a nihilistic avant-gardism, it powerfully challenges the notion of the chaos of urban Japan as a force to be dealt with rather than embraced. ■

What are you searching for in your work? Is it an expression of an ordering system?

The question of what is the best architectural order for contemporary and Modern architecture is very difficult. First, we have to recognise what exactly Modernism is. In my case, the starting point of Modernism is based on space and an architecture of openness and free-dom. My architectural Modernism evolved from how to erase things that repress freedom and openness. At the beginning of my architectural career, in the 1970s, the main objective for me was how to erase existing fiction, by which I mean the traditional and customary meanings of architecture, including the functional meaning. This subject, in spite of the passage of forty years, is still relevant to my work. For me, the meaning of architecture was created mainly by the local inhabi-tants. The existing customs and habits were things that disrupted or disturbed me and what I wanted to achieve. In short, I believed that old styles and old ideas of space were objects to be denied. So my architecture evolved from these starting points. For that reason, I frequently used a grid in both horizontal and vertical planes. A grid has no inherent meaning, it is a kind of sexless pattern. I wanted to erase or delete the meaning from the heart of architecture. Then from the late 1970s to the 1980s I focused on the transformation of architecture, by which I mean the metamorphosis of architectural forms. The stage I am at now, one that I reached gradually, is that even without using a grid, the old architectural ideas can still be deleted. At the present time, the subject that most interests me is how to create an environment with no meaning – an ambiguous, indistinct environment – and how people might, themselves, introduce meaning to such an environment. My present projects explore this facet.

So it is only recently that you have moved away from the grid as a method to erase existing meanings?
Even without using a grid I was increasingly conscious that it is possible to erase fictional or existing meanings from traditional architecture.

So it wasn't a question of there being an inherent problem with the grid itself, that through history had taken on some meaning in Japan or elsewhere?
I don't think different meanings exist in grids in each culture. The grid is only a geometrical pattern and it has no intrinsic meaning. However, when I use this geometry the problem with consistently applying the grid is that in actuality, during the construction, it forms a barrier to the building's functions. Though, in logical terms the grid has no inherent problems, when it is transformed into the real world it forms barriers. By overlapping walls or by moving them, architectural meanings can be erased. By pursuing such ways I believe that new forms can be discovered.

So your initial intention in constructing architectural forms based on grids in various forms was solely connected with the deletion of existing meanings?
Yes. In architectural consciousness, at present, the concept of classical construction is strong. But it is actually not necessary when people subjectively create

new sense and new meaning in architecture. Isn't it possible to freely make an environment, but one that is not like architecture? If people live in such an environment, then depending upon how they live there, they should be able to recover a human sense, and classical concepts of construction should no longer be needed.

But isn't it a concern that if all meaning is removed from architecture then people will feel no sensation at all?
That is the problem. That is why that is important. The word 'difference' exists, and when people first start to become conscious of a 'difference' they start to become conscious of meaning. Depending upon the disruption, if you like, this process of a consciousness of meaning starts. That feeling or sense marks the beginning of the appreciation of meaning. I feel that, the question of how to create this disruption or gap is crucially important.

It's my impression that an integral part of Japanese traditional architecture has been the thoughtful use of materials. Is there any meaning associated with the materials you use in your projects?
Architectural material is, for example, unclad concrete. People themselves are influenced in a sensory way through the qualities of these materials. But that is a surface type of sensory experience. The meaning and sense that I am thinking of is the one that emanates from inside a person, one I call a kind of internal nature or human nature. So, in that sense, an important subject is how architecture can itself bring out such an internal natural sense. People exist and find or establish their own self-meaning from the present cultural and social rules. The problem is that people's basic feelings of joy, fear, sadness are all depressed or masked by those social and cultural customs.

Japanese people, like most, see themselves as having certain unique qualities that are intrinsic to a question of defining themselves. Do you see your work as the expression of a particular 'Japanese'

The west facade of the Second Gymnasium at the Shibaura Institute of Technology (1986), Saitama. Fujii's largest completed project to date, it has two parts, an addition to an existing gymnasium and a new building on an adjacent site for Japanese martial arts. Special joint marks were made by chamfering the edges of the forming panels to form a 90 by 90 cm grid which flows through the building to appear on both interior and exterior surfaces of the building.

cultural sensitivity or quest? When you remove inherent meanings, does that include the part of Japanese identity that makes it unique?

No. There is no problem in erasing all of them, for Europeans or Japanese. It is very difficult to decide whether the sense Japanese people have and feel comes from 'this' specific aspect. The philosopher Tetsuro Watsuji [1889-1960] said people's sense was deeply influenced by the climate, by weather and the landscape. Europe and Japan their own particular climate. So from such variation of climate people's sense changes. Japan has its monsoon. Europe has its greenbelt. Many people say that climate is the clear basis of cultural variation. But what I am referring to is not such a sense like this but a more universal one. I want to make architecture that removes such a cultural sense; in particular, that which depresses the sense people have. I want to peel back and remove all culture so that people can again feel free to think as they like, and act when they like, on the basis of their own thoughts. My philosophy is easy isn't it? Even Socrates or Plato's philosophies were simple at the beginning of their theories. But those simple ideas are incubated, hatched, and grown up by society. So for me, too, if asked to spell out my philosophy, I cannot express anything at the moment other than such a simple idea.

One facet of Japanese traditional architecture is the use of the module based on the *tatami* mat. What does your grid module relate to?

The grid has an intimate relation with sense and perceptions of humans, in a word, a body. There is essentially no relationship between the grid and *tatami* mat or production modules. However, in reality, the production module is essential for architecture. In Japan, until the 1960s, the module was based on

90 cm by 1.8 m. This size is very convenient for mass production. When making panels, 1 m is kind of incomplete. In Europe you use 1 m, 2 m, 3 m, whole units I mean. But in Japan, 30 cm, or 60 cm, or 90 cm, can be made in a non-wasteful way, and the reason for this is that it is based on the old measurements of a *tatami* of 90 cm by 180 cm. 90 cm is a multiple of three. In Japan, these measurements seem suitable to make panels without waste. So my module is based on 90 cm, plus 60 cm and also 45 cm. In my work, multiples of three are common, based on production.

You want to remove all meaning don't you? So you didn't consciously reject the traditional modules as part of this quest?

No, that wasn't the case. Losing scale is important, but there is no specific importance to the proportions or dimensions of the Japanese traditional *tatami* module. It's because dimensions are nothing more than numbers, so depending upon their use, they change and lose any meaning. What is important is to erase scale, to lose a sense of scale.

In classical architecture, there is always a hierarchy

or an order to the space, which is expressed clearly in the spaces created. It was partially an expression of our understanding of our relationship with the world, so it was also a kind of social order. I see Japanese society as hierarchically based. Is your work an expression of a desire to break down Japan's social order?

There is no social message in my work, nor any hierarchy. It is enough if the people living there are able to freely generate their own message. Perhaps my message to society is that I want to design this kind of architecture.

In your recent work, what are you most concerned with?

Recently, I have been thinking that I don't want to consider everything solely from the point of 'architectural' concepts, I mean concepts of structure and construction, but rather think more freely about the environment in a broader sense, to create an 'environment' from such a stance, although whether you could call it architecture anymore I don't know.

Is The Passage in Matto an expression of this environmental work?

Well, yes. This is a passage isn't it. The passage expresses everything that I am thinking about in architectural terms, the space for human love, for human behaviour. Love is a complex thing isn't it? But even looking at your face is a kind of behaviour, feelings are also behaviour. What I would like to make is the space for such behaviour. I want to make space where people obey the intrinsic senses that they have.

You used inter-related grids in this project.
Yes.

Was that to negate meaning?

There is no meaning in geometry. What we human beings have been thinking of as geometric architectural division is the geometry of construction, the geometry of surveying or of building a structure up. The geometry that we have to investigate from now, on is based on our internal, human, natural behaviour. What is the geometry of this behaviour? I tried to express it in the Passage Project.

What will this new geometry look like?
It is as you will see it and feel it.

Will it be related to the new ordering systems in science?

I think that is somewhat exaggerated but it may be close to fractal or topological geometry.

Most people seem to see your work as part of Deconstruction.

Well, in the 1970s, transformation, or metamorphology, was the realisation of my architecture as a process of how to destroy the classical architecture and building. So in that sense it may have been deconstruction. The object of deconstruction was constructivism. Within construction, classical architecture contained human ideology or messages to God, for example, symmetry, integration or a centre. To destroy the architecture that contained such rules and to make free, open, space was what I was doing in the 1970s and the first half of the 1980s. If that is deconstruction, then that is ok by me.

The shifts in the grids you used at Matto – is there any rationale to their arrangement or location within the structure? How do you arrange these shifts or disruptions?

I want to make the form of these shifts correspond to human activity. It's a behavioural sequence, but can you imagine that if a person moves one way that the

The south facade of the Marutake Building (1976), Saitama, contains an internal geometric system and structure system that gives rise to two laws. One determines the connection of individual elements, the other the placement of groups of elements by producing common relationships that are associated by memory. The connective relationships occur as overlapping, layering and coupling, where adjacent elements produce a sense of linear continuity. Associative relationships occur as opposition, elimination and separation creating a sense of non-continuous space. Fujii says that reading such a project resembles the way one uses metaphor and metonymy in reading a text; that while reading all of the systems of laws one must be aware of the other system behind it.

wall would move with them. It is important that these shifts occur in the space, but in essence, if these shifts don't also take place within one's consciousness, then it means nothing. In order for these inner consciousness shifts to occur it is necessary to have shifts in the external factors of space and environment.

So what happens after people sense these shifts?
When people realise there is a shift they start to be conscious of it, and I think out of that, a sensation occurs. People start the process of sense about things from the point of not recognising them. If you look at a cigarette you instantly recognise it so there is nothing left to be conscious about, it's the end of the process. It's completely understood. When people cannot 'understand' a thing at all then finally all they can do is to rely on feeling.

There are innumerable sensations, aren't there. What are the ones you would like to elicit?
What I call a real sensation. By that I don't mean real as reality. Real is what I mentioned before as genuine feelings of anger, joy, unhappiness; sensations that human beings have had since early times. These sensations are repressed by present society. I want to release people from such constraints. So I recommend that people should allow their 'real' emotions to surface.

So that is unrelated to function in architecture?
Yes. It is not related to function. So it is vital to erase traditional concepts of architecture that instruct people to do something in a particular way.

How does your architectural work relate to the garden traditions in Japan?
Palace-style gardens in Western Europe occupied an ordered structural view of the world. There was an axis with the house's main room located on it and the views from that room reveal all the land one rules. In Japanese gardens, individuals have more scope for discovery; walking around the garden, are no straight views so greenery appears all around you. The greenery appears in layers rather than organised along a

straight line and so people are more inclined to use their imagination as to what the next vista may be, for example. That is the concept behind the Japanese stroll garden, which is based on Zen philosophy. This Zen basis for the stroll garden is well known of course. To stroll means to walk around, and in one sense Japanese stroll gardens are similar to the English Picturesque style of landscape. But our gardens, related to Zen, are more based on nature, the internal nature of humans.

So is that close to your own work?
It's close, but not so close to it.

So in that sense is it Japanese?
Well, in a way Japanese also means universal. So in that sense I would like to make architecture that integrates characteristics that are mutual to an English person or a Japanese person. Japanese architectural humanism is concerned with scale and materials that place human feeling and emotion at the centre of importance. Usually, architects don't use the word humanism in relation to emotions such as internal joy, or anger, or sadness; people instead use violence or avant-garde.

So how do you define your work? As a kind of humanism?
Well, deconstruction implies the destruction of the concept of construction, with its historical roots in classical architecture. Deconstruction is an experimental movement to destroy such classical architecture. We have to discover whether by using deconstructive architecture people can get a completely new – and real – sensation, as oppose to the sort of theme park sensation you would get from walking around Disneyland.

Are you interested in the relationship between your architectural works and the surrounding city?
I don't believe that I need the help of the surroundings. Just creating an environment is enough by itself. If my architecture cannot exist without the support of the

Projects T (1983).

surroundings then I must have failed. I think the concept of harmony is not a clear idea. Harmony or disharmony is just a simple feeling. In the architecture I make, if the people living there can be complete in themselves then the notion of harmony is unnecessary.

Do you believe that we can be optimistic about the future of Japanese architectural design? Most Western people are struck by the apparent chaos of Japanese cities.

Japanese chaos isn't so much chaos as confusion. For me the concept of chaos is a practical issue that doesn't force people. I think this concept of chaos is important for freedom and openness. But at present Japanese chaos isn't directed by human intention, but is like a garbage bag because people do nothing. We cannot say the Japanese state is in chaos, but it is a kind of 'pre-chaos' situation. A lot of architects who come here to visit Tokyo seem to be almost obsessed with the notion of chaos. I guess it is because the city seems to offer the potential for feeling completely free sensations. If it was a freedom based upon a planned system then that would be OK, but don't you think that if the freedom is based on an unstructured case where no-one has done anything, then it doesn't mean much. A hopeful world cannot be born out of the unintentional state of somewhere like Tokyo. It would be better if chaos was an intentional state. Without that then Japanese urbanism is hopeless. If a plan is used here then it is just a kind of nineteenth-century formula, based on nothing more than a grid plan. Even if they propose a new plan it is a kind of Parisian complete reconstruction with open space and lines of buildings.

I have thought a lot about this recently yet I cannot see that a new approach can emerge from the present situation. If you make this sort of architecture then, sure, a healthy and sanitary city is possible, but in such places there is nowhere where people can obtain a real feeling that touches the basic sensations of their soul. Aren't people just cheated by such a situation? I feel strongly that the Corbusian model of city planning, based on open space and sanitary amenity, on health and rationalism, has already been proceeded with too

far. We are not trying to make a safari park are we? Just a little greenery, like sparrow's tears as we say in Japan, is enough.

So what would be your ideal city space?

We cannot express it in anything other than ideological terms, but Le Corbusier's open space is not the warm enveloping space that we crave. There is no sign, or indication of warmth. Instead of open space, what I would like to do is to create space where there is a real human atmosphere. Although there may still be problems of scale I would still like to attempt this. There is no need for wide open spaces when smaller more enclosed ones will do. Walter Benjamin divided urban space into two groups, one based on rationally and functionally-organised cities where sleeping and work were segregated into two distinct areas and between them were leisure, amusement and shopping institutions. The other was like Naples, a twenty-four hour city where shopping, living and work were all combined. Benjamin was completely in awe of those types of twenty-four-hour cities and I would also like to try to think of a way to recreate something like that. Those rational bed towns and office centres are too cleanly divided and seem to be made in a numerical way. There may be good aspects to rationalism but aren't they outweighed by the negatives? I am not saying let's remake another Naples. But I do believe that it is beneficial to create types of cities where people's intrinsic sensibilities and sensations have the potential to be realised. I don't think we can say that those examples of modern urban planning like Brasilia and Chandigarh have been successful. For example, those tiny poor houses running alongside those wide contemporary roads, particularly in Chandigarh.

Although much has been lost in the post-Industrial Revolution era, if you go back further in time, is there some earlier model for your work?

There isn't a model, I guess. We have to go back and completely rethink from the beginning, from the source, again. I don't think that that is so difficult.

Where do you think that source might be?

When a baby is first born, it already has those 'real' feelings, but as it passes through life, through education, for example, that is gradually changed. I am not saying that traditional societies were better. Of course I don't want to get it wrong, but to return to the source, to go back and remake architecture is necessary. It is something that present-day young Japanese architects have to do, but it is my impression that they just see architectural magazines as fashion source books and imitate the projects that they see in them that they like. So that is why architects in Japan who want to develop architecture through returning to the source as the starting point for their work are so disliked. That is why I am so disliked by the architectural society in Japan!

What influenced you to explore the field of meaning and experience in architecture?

I lived in Milan for three years. I saw a lot of Roman and Renaissance architecture. That architecture is wonderful isn't it? It has been so closely calculated that it's as though it has been passed through the eye of a needle. It's as though they are always wearing close-fitting clothes. There is no freedom in such work. But looser clothing is OK for people, right? During the time I was there I looked at classical architecture from an oblique angle and thought about creating a freer approach and about how the scientific advancement and skill encouraged Modernism. But I decided to completely throw away all those things I had learned and to start again from the beginning. I also rejected Japanese traditional architecture – and why not as there was no reason to follow in its path? Although, of course, I have met other Japanese architects, I haven't really hung out with them. The only person I have kept a relationship with is the sculptor Shusaku Arakawa.

What would you like to focus on in the next ten years?

I want to do something to change traditional concepts of architecture to a concept of environment. I don't even mind if such things are called post-architecture. I don't feel obligated to confine my work to what is known as architecture. Not just architecture but the

surrounding land and landscape is all part of the environment. The human body per se is not what I would call the 'environment'. The external world is important for people but the problem is the relationship between the body and that world. I want to make an environment in which the human body is equal to its surroundings. If people want to associate such work with architecture rather than with the environment then I don't have a problem with that.

How would you define the word environment?

Environment is difficult isn't it? The word environment is being used everywhere. My definition of environment would be to say that it is the thing that human beings inherently have.

But aren't you concerned that natural elements hold even stronger associations for people than the man-made ones of architecture?

No, not at all. The environment that I refer to is the space-time that is generated in the human body by the relation with the external world, not nature. The old concept of architecture is no more useless for the generation of the space-time.

Do you think that this kind of revolution can come from architecture?

I think that it must be possible to achieve this. Architecture is something that generates people's behaviour, or even equals it. So the act of doing is more important than the fact that it is a person that is doing it. What I mean by person is not the person who might appear in a Balzac novel, or in the Japanese story *The Tale of Genji*, but rather someone who actually does something. Architecture is the one thing that should be most able to think about this human activity.

So you are optimistic about the future of architecture?

Rather than optimistic, to have hope is the key.

How is your work related to art?

When you go back to the source, to the beginning, you need some theory of direction to head for or some method. As we proceed towards this we gradually get closer to what someone like Donald Judd was doing. Primary things have such a character don't they? After removing any modifiers from a work, a pure and real object or method remains, and that is what makes art. So in that sense my work is sympathetic to art.

Can architecture be used as an expressive tool?

Architecture isn't something to be used as a means of expression like a picture or a novel but exists for the human body. So architecture is more like a piece of equipment; equipment to generate human sense. Architecture in olden times had a kind of moralistic ideology, like a pyramid that contained a message about God or the ruler of the time. Contemporary architecture has rejected that. It doesn't have any such role as a messenger for ideology, or aesthetics, or to transmit a standard notion of beauty to the public. Contemporary architecture is more like a type of equipment for the individual human body. Old 'architecture' is still connected to the Greek Parthenon. Do you still want to be connected to God through architecture? I have no need for that at all. I would rather be connected with joy than with God. We no longer need morals or a social message. If a message is needed then it is best made by the person living there. ■

HIROMI FUJII
1935 Born in Tokyo

Hiromi Fujii was interviewed in his university studio in Tokyo on 22 March 1997 and on 7 January 1999

Education:
1958 School of Architecture, Waseda University

Employment:
1958   Started work at Take Studio, Waseda University
1964-7 Studied in Milan and London and worked for Angelo Mangiarotti and Alison and Peter Smithson
1968   Established Hiromi Fujii Architect and Associates
1968   Lecturer, Shibaura Institute of Technology
1973   Associate Professor, Shibaura Institute of Technology
1977-80 Visiting Critic School of Architecture, Waseda University
1981   Professor of Shibaura Institute of Technology
1981-84 Chairman of Faculty of Architecture and Civil Engineering
1987   Harvard Visitors for Department of Architecture Lecture Series, Harvard University
1987-89 Chairman of Faculty of Architecture and Civil Engineering

Major Projects:
1973   Miyajima Residence, Tokyo
1975   Todoroki Residence, Chiba
1976   Marutake Building, Saitama
1979   Mochida Building, Tokyo
1980   Miyata Residence, Tokyo
1985   Ushimado International Arts Festival, Okayama
1986   Second Gymnasium at the Shibaura Institute of Technology, Saitama
1988   Mizoe House-I, Fukuoka
1988   Mizoe House-II, Project for GA Japan '88 Exhibition, Tokyo
1990   M-Guest House, Project for GA Japan '88 Exhibition, Tokyo
1991   Distribution for T-ZONE Exhibition, Japan Festival, London
1992   M.M. Project for GA Japan '92 Exhibition, Tokyo
1994   The Passage, Matto, Kanazawa Prefecture

Awards:
1991   Special Mention, 5th International Exhibition of Architecture Venice Biennale
1991   Best Exhibition of the Year Prize for Installation Distribution at Architectural Association, London

Exhibitions:
1978   A New Wave of Japanese Architecture, New York
1981   The House as Image: Post-Modern Architecture Louisiana Museum, Humlebaek, Denmark
1981   Series of Transfiguration, Linea 81, Gent, Belgium
1982   Hiromi Fujii – Architecture and Projects, Brussels
1987   Architecture of Hiromi Fujii, Columbia University, New York
1987   Hiromi Fujii – Recent Works, Harvard University, Boston
1989   Architecture of Hiromi Fujii, University of Kentucky, Tennessee
1989   'Nave of Signs' for Europalia '89, Japan, Transfiguration Exhibition, Brussels
1991   T-ZONE, Architectural Association, London Japan Festival

Publications:

Fujii, H. et al. (1971) *Contemporary Japanese Architect, Vol. 11,* Tokyo: San-ichi Shobo Publication Inc.

Fujii, H. (1971) 'A Note on the Negativity of Materialism Nos. 1-3', *A+U,* February-July

Fujii, H. (1971) 'Architecture of Negativity', *Toshijutaku* October

Fujii, H. (1972) 'Now What are we Asking of Architecture', *SD,* March

Fujii, H. (1972) 'Indication of the Visual Point of Absence', *SD,* August

Fujii, H. (1973) 'Meaning of Negativeness', *Shinkenchiku,* July

Fujii, H. (1973) 'Sympathy for Solid', *A+U,* December

Fujii, H. (1975) 'On Deep Structure', *Kenchikubunka,* April

Fujii, H. (1975) 'To Suspend from Suspension', *Toshijutaku,* Extra No. 9

Fujii, H. (1976) 'Zero Degree of Recognition', *Shinkenchiku,* July

Fujii, H. (1977) 'Liberation from Existence', *Shinkenchiku,* February

Fujii, H. et al. (1978) *Reconstruction of Contemporary Architecture No. 2,* Tokyo: Shokoku-sha Publication Inc.

Fujii, H. (1978) 'Architecture of Pleasure', *SD,* June

Fujii, H. (1978) 'Transformation of Architecture', *Kenchikubunka,* June

Fujii, H. (1978) 'Existential Architecture and the Role of Geometry: Oppositions', MIT Press Catalogue No. 10

Fujii, H. (1978) 'Quintessential Architecture', *GA Houses* No. 4

Fujii, H. (1979) 'Towards transformation' *Kenchikubunka,* October

Fujii, H. (1980) 'De-Composition', *A+U,* January

Fujii, H. (1980) 'Architectural Metamorphology', *Oppositions* No. 22

Fujii, H. (1980) 'Quintessential Architecture and Suspended Form', *Japan Architect,* November / December

Fujii, H. (1982) 'Intention to Meta-Architecture', *A+U,* Extra Number

Fujii, H. (1984) *Hiromi Fujii Miyata Residence,* Tokyo: Doho-sha Publication Inc.

Fujii, H. (1985) 'Deconstruction through Differentiation', *Japan Architect,* September

Fujii, H. et al. (1986) *Phase on Modern Architecture,* Tokyo: Kajima Publication Inc.

Fujii, H. (1986) 'Transformation, Trace and layering', *Shinkenchiku,* February

Fujii, H. et al. (1987) *New Space of Modern Architecture,* Tokyo: Kajima Publication Inc.

Fujii, H. (1987) *The Architecture of Hiromi Fujii,* New York: Rizzoli International Publication Inc.

Fujii, H. (1988) 'Towards New Space Structure', *Shinkenchiku,* November

Fujii, H. (1989) 'Dispersed Multi Layered Space', A.D. Vol. 58

Fujii, H. (1989) 'The Nave of Signs', *A.D.* Vol. 59

Fujii, H. (1991) 'Incompleteness as a Theme', Venice Biennale catalogue

Fujii, H. (1992) 'Untitled Architecture', *Shinkenchiku,* May

Fujii, H. (1992) 'Composing Through Distribution', *GA* Document No. 33

Fujii, H. (1993) 'Dialogue: Shusaku Arakawa and Hiromi Fujii', *Shinkenchiku,* March

Fujii, H. (1994) 'Dialogue: Shusaku Arakawa and Hiromi Fujii', *Shinkenchiku,* June

Fujii, H. (1994) 'Colours in Opposition', *Daidalos* 51

Fujii, H. (1996) 'Dialogue: Shusaku Arakawa and Hiromi Fujii', *Gendai-sisou,* October

Fujii, H. (1997) 'Dialogue: Shusaku Arakawa and Hiromi Fujii', *Kenchikubunka,* April

Fujii, H. (1998) 'Dialogue: Shusaku Arakawa and Hiromi Fujii', *Koudan-sha,* April

Fujii, H. et al. (1999) *Genetic Architecture,* Tokyo: Suisei-sha Publication Inc

conclusion

Japan is unique among Asian countries in that, despite its brief period of American occupation following the Second World War, it has never been colonised and so has become modernised through learning and incorporating Western and other Asian ideas itself. It has sometimes been a long and winding route from source to the genesis in Japanese design. But now at the start of the new millennium Japan rightly deserves to have the light shone on it and enjoy a moment of self-reflection with pride. As the work of the preceding designers shows, there is a wonderful range of thought, theory and completed works in Japan that has not always been given fair attention in the design press. Too often, publications on Japan have seemed to focus on the quirky storyline or the High-Tech image. I have often felt that it was too much of what we think we know about a distant culture and not enough investigative energy. It sometimes seemed there was an equally long road from Japanese design back to us. I hope that by bringing you directly into contact with the designers' words and thoughts it has brought alive a discourse on Japanese design. As I said at the beginning, this book is a simple story of the diversity of design in Japan. A simple story, maybe, but I hope very richly told. This book is a celebration of a unique culture and its experience with design. I hope that the individual stories and the collective themes that have been introduced will stimulate greater interest in Japanese design, in all its diverse forms.

If I can talk a little about myself to end with. Japan has always been a country that held the greatest fascination for me, even if slightly inexplicably so. Long before I had any notion of becoming a designer myself, the images and stories I heard about Japan filled me with curiosity. For a teenager in England it was a world I always knew that one day I would visit. I spent much of my early free time there visiting the traditional architecture and gardens but increasingly became fascinated with the incredible contemporary icons that were dotted, like good guys in a *film noir*, against the grainy backdrop of urban Japan. I guess I always wanted to know who were the figures who created such amazing work. From what marvellous minds did these projects develop? Where did their ideas come from? That really was the start of this book, an idle notion that became a search, a search that became a glorious infatuation. I don't know why you design, but for me it's a chance to be creative, to explore ideas and to realise an intangible part of oneself, in a form that will last. I hope that the consummated ideas and glorious notions of the designers introduced in this book spark the same enthusiasm for design in you that they did in me, that they show just what potential, what value, design can offer us all. ■

about the author

DAVID N BUCK
1962 Born in Moreton, England

Education:
1993   Master of Landscape Design Manchester University
        Manchester England
1995   Japanese Education Ministry Research Scholarship
        Kobe University Department of Architecture Kobe Japan

Employment:
1995-98 Landscape Architect, Nikken Sekkei Architects,
        Planners and Engineers, Osaka, Japan
1999-00 Landscape Architect, Colvin + Moggridge, England
2000-   Landscape Architect, Gustafson Porter, England
2000-   Founded '141'

Major projects:
In Japan for Nikken Sekkei
1995   Fuji Canon Research Park Landscape
1996   Osaka City University Media Center Plaza
1996   Rinku Town Gate Tower Building Roof Garden
1997   Moriguchi Park
1998   Osaka Dome Landscape
In England
2000   45:32 GARDEN London
2000   III-VI-II-V-I GARDEN Oxford
2000   SO WHAT GARDEN London

Competitions:
1994   Saitama Plaza Competition

© Tamiko Okamato

Publications:
Buck, D. (1994) 'Japanese Landscape Aesthetics' *Landscape Design*, April
Buck, D. (1996) 'Waterfront Redevelopment', *Landscape Design*, July
Buck, D. (1996) Kobe's Reconstruction, *Garten Landschaft*, December
Buck, D. (1996-98) Architecture and Design Columnist, *Japan Times Newspaper*
Buck, D. (1997) 'Media Plaza', *Japanese Landscape Design*, January
Buck, D. (1997) 'Kobe's Phoenix Plan', *Landscape Australia*, February
Buck, D. (1997) Shigeru Ban Portfolio (Introduction & Japanese-English Translation) Barcelona: *GG Publications*
Buck, D. (1999) Pre-Modern Design, *Japan Airlines Magazine*, February

pronunciation guide

As Japanese accent is a pitch accent, I have put the following marks to indicate rising pitch (¬) and falling pitch (Γ).

bun	bu¬n	ryotei	ryo:tei
chagoya	cha Γgoya	saburoku-jyuhachi	sa¬buroku- Γjyu:hachi
chashitsu	cha Γshitsu	sando	sando:
chinmoku	chinmoku	shaku	sha Γku
doma	do Γma	shi-i-teki	shi Γiteki
en	e¬n	shin-gyo-sou	shi¬n-gyo¬:-so¬:
engawa	engawa	shoin	sho¬in
furubiru	fu Γrubi¬ru	shoinzukuri	sho Γinzu¬kuri
gaiku	ga¬iku	shoji	sho:ji
garyu tensei	ga Γryu tensei	shokkaku	shok Γkaku
haiku	haiku	shuku-shaku	shu Γku-shaku
hanare	ha¬nare	sukima	su Γkima
ichimatsu moyo	i Γchimatsu mo¬yo	sukiya	su Γkiya
ikebana	i Γke¬bana	suibokuga	suibokuga
kaku	kaku	sumi-e	su Γmie
kawara	ka Γwara	sun	su¬n
kirei	ki¬rei	tachidomaru	ta Γchidomaru
ma	ma	tatami	ta Γtami
machiya	ma Γchiya	tatamiwari	ta Γtamiwari
ma no kenchiku	ma Γno kenchiku	torii	to Γrii
Meiji	Me¬iji	tsunagi no ma	tsu Γnagi no ma
minka	mi¬nka	urushi	u Γrushi
nagaya	nagaya	utsukushii	u Γtsukushi¬i
nakaniwa	na Γkaniwa	utsuroi	u Γtsuroi
roji	ro¬ji	washi	wa¬shi

photographic credits

index